City and Islington C˙   ...endence
283-309 G˙
Lor

£20.99

From Occupation to Independence

A Short History of the Peoples of the English-Speaking Caribbean Region

Richard Hart

Pluto Press

LONDON • ANN ARBOR MI

Canoe Press

University of the West Indies

BARBADOS • JAMAICA • TRINIDAD AND TOBAGO

First published in 1998 by Pluto Press
345 Archway Road, London N6 5AA

Copyright © Richard Hart 1998

British Library Cataloguing-in-Publication Data
A catalogue record for this book is available from the British Library

ISBN 0 7453 1382 5 hbk
ISBN 0 7453 1377 9 pbk Pluto Press
ISBN 976 8125 52 7 pbk Canoe Press

Library of Congress Cataloging-in-Publication Data
Hart, Richard, 1917–
    From occupation to independence: a short history of the
peoples of the English-speaking Caribbean region/Richard Hart.
        p.   cm.
    Includes bibliographical references (p.   ).
    ISBN 0–7453–1382–5 (hardcover)
    1. Caribbean, English-speaking—History. I. Title.
F2130.H37   1998
972.9—dc21   98–20613
                                                         CIP

Cataloguing in Publication Data (Jamaica)
Hart, Richard, 1917–
    From occupation to independence: a short history of the
peoples of the English-speaking Caribbean region/Richard Hart.
        p.   cm.
    Includes bibliographical references.
    ISBN 976–8125–52–7
    1. Caribbean, English-speaking—History. I. Title.
F2130.H37   1998   972.9—dc20

Designed and produced for Pluto Press by
Chase Production Services, Chadlington, OX7 3LN
Typeset by Stanford DTP Services, Northampton
Printed on demand by Antony Rowe Ltd, Eastbourne

To my four children and, to date, seven grandchildren
and
in memory of the pioneers who paved the way to independence
in the countries of the English-speaking Caribbean area

Contents

List of maps

Preface

In 1996 and 1997 I conducted study courses in London on the history of the peoples of the English-speaking Caribbean area. For each session the students were given a fact sheet containing information on the subject matter to be discussed. Looking at these, George Fisher, Haringey Council's Education Services Officer, suggested that they provided the basis for a book. That is how this book, containing an outline history of the peoples of these countries from their earliest occupation to their achievements of political independence, came to be written.

The enslavement of Africans and their descendants on the sugar plantations, their resistance and rebellions and their part in achieving the abolition of slavery are dealt with in outline. Elsewhere I have written extensively on these subjects and there is no need to go into these matters in detail here. Although systems of unfree status had also existed in earlier times in Britain and were known in Africa contemporaneously with the plantation slavery discussed in this volume, comparisons have been avoided. Suffice it to say that the Atlantic slave trade and slavery on the plantations of the West Indies were far more cruel and oppressive than any other forms of unfree status.

In 1958 the British government established a federation embracing most of the then British colonies in the region. In 1962 this federation was dissolved. As this experiment was short-lived and had no lasting effects, the coverage given to it in the final chapter has been relatively brief. Also limited has been reference to the Caribbean Labour Congress. This organisation was formed in 1945 to co-ordinate the efforts of popular organisations in the politically dependent territories to achieve political independence and the work of the trade unions in these countries to improve the workers' standard of living. To do justice to this organisation's contribution would require a separate study beyond the limited scope of this work.

This is not an economic history or a comprehensive history of the English-speaking Caribbean area, but it may provide enough background information to increase awareness of the origins and development of the peoples of the region and encourage a desire for a more detailed knowledge of their history. Should this be the case, the reader may wish to pursue further studies by consulting some of the works listed in the bibliography.

Indebtedness to the authors whose works have been cited is gratefully acknowledged. My thanks go also to Gad Heuman and Donald Wood for advice always readily given when I was in doubt on aspects respectively of Jamaican and Trinidadian history, and to Robert Hill, compiler and editor of the Marcus Garvey Papers, for generously making available to me his research on S.A.G. Cox and the National Club.

The assistance of my son Andrew Hart in preparing the maps, and suggestions from Roger van Zwanenberg, George Fisher and Jacqui McKenzie as to how presentation of the text might be improved, are much appreciated. Responsibility for any errors of fact or interpretation is entirely mine.

Richard Hart
London, May 1998

CHAPTER 1

Amerindian and European Penetration

There is some doubt as to where the first inhabitants of parts of Cuba and Hispaniola, and possibly other islands in the Greater Antilles, came from. These were a pre-agricultural, food-gathering and hunting people whom anthropologists refer to as Ciboneys or Siboneys, the name being derived from the word *siba*, meaning stone, in the language of the later migrants who replaced them. Survivors of these people were encountered in southwestern Hispaniola in Columbian times, but it has not been established whether they had migrated northwards from South America or southwards from Florida in southern North America. Similarities of items found at excavation sites in Florida and Siboney excavation sites in western Hispaniola have led to the belief that the latter may have been the case.[1]

The earliest evidence of human presence in the eastern Caribbean was located at an excavation site at Mill Reef in Antigua and has been dated at about 3100 BC. Excavations have revealed the existence in the eastern Caribbean islands of a primitive pre-agricultural people who may or may not have been of the same origin as the Siboneys. Anthropologists have called them the Ortoroid peoples, because evidence of their presence was discovered at Ortoire in Trinidad. Similar stone artefacts to those found at Ortoroid sites have been found in Venezuela.[2]

The aborigines of the Americas are usually referred to as 'American Indians', abbreviated to 'Amerindians'. The term 'Indian' arose because of a mistaken belief on the part of Christopher Columbus that the islands on which he made his first landings in 1492 were 'Indies', or islands off the coast of India. The first inhabitants of the Caribbean islands who had reached the evolutionary level of agriculture were probably migrants from northern South America. They are believed to have started their northward movement up the chain of eastern Caribbean islands about 5,000 years ago. The first migratory wave was followed by others. The pioneers of this movement were people who spoke a language or languages indentified by anthropologists as of the Arawakan group.

The Amerindians who first populated the Bahamas, Cuba, Jamaica, Hispaniola and Puerto Rico, and possibly also the Virgin Islands and Antigua, have been designated by anthropologists as

1

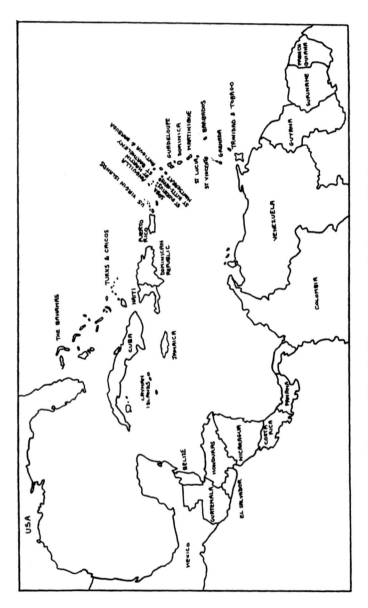

Map 1.1 The Caribbean region (© Andrew Hart)

Taino or Taino Arawaks. The later wave of Arawakan-speaking migrants who colonised the islands to the south of Antigua have been designated Igneri and may have been part of the South American tribe known today as Arawaks. Subsequently migrants from another tribe, calling themselves Calinago but called Caribs by the first European arrivals, from whom the Caribbean Sea takes its name, replaced the earlier migrants. These migrations took place over many hundreds of years. Arawaks and Caribs are among the aboriginal peoples who still inhabit northern South America.[3]

When the first Europeans arrived in the Caribbean, pioneering Taino Arawaks had long been established in the Bahama Islands, Cuba, Jamaica and Hispaniola. Arawaks had, however, been displaced by Caribs in eastern Hispaniola, Puerto Rico and, except for small numbers in Trinidad, in all the eastern Caribbean islands. That in some cases this displacement had taken place within a generation or two before the arrival of Columbus is confirmed by the report that on one of the eastern Caribbean islands it was noticed that the men and women spoke different languages. The probable explanation given for this is that Carib warriors, who had defeated the resident Arawaks, disposed of the men and took the women as wives.

Both the Arawaks and Caribs, while still relying for much of their food on hunting and fishing, were heavily dependent on agriculture. They also engaged in pottery-making, making dug-out canoes and wood carving. Those remaining on the South American mainland and the Caribs in the eastern Caribbean islands used bows and arrows, though this weapon was not used in the Bahama Islands, Cuba, Jamaica and Hispaniola.

On the Central American mainland the Amerindians were much more advanced than those in the islands or in South America. The Mayans, whose well laid out cities were in existence as early as the tenth century, engaged in trade, including trade by sea. It is possible that, centuries before the aborigines of the Bahama Islands discovered Columbus in 1492, there had been an outward movement into the Caribbean islands by the Mayans (see Map 1.2). This may explain the ball courts excavated in Puerto Rico. None of these ball courts was identical in construction with the ball courts in Central America, but they may indicate a higher level of development than either the Arawaks or the Caribs had reached. The discovery at the Bowden excavation site in Jamaica of a stone model of a piragua, or vessel with cabin, may or may not indicate that the sculptor was depicting a vessel of a more advanced level of construction technology than the Taino Arawaks were capable of.[4]

It would appear, however, that penetration of the Caribbean by a Central American civilisation, if it occurred, was interrupted a long time before the arrival of Columbus. The reason for this may

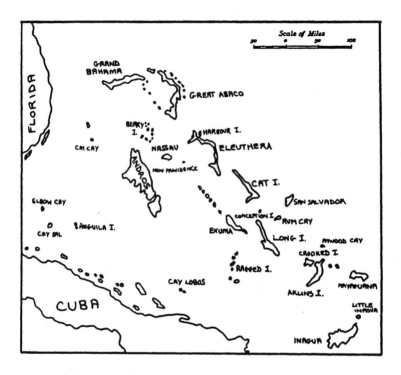

Map 1.2 The Bahamas, where the Amerindians first discovered
Columbus in 1492 (© Andrew Hart)

have been related to whatever it was that led to the abandonment
of several Mayan cities in the thirteenth century, the ruins of which
have been discovered by archaeologists. There is no certainty as
to the reason or reasons for these urban evacuations. During the
long history of Central American civilisations there had been
successive periods of efflorescence and decline. War and/or pestilence
may have been the cause.

Whether or not people from a Central American civilisation had
been there before them, it was the Spanish sovereigns who, in the
sixteenth and seventeenth centuries, claimed sovereignty over the
Caribbean islands, the adjoining mainlands and the sea that they
referred to, with Latin refinement, as their *mare nostrum*. In so doing
they, of course, ignored the claims of the peoples who, for centuries,
had occupied these lands.

The King of Portugal also claimed sovereignty over extensive lands
in the Americas. This came about initially through ignorance on
the part of Pope Alexander Borgia of the fact that the South
American mainland extended so far to the east. In the year after

the first voyage of Columbus to the Americas, anxious to avoid the possibility of conflict between the two great Christian maritime powers of the day, the Pope issued his famous Bull in which he divided all new lands discovered and to be discovered between the monarchs of Spain and Portugal.

This division of the spoils the Pope effected by drawing an imaginary line down what he thought was the middle of the Atlantic Ocean, 370 leagues west of the Cape Verde Islands. He then awarded all new lands 'discovered' to the west of it to Spain and to the east of it to Portugal. By the Treaty of Tordesillas in 1494, Spain and Portugal confirmed the Pope's award. Not until 1500 did they realise that part of South America, known today as Brazil, lay to the east of the line.[5]

The main activity of English and French seamen in the Caribbean during the sixteenth and early seventeenth centuries was piracy and illegal trade with the Spanish colonies. English and French attempts to establish settlements in northern South America in the first decade of the seventeenth century and English attempts to settle in St Lucia in 1605 and Grenada in 1609 failed, but Dutch merchants successfully established a trading post on islands in the Essequibo River, in what is now Guyana.[6]

In 1624 Thomas Warner, an Englishman financed by the London merchant Ralph Merrifield, arrived in St Kitts with settlers he had recruited in England and the English North American colony of Virginia. The merchant's intention was that the settlers should grow tobacco, cotton and other crops to be sent to England for sale. Some French settlers were already there, living with the Caribs, and other French settlers arrived soon afterwards. The Caribs were soon to regret their hospitality when the European settlers united in hostilities against them.

In 1625 Merrifield obtained Letters Patent, a form of land grant, not from the King of Spain but from the King of England. This authorised him to establish settlements on St Kitts, Nevis, Montserrat and Barbados. As a precaution, he obtained a noble patron, the Earl of Carlisle, and put up the money for Carlisle to apply for a royal grant of these and other islands. In 1627 the King purported to grant to Carlisle the islands of St Kitts, Nevis, Grenada, St Vincent, St Lucia, Barbados, Martinique, Dominica, Marie Galante, Guadeloupe, Antigua, Montserrat and several others, some of which did not exist, with authority to make laws for their government and tax the inhabitants. For this the King received £100 and was to receive one fifth of all gold and silver obtained. The right to tax the inhabitants was one thing, collecting taxes imposed was another. When Carlisle attempted to tax the settlers on St Kitts this provoked a mutiny. In 1628 Warner established a settlement on Nevis.

In 1627 John Powell, a ship's captain financed by the Courteen brothers, Anglo-Dutch merchants, took settlers to Barbados. The Courteens sent more settlers and by 1628 there were 1,600 Europeans on the island. Powell went to the Dutch Essequibo settlement and returned to Barbados with 32 Arawaks, who had agreed to teach the settlers how to grow cassava, maize, tobacco and other crops. He had promised the Dutch Governor that these Arawaks would be free and would be returned to Essequibo, but in Barbados they were enslaved. They did not regain their freedom and permission to return home until 1655.

Like Merrifield, the Courteen brothers acquired a noble patron, the Earl of Montgomery and Pembroke, who obtained a royal grant to the islands of Trinidad, Tobago, Barbados and another, non-existent, island. But Carlisle, who claimed that Barbados had already been granted to him, granted a lease of 10,000 acres of the island to the merchant Marmaduke Royden. In 1628 he appointed a Governor of the island, who arrived with 80 settlers. In 1629 Powell arrived with more settlers who were armed. They arrested Carlisle's Governor and seized much of the property of his settlers. There was eventually an out of court settlement between the rival merchants. The Lord Privy Seal, to whom the dispute between the two noblemen was referred, upheld Carlisle's grant.

For most of the time the Spaniards ignored the English and French settlers on the smaller islands, but in 1629 a Spanish fleet was sent to clear them out of the Leeward Islands. The settlement on Nevis was destroyed and the settlers taken off the island. On St Kitts the French settlers fled from the island and some of the English settlers surrendered, but others hid in the woods and returned to their farms when the fleet sailed. The French settlers also returned.

In 1629 members of the Puritan sect established a colony on New Providence (now Nassau) in the Bahama Islands. In the following year, Letters Patent were issued to 'The Governor and Company of Adventurers for the Plantations of the Islands of Providence, Henrietta and the adjacent islands ...'. Half the profits were to be retained by the settlers and half were to go to the Company. However, despite the strict religious principles of the colony's founders, the island had, within five years, become a base for pirates. Because of its proximity to their trade route to the isthmus of Panama, the Spaniards were more concerned about this colony than the settlements in the eastern Caribbean. They made an unsuccessful attack on the colony in 1635 and a more resolute attack in 1641, which destroyed it.

During this period the Netherlands was part of the Spanish Empire and the Dutch were Spanish subjects. Dutch merchants, who had developed extensive shipping and trading and become wealthy, resented and resisted Spanish control. By 1621, despite their subordinate status, the Dutch were at war with Spain and there was fighting at sea. In 1626, in addition to their Essequibo trading post, they established a settlement in the Guianas on the banks of the Berbice River. In 1634 they established settlements on the small islands of Curaçao, Aruba, Bonaire and St Eustatius, and in 1640 on Saba. In 1648 a peace treaty was signed with Spain, which recognised the independence of the Netherlands and the existence of the Dutch colonies.

In or about 1625 English and Dutch settlers had occupied St Croix. Some 20 years later they quarrelled and the English drove out the Dutch. Attempts made to colonise Tobago in 1634 and 1642 were abandoned because of Carib attacks. In 1635 the French 'Compagnie des Îles d'Amerique' was incorporated. This company financed settlements in Guadeloupe and Martinique. Subsequently, French colonies were established in St Barthelemy, St Martin, Grenada, St Lucia, the Saintes and Marie Galante.

The many English and French pirates, raiding Spanish shipping and Spanish ports in the Caribbean area, were encouraged by their governments. Colonial Governors issued Letters of Marque which were in effect licences to engage in piracy against other nations. Licensed piracy by English seafarers continued until 1670 when, by the Treaty of Madrid, Spain recognised the English colonies and the English agreed to revoke all Letters of Marque. This did not stop the pirate Henry Morgan from raiding Porto Bello later that year and, although subsequently arrested, he was knighted and became Lieutenant-Governor of Jamaica in 1674.[7]

CHAPTER 2

Thieves Falling Out

The European states that colonised the Caribbean region were acquisitive and aggressive. They inflicted great suffering on the aboriginal Amerindian peoples, in several islands to the point of extinction. They were also often at war with each other with the result that, until the first decade of the nineteenth century, there were frequent territorial changes of possession. To the few Amerindians on the Caribbean islands who survived, this incessant fighting over the lands stolen from them must have appeared to be a case of thieves falling out![1]

The principal contestants were Spain, England (later Britain), France and the Netherlands. In 1641 English settlers on New Providence (now Nassau) in the Bahamas were driven out by the Spaniards. By 1660 the English had taken Jamaica from Spain. The English and French settlers on St Kitts had divided the island, but when war was declared between France and England in 1666, the English settlers there surrendered to the French. The French also captured Antigua and Montserrat from the English.

In 1666, an English expedition from Barbados set out to capture the Dutch island of Tobago, only to find that English buccaneers from Jamaica had already occupied the island. The pirates agreed to hand over control of the island on condition that they would be allowed to sell the loot they had acquired in Barbados. Five months earlier other buccaneers from Jamaica, led by Edward Morgan the Deputy Governor, had captured St Eustatius from the Dutch. In 1667, the English recaptured Antigua and Montserrat, captured Cayenne from the French and Suriname from the Dutch. When the war was brought to an end in 1667, by the Treaty of Breda, the French and English returned the territories they had captured from each other and Suriname was returned to the Dutch.

There were further wars between England and the Netherlands from 1672 to 1674, during the course of which the English captured the Dutch islands of St Eustatius, Saba and Tortola and the Dutch captured Cayenne. There was war too between the Dutch and the French from 1672 to 1678, with the French recovering Cayenne and capturing Tobago in 1676. France and Spain were at war from 1673 to 1678, during the course of which, in 1675, a Spanish fleet expelled both French and English settlers from St Kitts. They, however, returned soon after the fleet's departure. This war ended with the Treaty of Nymwegen by which Spain recognised French ownership of the western part of Hispaniola. Saba and St Eustatius were returned to the Dutch in 1679 and Tortola in 1688.

In 1690, the English captured St Kitts, taking control of the whole island, and again captured St Eustatius. Six years later they returned this island to the Dutch. In 1696, the French, once more at war with Spain, attacked and plundered Cartagena on the mainland of South America. By the Treaty of Ryswick, restoring the peace in 1697, Spain conceded the French claim to western Hispaniola, which the new owners called Saint Domingue.

In 1702, England and the Netherlands declared war on France and Spain. France recaptured its half of St Kitts in 1702. In 1703, an English fleet landed a force on the French colony of Guadeloupe but was unable to hold it when French reinforcements arrived from Martinique. In 1706, a French fleet captured the English colony of Nevis and attacked the English half of St Kitts. Shortly afterwards Nevis was abandoned. A truce was agreed in 1712 and peace was restored by the Treaty of Utrecht in the following year.

By the Act of Union of 1707, which united England and Scotland, the English colonies had become British. One of the spoils of war obtained by Britain under the Treaty of Utrecht was the Asiento, a contractual right for a British company to supply slaves to the Spanish colonies for 30 years. Also under this treaty, France ceded to Britain its half of St Kitts. Treaties between these European powers tended however to last only so long as both sides found them convenient. Britain and Spain were once more at war in 1718 and again in 1727.

Ownership of the islands of Dominica, St Lucia and St Vincent had long been in dispute between Britain and France but neither had been able to establish successful colonies. The French were eventually willing to concede that Dominica and St Vincent belonged to the Amerindian Caribs, but contended that St Lucia belonged to them. The British government, however, continued to claim that all three belonged to Britain.

In 1739, Britain again went to war against Spain. A British naval expedition captured but later withdrew from Porto Bello on the isthmus of Panama and bombarded Cartagena. Another attack was made on Cartagena in 1741. Guantanamo at the eastern end of the large Spanish island of Cuba was also attacked.

France and Britain declared war on each other in 1744. They made peace, by the Treaty of Aix-la-Chapelle, in 1748, in which they agreed to declare neutral and remove all their nationals from the islands of Dominica, St Lucia, St Vincent and Tobago. However, in 1755, France established a colony in St Lucia, which was one of the causes of the outbreak of war in the following year. In 1759 the British captured the French colonies of Guadeloupe and Martinique and in 1761 occupied Dominica. In that year Britain also declared war on Spain and in 1762 captured Havana, carrying off enormous quantities of booty.

Peace was again restored early in 1763 by the Treaty of Paris, which provided for the restoration to France of Guadeloupe and Martinique, but conceded British ownership of Canada which had been in dispute. The treaty confirmed French ownership of St Lucia and British ownership of Dominica, Grenada and the Grenadines, St Vincent and Tobago. The treaty also restored Havana to Spain in exchange for the ceding of Spanish Florida in North America to Britain. Having been victorious in that war, Britain had obtained by far the greater part of the spoils.

In 1778, a French expedition from Martinique captured Dominica and later that year the British captured St Lucia. In 1779 the French captured Grenada, Spain declared war against Britain and the British made an unsuccessful attack on St Vincent. In December 1780 war broke out between Britain and the Netherlands. In January 1781 the British captured the Dutch colonies of St Eustatius, Saba, St Martin and St Barthelemy. In February the Dutch colonies of Demerara and Essequibo on the mainland of South America also surrendered. Later that year the French captured Tobago. In November they captured St Eustatius and St Martin and, shortly afterwards, Saba and St Barthelemy, all of which they returned to their Dutch allies. They also recovered and returned Suriname.

The French gave some assistance to the British North American colonists who were then in rebellion against Britain. In January 1782, they captured St Kitts and Nevis, and shortly afterwards also took Montserrat. In May, of that year a Spanish fleet captured New Providence in the Bahamas. In April 1783, a British force recovered New Providence. That year the French seized the British colony in the Turks Islands.

In 1783, the Treaty of Versailles was concluded whereby St Lucia and Tobago were restored to France, and France restored St Kitts, Nevis, Montserrat, Grenada and the Grenadines, St Vincent and Dominica to Britain. Spain agreed to return to Britain the Bahama Islands which it had captured and to allow British log-cutters to work in an area in Spanish Central America bounded by the Belize and Hondo Rivers.

By the Convention of London in 1786 it was agreed that British nationals would be evacuated from the Mosquito Coast (of Spanish Honduras and Nicaragua) and that in return the British log-cutters' Belize settlement could be extended southwards to the Sibun River and include St Georges Cay (Cayo Casina) near the mouth of the Belize River. It was further agreed that, as this was Spanish territory, no form of government and no plantations of sugar, cocoa and other like articles would be established.

It would appear, however, that this agreement, which was resented by the British settlers, was not properly enforced. They had extended their operations well to the south of the Sibun River and a form of government was indeed in operation under a Superintendent appointed by the British government. After this officer was removed in 1790, the settlement was governed for the next six years by magistrates elected by the settlers.

The French Revolution in 1789, which abolished the monarchy and established a republic, was profoundly disturbing to the British ruling class. They were concerned that republicanism posed a threat to the monarchical form of government everywhere and were also apprehensive about its effects in the French Caribbean colonies, where struggles between royalists and republicans were breaking out. Such fears were greatly increased when the French King, Louis XVI, was sent to the guillotine in January 1793.

In Saint Domingue, the largest and most prosperous of the French Caribbean colonies, in addition to disagreements between white royalists and republicans, there was dissatisfaction among the large free coloured section of the population at the discrimination to which they had long been subjected, and there was unrest among the slaves. In 1790 an uprising of free Coloureds was suppressed, but in May 1791 the revolutionary government in Paris declared that all free men in the French empire, of whatever colour, were in all respects equal. Then, on 22 August, a formidable slave rebellion commenced, which spread rapidly throughout the colony.

By the beginning of 1793 relations between Britain and revolutionary France had reached a breaking point and, on 1 February 1793, France declared war on Britain and the Netherlands. In April a British force captured Tobago. In June a British fleet landed troops on Martinique but had to withdraw. The British government instructed Major-General Maitland, then Governor of Jamaica, to occupy St Domingue and, with the complicity of the royalist planters, take possession of the island for Britain. In September, a British expeditionary force invaded the island. Maitland was appointed Governor of the colony and, with the arrival of reinforcements in May, the British forces were initially able to occupy a considerable area.

In 1794, Britain captured Martinique and Guadeloupe, but in 1795 again lost Guadeloupe to a French revolutionary force and also lost St Lucia. In that same year there was an uprising in Grenada, led by the mulatto plantation owner Julien Fedon, who freed his own slaves and formed them and other slaves into an army. Apart from abolishing slavery on the island, Fedon's objective was to return Grenada to republican France and for several months he controlled the greater part of the island. However, following the arrival of British reinforcements, assisted by Spanish troops despatched to their aid from Trinidad, Fedon's army was defeated. There was also fighting between the French and British in St Vincent in 1795 and 1796.

By the Treaty of Basle in 1795, much to Britain's displeasure, Spain ceded eastern Hispaniola to France. War between Britain and Spain began in the following year. Over the next two years the British fared badly in St Domingue, defeated by an army of free Coloureds and Blacks led by Rigaud in the south and an army of liberated slaves commanded by Toussaint Louverture in the north. Yellow fever also took its toll. In April 1798, they withdrew from Port-au-Prince. In October, defeated by the rebel slave armies, the last British troops were evacuated.

In 1795, the so-called Batavian Republic, established in Holland under French patronage, declared war on Britain. A British force was sent against the Dutch colonies in South America in 1796 and, in April, the authorities in Essequibo, Demerara and Berbice surrendered. In August of the following year Suriname also capitulated.

In 1797, British forces occupied Spanish Trinidad. The British fleet then attacked Puerto Rico, but was beaten off. In 1798, a Spanish fleet unsuccessfully attacked the settlement in Belize, following which the British government, which had hitherto acknowledged that this was Spanish territory, claimed the area as British. In 1800 Britain took possession of the Dutch island of Curaçao and in 1801 of St Eustatius and Saba.

In 1801, the British government turned its attention to the Caribbean possessions in the Virgin Islands of the less powerful Scandinavian states, taking St Barthelemy from Sweden and St Thomas, St John and St Croix from Denmark. In 1802, by the Treaty of Amiens, peace between Britain, France, Spain and the Batavian Republic was agreed. Trinidad was ceded to Britain and Britain returned all the French, Dutch, Swedish and Danish colonies taken during the late war. Nothing further was said about Belize, which remained under British control.

By the following year Britain was again at war with France. Napoleon Bonaparte, effectively in charge of France, was in control of the Netherlands and had also embarked on a vain attempt to restore French control and slavery in Saint Domingue. Although Toussaint Louverture had been in command of the island for some years, he had claimed to be ruling on behalf of France. However, with the French invasion, a war of liberation by the former slaves commenced. This was terminated successfully under the leadership of Dessalines in 1804 with the defeat of the French and the establishment of an independent republic.

Meanwhile, in 1803, British forces had captured St Lucia, Tobago, Essequibo, Demerara and Berbice. In 1805 they captured Dominica. In 1807, Britain declared war on Denmark and again occupied St John and St Croix. In 1808, a Spanish force from Puerto Rico attacked Santo Domingo and in 1809, aided by the British, re-established Spanish control of the eastern part of Hispaniola. Also in 1809, a British force captured Martinique and a joint British-Portuguese force captured Cayenne. In January 1810, a British force took Guadeloupe and St Martin, Saba and St Eustatius.

In 1814, a defeated Napoleon was compelled to abdicate. By the Treaty of Paris Britain agreed to restore all the captured French colonies except St Lucia and Tobago, and France agreed to concede that the eastern part of Hispaniola was Spanish. The new black Republic of Haiti in western Hispaniola was ignored in the negotiations leading to the conclusion of this treaty, but was in no position to dispute the Spanish claim. The Netherlands ceded Essequibo, Demerara and Berbice to Britain but retained Suriname. The Treaty of Paris was confirmed at the Congress of Vienna in 1815, formally bringing the Napoleonic Wars to an end.

Britain had emerged as the dominant naval power and thereafter no further wars were fought between the European powers to effect exchanges of Caribbean territory. What were the factors that led these European states to a consensus that stability in this hitherto volatile region was desirable?

One factor may have been that there had been an increasing disposition on the part of the subject populations of the larger colonies in the Americas to opt for the alternative of self-rule. In 1781 a combined American and French force had led to the defeat of the British at Yorktown, effectively ending any prospect of Britain retaining control of her North American colonies and leading, in 1787, to the establishment of the United States of America. In 1804 France, then at war with Britain, had lost Saint Domingue to the rebel slaves and seen the establishment there of an independent black republic. Spain had had to reconcile herself to the independence of Venezuela in 1811 and the loss of New Grenada (including Colombia and Ecuador) in 1819.

Another consideration may have been the growing strength and influence in the region of a new power, the United States of America, determined to place a limit on further European penetration of the Americas. This had led ultimately to the promulgation by a US President in 1823 of the Monroe Doctrine which stated explicitly: 'that the American continents ... are henceforth not to be considered as subjects for future colonization by any European power' and that European interference in the Americas would be regarded as an unfriendly act.

A third factor may have been that the Caribbean islands had declined in importance as sources of wealth, to the point that it was no longer worth the trouble and expense of engaging in warfare to effect a redistribution of their ownership.

CHAPTER 3

Sugar and Slavery

Although Columbus had brought sugarcane plants to the West Indies from the Canary Islands, sugar production for export to Europe had not been developed on a significant scale in the Spanish colonies. Spanish monarchs may have refrained from encouraging sugar production in the Caribbean area because sugar was already being produced in Andalusia in southern Spain. The Portuguese, on the other hand, had developed sugar plantations on the island of São Tomé off the west coast of Africa and had brought with them to Brazil the technique developed there of producing good quality sugar.

In 1581, a Spanish king had become heir to the throne of Portugal and, until the Portuguese succession was restored in 1640, Portugal and the Portuguese colonies had been ruled by the Spanish sovereigns. During the greater part of this period the Netherlands had also been part of the Spanish empire and many Dutch settlers had gone to Brazil. There they had learned how to make good, marketable sugar. After Portugal ceased to be part of the Spanish monarch's domains, life for the Dutch settlers in Brazil became difficult. In the 1640s, they were being forced to leave the country.

In 1649 some of these exiles were allowed to settle in Barbados. Others were admitted to the French colonies. Some said that it was from these people and the slaves they had purchased from the Portuguese that the English and French colonists learned the technique of making good sugar. Others said that people went from Barbados to Brazil in the early 1640s to learn the technique. Before they had learned how to make good sugar, wrote Richard Ligon (who went to Barbados in 1647 and wrote in 1653), their sugars were 'so moist, and so full of molasses, and so ill cur'd, as they were hardly worth the bringing home for England'.[1]

In the English colonies sugar was first produced for shipment to England in Barbados and then in Antigua. It was not produced in Jamaica for this purpose until after the arrival of Thomas Modyford as Governor, in 1664. Modyford, who owned a sugar plantation in Barbados, is said to have brought 800 settlers from Barbados, many of whom had sugar-making experience.[2]

Although some large land grants were made to favoured individuals, the original colonisation plans for the eastern Caribbean and for Jamaica had been to populate these islands mainly with farmers who would work their own small farms, assisted perhaps by one or two indentured servants. In Jamaica, for example, the original land grants were of 30 and 35 acres. The settlers were expected to grow crops which could be sold profitably in Europe.

At first the principal exports had been tobacco and cotton, but in most colonies sugar soon proved to be by far the most profitable crop. The production of sugar required expensive milling machinery to express the juice from the canes and equipment for boiling and clarifying the juice. To justify such a large capital investment the producer had to be sure of a large supply of canes. But the canes have to be milled soon after they are cut or they lose their sugar content and fermentation sets in, and there were no railways or good roads in those days by which canes could be carried over long distances. The lands on which the canes were planted therefore had to adjoin the mill. This dictated the need for plantations rather than small farms. As the sugar plantations increased, land grants became bigger and many of the small farms were swallowed up.

Sugar plantations required a large labour force. As the Amerindians were extinct or reduced in numbers, labourers had to be recruited from outside (see Figure 3.1). Some labour was obtained from the British Isles as indentured servants. These were convicts sentenced to serve for a term in the colonies, Welsh and Irish rebels similarly sentenced, debtors sold into service by their creditors and others wishing to emigrate who sold themselves into service for the price of their passage. But they were not numerous enough to satisfy the needs of the sugar plantations. Also, they were unaccustomed to working in a hot climate and their indentures were temporary – from three to at most seven years.[3]

West Africa, which was closer to the Caribbean than Europe, was densely populated with people accustomed to agriculture in a similar climate, but the Africans had no desire to leave their homelands in search of employment. If they were to be recruited, it could only be done by force. The Europeans therefore revived slavery, a form of labour exploitation which, though still known on the Iberian peninsula at the time that Columbus made his first voyage to the Caribbean, had long ceased to exist in England.[4]

The rapid development of sugar production was accompanied by a dramatic increase in the populations of the sugar colonies and an alteration in their ethnic compositions. In Barbados there were 18,600 Whites and 6,400 African slaves in 1643; by 1724 there were 18,295 Whites and 55,206 African slaves. By 1812, four years after the slave trade had ended, the white population was down to 13,794 but the number of slaves had increased to 69,132 and there were 2,613 free persons of African or partly African descent. In Jamaica, where there had been 7,768 Whites and 9,704 African slaves in 1673, there were 7,648 Whites, 74,525 slaves and 865

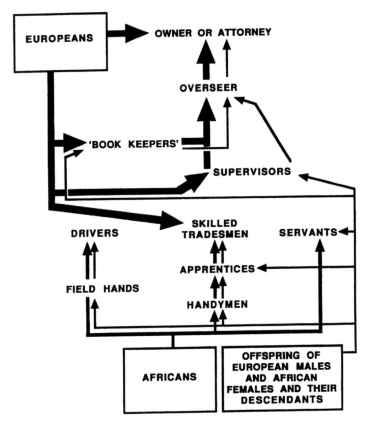

Figure 3.1 The sugar plantation – ethnic input and stratification

free persons of African or partly African descent by 1729. The story was similar in all the sugar colonies. This is illustrated in the population statistics (see Table 3.1).

Africans were enslaved not because they were black but because, being nearest to the plantations, they were cheaper to transport, were available in greater numbers and were accustomed to agricultural labour in a hot climate. But this does not mean that race and complexion were unimportant considerations. The slave trade and slavery involved inhuman cruelty and it was easier to justify such cruelty when it was employed against people who were so different in appearance to their oppressors that it could be alleged that they were a lower form of human life or not human at all. Such allegations were indeed made by the spokesmen for the slave traders and slave owners, while pointing out the economic advantages to be derived from enslaving Africans.[5]

18   FROM OCCUPATION TO INDEPENDENCE

Table 3.1 Populations to the End of the Slave Trade[6]

Country	Year	Whites	Free African & Coloured	Slaves
Barbados	1643	18,600		6,400
	1724	18,295		55,206
	1757	16,772		63,645
	1788	16,127	2,229	64,405
	1812	13,794	2,613	69,132
Antigua	1707	2,892		12,892
	1729	4,088		23,611
	1756	3,412		31,428
	1788	2,590	1,230	37,808
St Kitts	1707	1,416		2,861
	1720	2,740		7,321
	1729	3,677		14,663
	1756	2,713		21,891
	1788	1,192	1,908	20,435
Dominica	1763	1,718	500	5,872
	1780	1,066	543	12,713
	1812	1,525	2,988	21,728
Grenada	1700	251	53	525
	1788	996	1,115	23,926
St Vincent	1763	1,138		3,430
	1788	1,450	300	11,853
Jamaica	1673	7,768		9,504
	1729	7,648	865	74,525
	1774	12,737	4,093	192,787
	1801			307,094
	1809			323,714

The land required for a plantation could be obtained from the Crown at relatively little cost – a 'quit rent' of ½d per acre. A substantial capital investment was nevertheless required. Lord Vaughan estimated that in 1676 the cost of establishing a sugar plantation in Jamaica, with 1,000 acres of land, would be £5,000. In 1690 Sir Dalby Thomas estimated that a plantation in Barbados, with 100 acres in canes with 50 African slaves, seven white indentured servants, sugar works, equipment and livestock, would cost £5,625. In 1777, the planter historian Edward Long estimated the cost of establishing a plantation of 300 acres in Jamaica with 100 slaves, equipped to produce 100 hogsheads of sugar and 50 puncheons of rum, at £14,029, that of a plantation of 900 acres with 300 slaves, making 300 hogsheads of sugar and 130 puncheons of rum at £39,270.[7]

In several aspects a sugar plantation was a capitalist enterprise. Production was by the combined labour of a large number of workers brought together in the workplace, the product was not for consumption by the producers but was a commodity for sale, and the proceeds of sale of the product were appropriated not by those who produced it but by their employer. Where the sugar plantation differed from an ordinary capitalist enterprise was that, instead of purchasing the labour time of the worker, the owner purchased the worker himself and the incentive used to encourage work was not remuneration in the form of wages but the use of force, or fear that it would be used.

In the Bahama islands, unlike most of the other islands in the Caribbean area, the production of sugar for export was not undertaken. The plantations developed there initially concentrated on growing cotton. A boom in cotton production in the late eighteenth century was further stimulated when, in 1787, Nassau on New Providence was declared a free port for trade with the French and Spanish colonies. But the cotton boom was short-lived. A combination of soil exhaustion and depredations caused by the chenille and red bugs led to the abandonment of many plantations.

The collapse of the cotton plantation system by 1800 left slave owners with slaves whose labour they could no longer profitably exploit but for whom there were not many purchasers. This led to the increasing use of a system of so-called self-hire. Many slaves were turned out to find jobs for themselves, subject to the requirement that they pay over to their owners a percentage of their wages. As employment opportunities were scarce in the out-islands this led many slave owners to transfer their slaves to Nassau. Although the self-hire system was not unknown in other colonies, it was more prevalent in the Bahamas than elsewhere.[8]

Some Bahamian slave owners were able to sell their slaves in Trinidad and Demerara where, in the first three decades of the nineteenth century, the sugar planters were experiencing a shortage of labour. It has been estimated that between 1808 and 1825 more than 3,000 slaves were exported from the Bahamas to other colonies. One planter migrated with his slaves to Trinidad to establish his own plantation.[9]

CHAPTER 4

Slavery and Exploitation

Both the trade in slaves and the production of sugar were immensely profitable. But all the wealth derived from the slave trade and most of the wealth derived from the plantations was accumulated in Britain. Manufactures, firearms and intoxicating liquors were shipped out from Britain to be exchanged for Africans, who were then shipped to the sugar colonies. The same ship then returned to Britain with cargoes of sugar and rum (see Map 4.1). As Eric Williams has shown in his classic *Capitalism and Slavery*, this wealth transformed the ports of Bristol and Liverpool into thriving cities and financed much of the development consequent upon the industrial revolution.

At first the European slave traders obtained their human cargoes by raiding villages on the west coast of Africa. This practice was, however, soon abandoned when the traders found that they could obtain many more slaves by purchasing the prisoners captured in

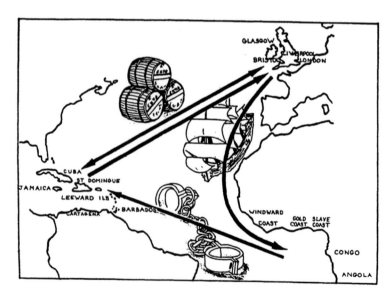

Map 4.1 The triangular trade (© Andrew Hart)

local wars. They then adopted the practice of making alliances with local rulers whom they armed and encouraged to make war on their neighbours. So notorious did this become that the English Prime Minister, William Pitt, felt obliged to condemn it. During a debate on the slave trade in Parliament in 1792, he referred to 'those dreadful enormities on that unhappy continent,' and said: 'I have no more doubt that they are British arms put into the hands of Africans, which promote universal war and desolation ...'[1]

The losses of life in the slave trade were enormous. In the wars to obtain captives for sale to the traders as many were killed as were captured alive. For the Atlantic crossing, which in the days of sailing ships could take months, the slaves were shackled in crowded, insanitary conditions in the holds of the slave ships and only brought up on deck for air and exercise in batches when the weather was fair. Between 1680 and 1700 the loss of life on ships of the Royal African Company was estimated at 23.4 per cent. Although mortality at sea decreased during the eighteenth century, a Privy Council enquiry in 1789 disclosed an average mortality rate of 12.5 per cent, with a further loss of 4.5 per cent between the arrival of the ships at their destinations and the sale of their cargoes.[2]

On the plantations the slaves went through a process known as 'seasoning'. This was to accustom them to the plantation routine and the use of tools and equipment with which they might not be familiar, to enable those suffering from melancholia as a result of their traumatic experience to recover their will to live, to curb any spirit of rebelliousness or resistance, and to accustom them to raising their own food on plots of land allotted to them for this purpose. Evidence presented to the same Privy Council enquiry disclosed that there was a further decrease by deaths during the seasoning period of 33 per cent.

Driven by frequent use of the whip in the fields, labour on the sugar plantations was onerous and exacting and the average life expectancy of the slaves was short. The slave trader John Newton, who on retiring from his seafaring career became an Anglican parson and an abolitionist, wrote:

> One thing which I cannot omit, which was told to me by the gentleman to whom my ship was consigned, at Antigua, in the year 1751, and who was himself a planter. He said, that calculations had been made, with all possible exactness, to determine which was the preferable, that is, the more saving method of managing slaves: 'whether, to appoint them moderate work, plenty of provision, and such treatment as might enable them to protract their lives to old age? Or,

> By rigorously straining their strength to the utmost, with little relaxation, hard fare, and hard usage, to wear them out before

they became useless and unable to do service, and then to buy new ones, to fill up their places?'

He further said, that these skilful calculations had determined in favour of the latter mode as much the cheaper; and that he could mention several estates in the island of Antigua, on which it was seldom known that a slave had lived above nine years.[3]

Giving evidence before a parliamentary committee in 1791, Henry Coor, a millwright who, with his jobbing gang of slaves, had serviced sugar plantations in four parishes in Jamaica for 15 years, said:

> It was more the object of the overseers to work the slaves out, and trust for supplies from Africa ... I have heard many overseers say, 'I have made my employer 20, 30 or 40 more hogsheads per year than any of my predecessors ever did; and though I have killed 30 or 40 Negroes per year more, yet the produce has been more than adequate to that loss.'[4]

More men than women were transported as slaves. Between 1673 and 1723 the Royal African Company brought 18,821 males and 11,910 females to Barbados and the ratios of the sexes imported into the other sugar colonies showed a similar bias. This disparity appears, however, to have been rectified by nature with the passage of time. In 1801 there were 34,324 female and 29,872 male slaves in the colony. In 1832 there were 43,738 females and 37,762 males, the respective percentages having remained at approximately 53.5 for females and 46.5 for males.[5]

On most sugar plantations field workers were divided into three gangs. The first gang was composed of those slaves, male and female, who were reckoned to be most capable of performing the heaviest tasks, such as digging cane holes and cutting cane. The second gang was composed of those performing less exacting but often still onerous tasks. The third gang, consisting mainly of children whose ages might range from five or six to twelve years and sometimes elderly slaves, performed the lightest tasks such as weeding, collecting grass for the livestock and carrying water for the first and second gangs.

Plantation owners did not however regard women as 'the gentler sex'. Many women were placed in the first gang, where it was not unusual for them to outnumber the men. On the Newton plantation in Barbados, for example, there were 87 females and 84 males in 1740 and these numbers had been increased to 128 females (62 women and 66 girls) and 81 males (36 men and 45 boys) in 1776; 51 of these women were in the first gang and 17 of the girls were in the second gang. On the Seawell plantation in 1803 there were 20 men and 34 women in the first gang.[6]

In Jamaica, where the numbers of male and female slaves were approximately equal in 1817, males exceeded females among those born in Africa, as was to be expected in view of importation policy, but females outnumbered males among those born in Jamaica. In the total slave population there were, by 1829, 96.4 males to every 100 females and by 1832 the number of males per 100 females had decreased further to 94.5. On the Irwin plantation in 1821, although the males (135) still outnumbered the females (124), females outnumbered males in the first and second gangs. There were 46 women and 37 men in the first gang and 23 and 16 women and men respectively in the second gang.[7]

There was no overall natural increase in the slave population of Jamaica or most of the other sugar colonies during slavery, where increases in the total numbers of slaves were attributable entirely to importations from Africa. A natural increase did, however, commence in Barbados after the enactment of a law in 1807 prohibiting further importations of slaves.[8] The planter historian and slave owner Edward Long expressed the view in 1774 that slaves would be more likely to reproduce in conditions where the labour they were required to perform was less exacting.[9]

Although there was at no time in Jamaica an overall natural increase in the slave population, there were areas in which, in the nineteenth century, natural increases occurred. Giving evidence before a select committee of Parliament in 1832, William Taylor, a manager of properties in Jamaica with 15 years' experience, stated that increases generally occurred on coffee plantations and livestock pens, where the labour was less intense, while decreases occurred on most sugar plantations. He attributed the heavy mortality on sugar plantions to cane hole digging, night work and the use of the whip.

Taylor, however, acknowledged that on sugar plantations in Vere there had been a natural increase. He thought that this was because the very fertile nature of the soil there considerably increased the possible number of 'ratoons' or regrowths without replanting, thereby reducing the amount of intensive labour required, and that the dryness of the soil meant that the slaves' feet were less likely to develop sores.[10]

The excess of deaths over births in the slave populations of the sugar colonies was remarkable. The total number of slaves imported into Jamaica is estimated to have been approximately one million, of which number some 200,000 were re-exported – a net absorption of approximately 800,000. During the period of slavery an unknown number of children were born to slave women. When slavery was abolished, the number of surviving slaves was found to be 311,070. At that date there may have been as many as 50,000 free men and women of African and partly African descent. This leaves well over 400,000 to be accounted for.[11]

The post-emancipation population statistics provide a revealing contrast to the previous period. No sooner had slavery ended than the populations of the British West Indian colonies began to increase. The increases recorded in Jamaica, are fairly typical of the rate of increase in the region.

Table 4.1 Post-Emancipation Populations (Jamaica)

1834	377,433	1861	441,264	1871	506,134
1881	580,804	1891	639,491	1911	831,383
1921	858,118	1943	1,237,063	1949	1,388,917
1960	1,609,814	1982	2,095,878	1991	2,435,800

CHAPTER 5

Resistance and Rebellion in the Seventeenth and Eighteenth Centuries

Although a majority of those enslaved may have felt that there was no alternative to adapting themselves to their situation, everywhere and always there were substantial minorities who were unwilling to do so. Resistance was offered in many ways. Minor resistance included inducement of abortions by some women to ensure that they did not bear children enslaved from birth, and illnesses induced by eating dirt and in other ways. Individual escapes were often attempted. Sometimes groups of slaves absconded temporarily, letting it be known, through a sympathetic intermediary, that they would return to their owner's service if promised less severe treatment or increased rations.[1]

Higher forms of resistance took the form of mass escapes, rebellion or conspiracy to rebel, and guerrilla warfare. The scope for these was of course greater in the larger colonies and those with mountainous hinterlands in which escaped slaves could take refuge. As might be expected, rebellions and guerrilla wars waged by escaped slaves were most numerous and extensive in Jamaica and in the Dutch colonies of Berbice and Demerara (subsequently amalgamated to form, with Essequibo, the colony of British Guiana). But even in Barbados, where there were no mountains, and in the smaller islands, many rebellions and conspiracies for rebellion occurred. That higher forms of resistance should have occurred throughout the region is remarkable.

Between 1657 and 1660 the Barbados militia was engaged in eradicating 'divers rebellious and runaway negroes'. A conspiracy in 1675 resulted in the leader Kofi ('Cuffee') and 51 others being sentenced to death: six were burned alive, eleven were beheaded and five awaiting trial took their own lives.[2]

After the expulsion of the Spaniards from Jamaica in 1660, slaves who had escaped from them before and during the fighting, resisted re-enslavement and established their own settlements. The leader of one of these settlements, whose name was Lubola but who was called Juan de Bolas by the English, made peace with them and accepted a grant of lands. Appointed a magistrate, he agreed to act against other settlements of escaped slaves, but was defeated and killed by the leader known as Juan de Serras.[3]

In 1673, in the parish of St Ann, 200 slaves, introduced by the English, escaped to the central mountains. In 1675 martial law was declared and 35 slaves were executed for conspiracy. In 1676, a minor rebellion was suppressed in St Mary, and in 1678, another rebellion was crushed at Caymanas in St Catherine. In 1683, a conspiracy involving 180 slaves in Vere was betrayed. In 1685, following a rebellion at Guanaboa Vale, St Catherine, 63 rebels formed a guerrilla band which was dispersed in 1686. Another guerrilla band was formed in the northeast in 1686.[4]

In 1687, a rebellion in Antigua was suppressed. One leader was burned alive, another had his leg cut off.[5]

In 1690, a formidable rebellion occurred at Suttons, Clarendon, in Jamaica involving 500 slaves. After failing in their attempt to hold the plantation, 150 survivors escaped with arms taken from the plantation and established themselves in the central mountains. In 1704, the Governor reported a 'small insurrection' of 30 slaves. Twelve rebels were killed, their leader was executed and the others were transported for sale off the island.[6]

In Barbados a paramilitary force, organised by Hammon, Ben and Sambo, was supressed soon after the revolt commenced in 1692. The leaders and 92 conspirators were executed. Four, sentenced to be castrated, died as a result of the operation and 14 died in prison. Six Irish indentured servants were said to have been involved in the conspiracy.[7]

Leading conspirators in Nevis in 1725 were executed. In Antigua conspiracies were frustrated in 1728 and 1737, 69 conspirators being executed, 58 chained to stakes and burned and 130 imprisoned. All 49 Whites on St John, Virgin Isles, were killed in a rebellion 1733.[8]

Settlements of escaped slaves in Jamaica provided a refuge for others. These 'Maroons', as they came to be called, often raided the plantations and became a serious problem. In 1728, the local militias, aided by troops supplied by the British government, embarked on a campaign to re-enslave or annihilate them. Known as the First Maroon War, this campaign lasted for ten years and ended in 1739 with peace treaties which conceded freedom and lands to the inhabitants of the two largest Maroon 'towns'. Thereafter, the Maroons ceased to provide a refuge for runaways and were used as mercenaries to aid in suppressing slave rebellions and rewarded for capturing runaway slaves.

In 1760 two major slave rebellions in Jamaica were suppressed. The first, led by Tacky in St Mary, was isolated and contained before the second, in Westmoreland, broke out. Tacky was killed by a Maroon, another leader was burned alive, two were starved to death suspended on a gallows, 400 were executed and 600 were transported for sale to log-cutters in the Bay of Honduras. A minor uprising at Manchioneal was also suppressed and there were abortive conspiracies in four other parishes. In St Mary in 1765 another uprising which had started prematurely was suppressed: 13 conspirators were executed and 33 transported.

A rebellion in Berbice in 1763 became a national liberation struggle. The Dutch were driven down the river to the coast. From Fort Nassau the rebel leader Kofi, signing the letter as 'Governor of Berbice', proposed to the Dutch Governor the partition of the colony, the southern half to belong to the Blacks. When internal dissensions developed the Dutch, in alliance with Kofi's opponents and with reinforcements from Holland, re-established their control. Rather than surrender Kofi committed suicide.[9]

Conspiracies were discovered and frustrated in Montserrat in 1768 and in St Kitts in 1770. In Tobago slave rebellions were suppressed in 1770, 1771 and 1774.[10]

A letter from the settlement of log-cutters on the Bay of Honduras to the Governor of Jamaica in 1765 reported that slaves belonging to a resident, lately arrived from Jamaica, had rebelled, killing their owner and several others and sinking a vessel on the New River. These men, the writer said, 'still continue in Rebellion and have entirely stopped the communication of the New River, altho there are not above ten or twelve men able to carry arms amongst them ...'

Another slave revolt occurred in this Central American colony in 1768. A memorial from a London merchant doing business there recorded:

Matters are come to this miserable pass, that Twenty three British Negroes, Armed, had gone off from the New River to the Spaniards, and many more were expected to follow them; so that business of every kind was at a dead Stand. All his Majesty's Subjects there being reduced to the ... necessity of protecting their Houses from being plundered, and themselves from being slain ... some of the Baymen have already quitted the Country, more of them are preparing to follow ...[11]

The most formidable slave rebellion in the Bay of Honduras settlement, which later came to be known as British Honduras, broke out in May 1773 on the Belize River. Captain Davey, the officer in charge of the force sent to suppress the uprising, reported to Admiral Rodney:

The Negroes ... had taken five settlements and murdered six White Men and were join'd by several others the whole about fifty armed with sixteen Musquets Cutlasses, etc. Our people attacked them ... but the Rebels after discharging their Pieces retired into the woods and it being late in the afternoon we could not pursue them.

Davey added that 14 slaves subsequently surrendered and that he was organising a militia of three parties of 40 men each to 'surround and destroy' the remainder who would provide 'an Asylum for all the Negroes who choose to run away from their masters'.

As the rebels were still at large on 8 August, Admiral Rodney sent the HMS *Garland* to the Bay, but with no greater success. In October, the Admiral was informed that 19 surviving rebels were endeavouring to reach the Spaniards. Eleven of them did complete the journey of about 100 miles to Rio Hondo, where the Spanish commandant Bacalar gave them refuge and refused to return them. Escaping British slaves were always freed by the Spaniards on professing conversion to the Roman Catholic Church.[12]

In 1776 an uprising in Westmoreland, Jamaica, was suppressed and 'Thirty of the ring-leaders were executed.'[13] By 1785 escaped slaves in the mountainous island of Dominica, known as 'Negres Marons', had established so many free settlements that they had become a serious threat to the plantation owners and the government in many areas.

One of the most formidable rebel leaders was Balla. Maroons from Balla's camp plundered the Rosalie plantation, which they held for two days before withdrawing. Raids on other plantations were carried out by different Maroon bands. To suppress the Maroons the Assembly resolved to establish a 500-strong military force. The campaign against them continued for several months in the latter part of 1785 and the early part of 1786, during which time most but not all of these rebel settlements were dispersed. The leaders of two of the settlements, Cicero and Balla, were captured and sentenced to die publicly on a gibbet. Balla took a week to die.

On 16 April 1786, Governor John Orde reported to the British Secretary of State that:

> good fortune has given us possession of the principal Runaway Chief, Balla, many of his followers are killed and taken, many have surrendered and the rest are greatly dispersed and distressed.

He reported that Balla met his death defiantly, bidding his five-year-old son to remember that 'the Beckeys or White Man had killed his father'.[14]

On 20 January 1791, a major slave rebellion commenced at Grand Bay in Dominica, under the leadership of Louis Polinaire, a free mulatto from Martinique. Polinaire was believed to have been inspired by the revolution that had broken out in France, but the claims put forward by the rebels were specific and unique. They demanded more free days on which they could work for themselves in addition to their traditional half-day Saturdays and Sundays.

The rebellion was suppressed and Polinaire, his whereabouts betrayed by a Carib, was captured and placed on trial. He was found guilty by a jury of French and English residents and on 7 March 1791 the macabre sentence – that he be disembowelled and have his body cut into four quarters – was carried out.[15]

In 1795 Julian Fedon, a mulatto plantation owner in Grenada, freed his own slaves and organised an army, consisting of pro-French residents and the freed slaves, to drive the British out of Grenada. Other slaves joined the rebellion. After holding most of the island for some months, probably with the intention of returning it to French control, Fedon was defeated when British reinforcements arrived.[16]

There had been hostilities between the 'Black Caribs' of St Vincent and the British, which had lasted for five months and had ended with a treaty in 1773 reserving part of the island for Carib settlement. These Black Caribs were descendants of Amerindian Caribs and African slaves shipwrecked in 1675 and others who had escaped from neighbouring islands. In 1795, hostilities recommenced. Their leader Chatoyer was killed and the 5,080 survivors were removed to the Bay of Honduras.[17]

In August 1795, an attack was made on the Trelawny Town Maroons, one of the five free communities in Jamaica. These hostilities, known as the Second Maroon War, ended five months later when the undefeated Maroons signed a peace treaty. Having laid down their arms they were then, in violation of the treaty, deported to New Brunswick, Canada and thence to the settlement for former slaves in Sierra Leone. In 1798 a group of escaped slaves, established in the former territory of the Trelawny Maroons, was discovered and dispersed.[18]

Where freedom fighters successfully conducted guerrilla warfare, as in the case of the First Maroon War in Jamaica and the Maroon wars in Suriname, these were partial victories, achieving freedom for only a small minority of those enslaved at the time. The numerous other conspiracies and rebellions that took place throughout the Caribbean area in the seventeenth and eighteenth centuries all ended in defeat. But these struggles were nevertheless significant in that they kept the torch of liberty burning in the hearts of oppressed men and women and demonstrated their determination to be free.

Had so many of the enslaved not fought for their freedom, the voices of those who condemned the slave trade and slavery would have been heard to less effect. The slave traders and slave owners who were profiting from the discomforture of their fellow human beings would have been able to assert, with some degree of plausibility, that those who it was alleged were suffering the indignities and tribulations of enslavement were not dissatisfied with their situation.

CHAPTER 6

British Abolitionists

At the beginning of the nineteenth century momentous events were unfolding in the Caribbean. What had commenced in 1791 as yet another slave rebellion, in the western part of the French colony of Saint Domingue, had escalated into a war of national liberation. This came to a victorious end when, in 1804, the armed slaves, under the leadership of Dessalines, defeated and expelled the French and proclaimed the establishment of an independent republic.[1]

Meanwhile, in Britain, a movement advocating the abolition of the slave trade had been steadily gaining support. The Abolition Society had been formed in 1787 by a committee of eleven men, nine of them Quakers. They all disapproved of slavery but, for tactical reasons, decided to confine the society's objective to obtaining legislation by Parliament making trading in slaves illegal. At their inaugural meeting only one of their number, Granville Sharp, had advocated that they should also call for the abolition of slavery.[2]

Not surprisingly, those with a direct interest in the slave trade were strongly opposed to slave trading being declared illegal, but the reactions of the owners of sugar plantations in the old-established sugar colonies and the members of their parliamentary lobby was more equivocal. On the one hand, they would have liked the importation of slaves to continue. On the other, they saw in the abolition of the slave trade the possibility of restricting the development of competitors in Trinidad, Demerara, Berbice and Essequibo, colonies recently acquired by Britain from Spain and Holland.

In Trinidad, occupied by Britain in 1797 and formally ceded in 1802, there had been little sugar production under the Spaniards although the soil and climate there were ideal. Sugar produced on the plantations developed there after the British occupation would have entered the British market with the same preferential customs duties as were payable on sugar produced in the older colonies. The same applied in the case of the Dutch colonies of Berbice, Demerara and Essequibo, occupied by British forces in 1804, where there was ample opportunity for the expansion of sugar production. Greater quantities of sugar entering the British market could result in a reduction of the prices paid for sugar.

On balance, sugar producers in the older colonies concluded that abolition of the slave trade might be to their advantage, both as regards their sales in Britain and also in terms of their re-exports to the continental market. It would prevent potential competitors in Trinidad and the Guianas from acquiring the labourers they needed. Also, if Spain and Portugal could be persuaded to abandon the slave trade, this would slow down the rate of expansion of the sugar industry in Cuba, the rapid development of which had commenced only in the last two decades of the eighteenth century, and limit the quantity of sugar produced in Brazil.

These are the factors that explain the support of some of the plantation owners in the British Parliament for the legislation enacted in 1807 prohibiting importation of slaves into the British colonies and the legislation in 1811 making participation by a British subject in the slave trade a criminal offence. It also explains in part the pressure brought to bear on Spain and Portugal by Britain to follow the British example.[3]

There had always been individuals in Britain who, on humanitarian grounds, had been opposed to slavery as well as the slave trade. However, prior to the remarkable industrialisation which occurred in Britain in the closing decades of the eighteenth and early in the nineteenth century, such people had lacked the financial resources to promote the cause of abolition on a scale that could compete with the pro-slavery propaganda of the slave trading and slavery interests.

The industrial revolution, which transformed Britain from a society in which wealth was shared between the landed aristocracy and the merchant class to one in which wealth was also being acquired by a new class of factory owners and investors who financed industrial development, gave rise to liberal ideas. Spokesmen for this new class advocated freedom of movement from the countryside to the towns, the unrestricted right of employers to agree wages with their employees without state or guild regulation, social mobility irrespective of birth and other so-called 'bourgeois freedoms'.

Members of this new industrial bourgeoisie were opposed to what they regarded as fetters on the development of capitalism which had been inherited from feudal times – restrictions on movement from one place of residence to another, price and wage fixing legislation, monopolies and a rigid class structure which inhibited social mobility. They also resented the exclusion of their representatives from participation in the law making institutions. Prior to the Reform Act of 1832, industrial cities such as Manchester had no representation in Parliament.

Because slavery was a system that prevented the movement of labour in search of employment and excluded the possibility of contractual relations between individual employees and their employers, many members of this new class were ideologically opposed to it. They also had a practical reason for their opposition to slavery. As slaves did not receive wages, their purchasing power was limited or non-existent and this was an impediment to the expansion of the market for manufactured goods. Members of this class were therefore prepared to finance campaigns for the abolition of the slave trade and slavery. This altered the balance of forces, enabling opponents of slavery to compete with the propaganda of their adversaries on equal terms.

In 1823 an organisation was formed to promote legislation for the abolition of slavery. But because many leading British abolitionists were property owners – Thomas Fowell Buxton was the owner of a brewery and William Wilberforce was a banker – they did not want abolition to be accompanied by social upheavals that would endanger lives and property. They therefore did not wish the slaves to participate in the abolition process as had occurred in Haiti, where the slaves themselves had brought their enslavement to an end. Although the organisation was popularly known as the Anti-Slavery Society, its formal name was 'The Society for the Mitigation and Gradual Abolition of Slavery'.

As its name implied, the Society envisaged a very gradual programme. This was explained in the House of Commons by Buxton in May 1823. He proposed that all parties should agree on a date after which all children born would be born free. Those who were already alive on that date were to remain slaves for their natural lives unless freed individually. They were, however, to have the right to purchase their freedom, or have it purchased for them, at their market value. This right of purchase, which did not exist in the British colonies, was in accordance with Spanish and Portuguese law and practice.[4]

This proposal, gradual as it was, was withdrawn by Buxton when the government agreed to sponsor a resolution accepting in principle the desirability of the abolition of slavery. The resolution, introduced on behalf of the government by George Canning and approved unanimously by Parliament, was as follows:

> That it is expedient to adopt effectual and decisive measures for ameliorating the condition of the slave population of his Majesty's colonies.

> That through a determined and persevering, but at the same time judicious and temperate inforcement of such measures, this House looks forward to a progressive improvement in the character of the slave population such as may prepare them for a participation in those civil rights and privileges which are enjoyed by other classes of his Majesty's subjects.

That this House is anxious for the accomplishment of this
purpose at the earliest period that shall be compatible with the
well-being of the slaves themselves, with the safety of the
colonies, and with a fair and equitable consideration of the
interests of private property.[5]

In presenting this resolution Canning argued against early
emancipation and no timetable for abolition was suggested. How
many years would have elapsed before the conditions imposed
would have been considered to have been fulfilled is a matter for
speculation. Buxton's gradual plan would have taken at least 50
years for its completion. Canning's more nebulous formula could
have taken even longer.

And yet in 1833, a mere ten years later, legislation providing for
the abolition of slavery was approved by Parliament.[6] Clearly
something must have been happening to disturb the complacency
of the British abolitionists and bring about a remarkable change
of mind on the part of the legislators. This will be discussed in the
next chapter.

CHAPTER 7

Nineteenth-Century Slave Rebellions and Emancipation

In 1795 the British government set about the establishment of several black West India Regiments under the command of white officers, consisting mainly of slaves pressed into military service. The regiment stationed at Cabrits in Dominica at the beginning of the nineteenth century, consisting of 500 men, was the 8th West India Regiment. Although these soldiers were slaves, they were supposed to receive a regular soldier's allowance, but payment of this was irregular. Another cause of complaint was that the Governor made use of these soldiers as labourers on his privately owned plantation.

In April 1802, members of the regiment in Dominica rose in rebellion, taking control of Fort Shirley and the surrounding hills. Marines were landed from a British warship and the rebellion was suppressed, although some of the rebels escaped and took refuge with Maroons who still maintained free settlements in the mountains.[1]

Many of the Africans taken from ships illegally trading in slaves which had been intercepted by the British Navy were recruited into the British West India Regiments. In 1808 a mutiny by slaves described as 'Coromantins' and 'Chambas', who had been pressed into service in the West India Regiment stationed at Fort Augusta in Jamaica, was suppressed. Two of the white officers and 15 of the mutineers were killed.[2] In 1816, there were fears of mutiny among Africans who had been similarly recruited for the 2nd West India Regiment stationed in the Bahamas.[3]

In Dominica, unlike Jamaica and Suriname, there had been no treaty of peace with the Maroons, some of whom had avoided capture and continued to maintain their illegal and precarious freedom in the mountains. In 1810 the Assembly noted that Maroon activity was again on the increase in the parishes of St Joseph and St Peter and that there was a settlement of 20 huts in St Patrick. When this was attacked the huts were burned by the escaping Maroons.

In July 1812, there was a rebellion involving over 75 slaves on Castle Bruce plantation and the rebels escaped to the woods. The total number of Maroons on Dominica at this time was estimated to be about 800. A member of one of their several settlements was identified as Jacko, who had been a rebel leader 40 years earlier. In 1812, Governor George Ainslie issued a proclamation offering a free pardon to those Maroons who would surrender. In the event however, either because they mistrusted the offer or because there had been no promise of freedom, the offer was not accepted.

Intense military action was pursued against the Maroons in Dominica over the next two years. By the end of 1814 many had been killed or captured and there were many executions. Eleven of those executed were decapitated. Some who had surrendered were pardoned and returned to slavery with their former owners. 'Marronage' in Dominica was thus brought to an end.[4]

While the participants in the mutinies after the turn of the century, and also those participating in the formidable conspiracy among Ibo slaves in St Elizabeth, Jamaica, in 1815 were Africans, almost all the principal organisers of the subsequent rebellions and conspiracies in the region had not been born in Africa but were creoles, born into slavery in the West Indian colonies.

The slave rebellions that occurred in the British colonies in the nineteenth century, following as they did in the wake of the Haitian revolution, had a decisive effect on the movement for the abolition of slavery. But a distinguishing feature of these rebellions and conspiracies was that the principal objective of the organisers was to achieve, within their respective countries, the abolition of slavery and the elevation of the slaves to the status of wage earners or independent farmers. Severance of the colonial relationship with Britain was not one of their demands.

Of all these colonies, Barbados was topographically the most unsuitable for rebellion. In their report on the events that occurred there in 1816, the African Institute, a pro-abolition organisation in Britain, emphasised this:

> there are no mountains, no fastnesses, no forest. European foot and even horse, can traverse it in all directions.[5]

Yet, despite these difficulties, some 5,000 slaves participated in what proved to be a major rebellion. Only one African, Bussa, was among the leaders. The other leading rebels – King Wilshire, Dick Bailey, Johnny and other men, and Nancy Grigg – were all creoles.

The rebellion was of course suppressed. According to the Governor's report, about 50 slaves were killed in action, 144 were executed under martial law, 70 were sentenced to death and 123 to transportation. Other estimates put the casualties of the rebels much higher. The commander of the Christ Church parish militia stated that his men alone had killed 40 rebels in two days.[6]

In 1823 there was a rebellion in Demerara involving some 14,000 slaves. The principal leaders were Jack Gladstone, Telemachus and Quamina. The rebellion was suppressed and the leaders were captured. Also imprisoned was the Reverend John Smith, a white missionary opponent of slavery who was falsely accused of inciting the slaves to rebellion. To save his own life, Gladstone gave perjured evidence against Smith. Telemachus and Quamina, who refused to do so, were executed. When the missionary died in prison, his ill-treatment occasioned widespread condemnation. Because of this the rebellion received far more attention in Britain than would have been the case if the only persons to lose their lives had been rebel slaves.[7]

In 1823 a conspiracy was discovered in the central Jamaican parish of St George (later divided between St Mary and Portland), resulting in the hanging of six and the transportation of eight of the alleged conspirators. In the following year, in the far western parish of Hanover, the discovery of a conspiracy led to the hanging of six and the transportation and flogging of others. In the east of the island four members of a rebel band were hanged.

At the end of December 1831 the Emancipation Rebellion, the best organised and most significant of all the many slave rebellions that occurred in the region, commenced in western Jamaica. This was led by Sam Sharp and involved an estimated 20,000 slaves. It was suppressed, but the last embers were not extinguished until April of the following year: 214 rebels were killed in action and some 750 slaves and 14 free blacks were convicted, most being sentenced to death. Others were sentenced to receive from 200 to 500 lashes of the whip. There was also unrest in other areas. At the eastern end of the island three rebels were sentenced to have their heads cut off and exhibited.

Sharp's plan was for an initial strike of the slaves on the various plantations who would refuse to do any more work unless their owners would agree to pay them wages. Only in the event of the latters' refusal to do so were the slaves exhorted to fight for their freedom. Sharp's agents, among whom was a free black man, spread the word that it had already been decided in England that the slaves were to be freed and that the local Whites were delaying the implementation of the decision.

Whether Sharp really believed this it is difficult to say. He was literate and very intelligent and had information about the abolitionist movement in Britain through the Baptist missionaries and abolitionist literature. It is possible that his encouragement and dissemination of this already widespread belief was a means of broadening support for his plan.[8]

Although the Emancipation Rebellion in Jamaica was suppressed, the post-rebellion atmosphere among the slaves was such that things would never be the same again. The Methodist Minister Henry Bleby, a contemporary of these events, observed the manner in which many of the convicted rebels faced their execution:

The undaunted bravery and fortitude with which many of the insurgents met their fate formed a very remarkable feature of the transactions of the period, and strikingly indicated the difficulty attendant upon the maintenance of slavery, now that the spirit of freedom had gone abroad, and many of the Negroes had learned to prefer death to bondage.

I have seen many led out to die, who were as calm and undismayed in walking to the scaffold as if they had been proceeding to their daily toil. There was nothing that had the appearance of bravado; nor was there aught like effort to get up a scene, or make a display of heroism; yet the eye was undimmed; not a lip trembled; no muscle of the face could be seen to quiver, but, with dignified bearing of men untroubled with misgivings as to the justice of their cause, they yielded themselves to their doom.

In custody awaiting execution in the gaol at Montego Bay, Sharp was interviewed by Bleby, to whom he made his famous statement: 'I would rather die on yonder gallows than live in slavery!' He faced his execution with dignity on 23 May 1832.[9]

There can be no doubt that it was the cumulative effect of the nineteenth-century slave rebellions and conspiracies in the region, particularly the rebellions in Barbados in 1816, in Demerara in 1823 and, above all, the rebellion in Jamaica in 1831–32, that forced both the British abolitionists and the British government to revise their approach to the issue of the abolition of slavery. In 1833 the British Parliament enacted legislation which formally brought slavery to an end throughout the British Empire on 1 August 1834.[10]

The 1833 legislation converted the slaves into so-called 'apprentices'. Those who were engaged in agriculture (the so-called 'praedials') were required to work for their former owners free of charge for 40.5 hours per week for six years. Those engaged in other types of work were similarly bound for four years. If required to work after their 40.5 hours of free labour, they were to be paid for their services at rates of pay to be agreed with their employers. Local legislatures were free to shorten the period of the apprenticeship.

The slave owners in Antigua saw no merit in the apprenticeship scheme. They reckoned that, on that small and fully developed island, their slaves would have no alternative but to seek employment with their former owners. The Antigua Assembly accordingly decided not to introduce apprenticeship but to proceed to complete emancipation on 1 August 1834. A similar motion in Montserrat was lost on the casting vote of the Speaker.

In the other colonies the local Assemblies accepted the scheme, but because of the widspread resistance of the apprentices it proved unworkable. In St Kitts, in 1834, many apprentices rose in rebellion. The British government advised the local Assemblies to shorten the period. This they proceeded to do, enacting legislation terminating the apprenticeship as of 1 August 1838.

Bleby gave an assessment of the significance for the abolition of slavery of the rebellion that had occurred in Jamaica:

> The revolt failed of accomplishing the immediate purpose of its author, yet by it a further wound was dealt to slavery, which accelerated its destruction; for it demonstrated to the imperial legislature that among the Negroes themselves the spirit of freedom had been so widely diffused, as to render it most perilous to postpone the settlement of the most important question of emancipation to a later period.
>
> The evidence taken before the Committee of the two Houses of Parliament made it manifest, that if the abolition of slavery were not speedily effected by the peaceable method of legislative enactment, the slaves would assuredly take the matter into their own hands, and bring their bondage to a violent and bloody termination.[11]

Referring to the abolitionists' plans for termination of slavery, an Army officer engaged in the suppression of the rebellion arrived at much the same conclusion from a different perspective:

> It will not be surprising that so propitious a circumstance as the late rebellion should be seized with avidity for their furtherance and immediate accomplishment. A bill was brought into Parliament ... by which it was enacted that 'all slavery should cease throughout the British dominions on the first of August 1834'.[12]

Bleby and Senior made reference only to the rebellion in Jamaica and may not have been aware of the full extent or effect on public opinion in Britain of what had occurred elsewhere. While the Emancipation Rebellion in Jamaica was the final and decisive event, the nineteenth-century rebellions and conspiracies in the region as a whole undoubtedly had a cumulative effect on British policy. These rebellions and conspiracies gave the issue of abolition an urgency which it would not have had, had they not occurred. Slavery was abolished by parliamentary legislation, but it was the rebellious slaves who expedited the process and dictated the necessity for emancipation in accordance with a precise timetable.

CHAPTER 8

Restricted Acquisition of Land

As Karl Marx pointed out, important social reorganisations in history are preceded and accompanied by conflicts between different social strata or classes. He called this the 'class struggle'. Sometimes such social conflicts are resolved by the total victory of one class over another; sometimes there is a compromise resolution.

The abolition of slavery is a good illustration. It was preceded and accompanied by a conflict between slave owners and slaves. In the case of the Haitian Revolution the dominated class, the slaves, not only forcibly abolished slavery but also expelled the slave owners, expropriated their property and took control of the state.

In the case of the abolition of slavery in the British colonies the conflict was also resolved by the abolition of slavery, but the ownership of property (other than property in human beings) remained as it had been before, as did the control of the state. Although the slaves, by their revolutionary activity, had made abolition unavoidable and expedited the process, abolition was effected by legislation which left the ownership of land and the control of the state in the same hands as before. As the former slave owners remained dominant, the state concerned itself with the task of ensuring that the plantations remained profitable.

Measures were adopted to ensure that the plantations continued to have at their disposal an adequate supply of labour, albeit wage labour rather than slave labour. One of the ways in which this was done was to discourage the former slaves from leaving the plantations by making it as difficult as possible from them to acquire lands which they could farm for themselves.

As early as 1834, foreseeing the possibility that when their apprenticeship ended workers might acquire land and aware that in Jamaica there were extensive unused lands owned by the government, the Governor of Jamaica warned the Assembly:

> With our present prospects, I think it very injurious that these tracts should remain without owners, as I feel assured that a vast number of apprentices as they get liberated by purchase, or become finally free in 1840 will retire to these tracts, as squatters, in preference to paying rent for land on the Estates on which they have heretofore lived.[1]

The Secretary of State for the Colonies was equally alive to this possibility. He was aware that, in addition to potential squatters, there would be former slaves who, by selling some of the food crops and livestock raised on the provision grounds that had been allotted to them during slavery to enable them to feed themselves, had accumulated savings which would enable them to buy land. In a despatch sent to Colonial Governors in November 1836 he therefore advised that:

> it will be necessary to prevent the occupation of any Crown lands by persons not possessing a proprietory title to them, and to fix such a price upon all Crown lands as may place them out of the reach of persons without capital.[2]

In British Guiana this policy was implemented by setting a high minimum price on the sale of Crown lands, thus placing them beyond the means of the recently emancipated slaves.[3] In Trinidad, when slavery was abolished, there were still over one million acres of undeveloped Crown lands. The policy adopted there to prevent the former slaves from acquiring land was to fix the minimum quantity of Crown land that could be acquired by purchase at 340 acres. This was later increased to 680 acres.[4]

In the area adjoining the Bay of Honduras much land was available and, although the area had not yet been formally claimed by Britain, it had since 1817 been the practice to make free land grants to British settlers. After the abolition of slavery the Colonial Office gave instructions that lands should be sold because the gratuitous granting of land discouraged 'labour for wages'. Presumably the payments required were beyond the means of the recently emancipated slaves. As Nigel Boland records: 'This strategy to keep Crown land away from the former slaves was successful as no such land was sold in the period up to 1855 and, by 1868, the total amount of Crown land sold was said to be "utterly insignificant".'[5]

In the late 1820s the amount of plantation land available for sale or lease had increased. This was associated with the decreasing profitability of sugar production. Within five years of the end of the Napoleonic Wars in 1815, which had considerably boosted sugar prices, prices paid for sugar exported to Britain had started on a downward slide, which continued throughout the nineteenth century.[6]

The situation was particularly acute in Jamaica where, in 1832, almost one fifth of all plantations were in receivership or had been possessed by mortgagees. Although, initially, sales and foreclosures did not involve the break-up of plantations into smallholdings, this was no longer always the case by the end of that decade.

The British government may have expected that the compensation money, awarded to slave owners for the loss of their slaves, would enable the plantations to make the transition to the payment of wages; but in the event, much of this money remained in Britain in the hands of mortgagees and other creditors. In the case of Jamaica 15 per cent of the compensation money was paid directly to 23 British merchant firms with whom the plantation owners had maintained running accounts. Many of these merchants, uncertain of the consequences of abolition, were reluctant to renew credit arrangements with the plantation owners.[7]

In 1846 Parliament enacted the Sugar Duties Act, the effect of which was to accelerate the abandonment of sugar production and the availability of land for sale. Much of the former prosperity of the sugar plantations had been dependent on the fact that sugar produced in the British West Indian colonies had entered the British market on payment of considerably lower customs duties than sugar imported from other sources. The Sugar Duties Act, inspired by Britain's adoption of free trade policies, progressively reduced this duty preference from 1848 until it was abolished in 1852. Representations by the plantation lobby secured a postponement of the final stage of the duty equalisation until 1854, but thereafter the same duties were payable on sugars from whatever their source.

Although the crisis within the sugar industry resulted in some of the less efficient plantations being taken over by more efficient ones and some amalgamations did occur, even the most efficient planters were understandably hesitant to expand at this time. It therefore became increasingly difficult to sell plantations as going concerns and many landowners, forced to abandon sugar production, found that they could only dispose of their land by dividing it up and offering it for sale in small plots.

Another factor facilitating the sale and purchase of land in the post-emancipation period was that some slaves, albeit a minority, had been able to save some money. On most plantations plots had been allocated to slaves from the cultivation of which they had been required to raise their own food. Despite the deprivations involved, industrious slaves had been able to raise crops and small stock for sale. Money thus earned was used to purchase or lease land. In some colonies the nonconformist churches organised land settlement schemes for their members.

Despite all the difficulties, many former slaves did acquire smallholdings. One way to acquire land was to 'squat' on undeveloped Crown land owned by the state. Gisela Eisner has estimated that by 1846 the total number of illegal squatters in Jamaica was 10,000 or more. But it would seem that more holdings were acquired by purchase than by squatting. According to Thomas Holt, the total number of freeholds 'settled and legally registered' by 1845 was 20,724.[8]

In Jamaica the number of freehold properties of under 40 acres assessed for taxes rose from 2,014 to 7,818 in the first two years following emancipation. The nonconformist churches purchased land which they sold to their members. In 1845 the Baptist missionary William Knibb reported that the 1844 census showed 'full nineteen thousand persons, formerly slaves, who had purchased land on which they were erecting their own cottages'.

According to Lord Olivier:

> The original exodus from the sugar estates created populous settlements in the Darliston Mountains of Westmoreland and the adjoining district of St Elizabeth, in the southern uplands of Manchester, in the mountains of Upper Clarendon, of St Catherine and of the adjacent part of St Andrew, in the Port Royal Mountains, the Yallahs Valley and the hills adjoining and dividing the copious rivers of St Thomas, in parts of St Ann's, most extensively in the Dry Harbour Mountains ... and in some of the less accessible but very fertile interior parts of St James and [in] ... Hanover.[9]

In the period following the abolition of slavery it is probable that some of the former slaves wished to leave the vicinity of the plantations on which they had suffered the oppression and indignity of enslavement. Such individuals may therefore have found the idea of establishing themselves on remote Crown lands attractive, despite the formidable task of clearing and cultivating undeveloped mountain land. Others, wishing to distance themselves from the plantations, may have migrated to the towns in search of employment.

It is, however, unlikely that a majority of the former slaves who remained in the rural areas wished to establish themselves on holdings far removed from the plantations. If they could do so, they wished to achieve some independence by acquiring land on which they could build their homes and grow crops. But because of the small size of the holdings that they were able to acquire, they needed to supplement their incomes by part-time employment.

Those former slaves who remained in the rural areas but could not acquire land were, of course, wholly dependent on wage labour, but most of those who did acquire land were willing to work part-time on the plantations. What ensued during the post-emancipation period was a struggle between the plantation owners and their full-time or part-time employees over the rates of pay. Still convinced that the prosperity of the plantation owners was essential to the prosperity of the colonies, both the British and Colonial governments turned their attention to ensuring that the labour of the former slaves would be available to the planters as cheaply as possible.

In Trinidad the official policy of restricting access to land was modified in the late 1840s. The Governor, Lord Harris, decided in 1847 to regularise the squatting that had occurred by a proclamation that all squatters who had been in possession of land since 1838 could purchase their holdings at six shillings per acre and that those whose occupation was more recent could purchase theirs at £1 per acre. Squatters who failed to take advantage of these facilites were to be liable to dispossession.

Only 295 persons took advantage of the offer but there were so many squatters that there was little or nothing that the government could do about it. In 1869 the policy of restricting access to Crown lands by purchase was finally abandoned with the enactment of an Ordinance authorising sale of parcels of land of not less than 5 acres at £1 per acre.[10]

In the region as a whole a policy of encouraging the development of a peasantry was not adopted and there was no recognition of the fact that such a policy would be economically advantageous and make for social stability until it was recommended in the report of the Royal Commission of 1897.[11] Significantly, this policy was recommended only after an alternative supply of cheap labour had been found in the importation of indentured labourers from India.

CHAPTER 9

Worker–Employer Relations after Abolition

During the apprenticeship period plantation owners were required to allow the apprentices to occupy the huts and cultivate the provision grounds that had been allocated to them as slaves, but wages for time worked in excess of the 40.5 hours' free labour they were required to give were a matter for negotiation. In Jamaica, employers offered different rates of pay for work-days of different lengths of time, ranging from 8 to 10 hours. Pay varied from one shilling to 1s 8d, the rate most commonly paid being 1s 6d per day.[1] After total emancipation in 1838, most plantation owners tried to reduce wages, either by lowering the daily rate or by charging a rent for the huts and/or provision grounds on their land. This led to disputes between workers and employers.

Several factors have to be taken into account in assessing the relative bargaining power of the workers and the employers. The acquisition of land by many former slaves and the migration of others to the towns reduced the number of workers available to the plantations, thereby strengthening the bargaining power of those who remained. But the law favoured the employers. They had the right to evict, from their huts and provision grounds, workers who would not give the number of days' work required of them or accept the terms offered. Governments were concerned to assist the plantations to prosper by keeping the level of wages as low as possible and enacted legislation to prevent the workers from engaging in strikes and forming organisations to bargain for increased wages. Despite this, workers did go on strike.

The first Masters and Servants Law, regulating relations between employers and employees, was enacted in Antigua, where the Assembly had dispensed with the apprenticeship system in 1834. In 1838 a Masters and Servants Act, modelled on the Antigua Law, was enacted in Barbados, popularly known as the 'Contracts Law'. This provided that any worker employed for five consecutive days was deemed to have agreed to be hired for one year and could only terminate his hiring on one month's notice. If the worker resided on the plantation, the consequence of terminating his contract was the termination of his tenancy and eviction. According to Hilary Beckles, the law

> provided for ... control of the hired worker during working hours ... the legislation transcended mere labour supply considerations and touched upon issues of public order. If a worker behaved in a manner considered ... insubordinate he could be evicted ... without wage compensation, and imprisoned ... workers could be imprisoned for foul language, gambling or forming illegal combinations.

As originally enacted, this law was disallowed on the advice of the Governor, but was re-enacted in 1840 in a somewhat less oppressive form.[2]

The preamble of a law enacted in Jamaica in 1839 stated:

> all combinations for fixing wages and for regulating and controlling the mode of carrying on manufacture, trade, or business, or the cultivation on any plantation, estate or pen, are injurious to trade and commerce, dangerous to the tranquility of the colony and especially prejudicial to the interests of all who are concerned in them.

That this law was particularly designed to prevent strikes is evident from the following clause:

> if any person shall ... force or endeavour to force any other person ... employed in agriculture or in any manufacture, trade, or business, ... domestic service, or as a boatman, or porter, or in any other occupation ... to depart from his hiring, employment or work, or prevent or endeavour to prevent any such person ... from hiring himself ... or from accepting work or employment ... every person so offending, or aiding, abetting, or assisting therein, shall on conviction thereof ...be imprisoned ... or ... imprisoned and kept to hard labour and solitary confinement for any time not exceeding three months ...[3]

Enacted in 1841 the Masters and Servants Act provided:

> (1) If any servant in husbandry, or any mechanic, artificer, handicraftsman, field or other labourer, person employed in droghers or other person, or any household or other domestic servant, body servant, or any other class of servant shall contract with any other person to serve him ... shall not enter into or commence his service according to his contract ... whether the same shall be in writing or not in writing –

> (a) shall absent himself from his service or employment before the term of his contract shall have been completed ... unless for some reasonable excuse ...; or

(b) shall neglect or refuse to fulfil the same; or

(c) shall be guilty of any other misconduct ... or ill-behaviour ...

every such offender ... shall be liable to a penalty not exceeding three pounds, or to be imprisoned with or without hard labour for ... not exceeding thirty days.

(2) The Justices ... may in addition ... abate the whole or any part of the wages due to such servant and direct the same to be retained by ... the employer ...[4]

In Jamaica, in the first few months after the advent of full freedom, plantation owners offered rates of 7–9d per day and demanded rents, either in cash or in the form of two days' free labour. Workers, for their part, generally demanded 1s 6d per day and lower rents, or in some cases free occupation. In August and September 1838 Lionel Smith, the Governor of Jamaica, was so alarmed at the prospect that no work might be done on the plantations that he addressed meetings of workers in several parishes in the south of the island. He suggested that they accept a rate of one shilling per day and agree to pay a rental of two shillings per week. The workers, for the most part, refused to agree to this.

On one plantation the workers' spokesman respectfully informed the Governor that they would not work for less than 1s 6d per day if they had to pay rent. Faced with this determined attitude, the Governor took the unusual step of using his influence to persuade employers to agree to pay one shilling per day if huts and provision grounds were provided rent-free and 1s 6d if they were not. On plantations on the northern side of the island, where workers were holding out for the same terms, the missionaries and stipendiary magistrates persuaded the employers to agree to similar terms to those negotiated by the Governor.[5]

Despite these negotiated settlements, many plantation owners continued to resort to rent increases and evictions as a means of intimidation. In some cases this provoked strikes. In St James, where the employers had reduced by 33 per cent the wages offered, a strike achieved restoration of the previous rates.[6]

In Trinidad, because of the shortage of labourers and the competition for their services before the importation of indentured labourers had solved that problem, wages in the sugar industry had been higher than in most other Caribbean colonies. In 1838 unskilled labourers were earning 1s 5½d per day. But in 1841 the employers got together and agreed to fix the daily rate for the 1942 crop at 1s 3d. When the workers refused to accept this, the employers were forced to increase the wages offered. In 1842, most plantations were forced to pay 2s 1d per day. Another attempt was made to reduce wages at the end of 1844 but after a six-week strike the former rate was restored.[7]

These conflicts between the plantation owners and their recently freed slaves occurred in most of the sugar colonies in the Caribbean area. In British Guiana there was a strike in 1842 which lasted 12 weeks and resulted in victory for the workers. Another strike, in 1848 which lasted for 14 weeks, ended in failure.[8]

In Jamaica there was a strike for increased wages in Trelawny in 1845. The *Falmouth Post* of 28 January reported:

> the planters of this parish are likely to experience considerable difficulty ... in taking the present crop off the ground, in consequence of the demand of the labourers for an increase of wages. Most of the estates are ready, or making preparations, to 'go about', but will be unable to do so until the existing differences are settled, in the meantime the people are idle. The sum asked for loading a cart with canes and taking it to the mill, is 1s.6d., which is exactly 50 percent more than was paid last year. We have been informed by a gentleman ... that a few days ago he spoke to upwards of fifty persons who had struck work ...[9]

What finally persuaded the sugar planters that, come what may, they would have to reduce the wages paid to their workers was the crisis caused by the imperial Sugar Duties Act of 1846. This Act created a serious financial crisis in the colonies and affected the ability of the sugar planters to pay higher wages. At the same time, the increasing availability after 1845 of imported indentured workers, whose rates of pay were lower than the prevailing rates, reduced the bargaining power of the workers. (The introduction of indentured labourers will be considered in the next chapter.)

In all the sugar colonies of the British Caribbean area the Sugar Duties Act led to a reduction of wages, as did the employment of indentured labourers wherever they were introduced. In Trinidad the plantation owners were able to reduce wage rates to 1s 3d (30 cents) per day.[10] In the 1860s the West Indian sugar industry suffered yet another blow with the development of beet sugar production in Europe. Beet sugar entered the British market on equal duty terms with cane sugar. Also, European governments subsidised its production by payments, called 'bounties', on all beet sugar exports.

The effects of these factors on the economies of the sugar colonies was devastating. Sugar production, on which their prosperity had depended, declined. Many smaller plantations were amalgamated and some abandoned sugar cane cultivation. At the same time modernisation, including the use of steam power, was forced on those sugar producers who survived and the first of the larger factories, known as 'centrals', were established.

A resulting adverse consequence was widespread unemployment. Giving evidence before a Jamaican government commission in 1877 a witness, William Lee, described the situation in the capital:

> After the Sugar Bill came into operation ... there was not a day's work to be done for a carpenter or bricklayer throughout the length and breadth of the city. Many thousands of trademen and labourers were forced to seek employment elsewhere; they went to the Isthmus and completed the Panama Railway, and nearly all of them died there, indirectly the victims of the free traders and sugar refiners of England ... there is not now in Kingston enough work for one quarter of the honest and industrious poor ... who would be willing to work.[11]

Employment opportunities were also severely reduced in the rural areas of Jamaica. Despite this, there were strikes on sugar plantations in the western parishes in 1864.[12] Unemployment and underemployment were also high in the other British colonies in the Caribbean area, resulting in unrest and dissatisfaction.

When the Morant Bay Rebellion, an uprising of peasants and agricultural workers, occurred in eastern Jamaica in 1865, this demonstration of the fact that the disfranchised masses were capable of decisive action alarmed the ruling planter and merchant elites in all the older British colonies which, up to then, had enjoyed powers of internal self-government. This event, and its repercussions throughout the region, are related and discussed in Chapters 13 and 14.

CHAPTER 10

The Use of Indentured Labour

Before and during the apprenticeship period, most plantation owners were expecting that freedom would have disastrous effects. They anticipated that many workers would be reluctant to work on the plantations on which they had been enslaved and that to attract workers they would have to pay wages higher than they could afford. The planters realised that one of the most effective ways of ensuring a supply of labour for the plantations would be the importation of labourers from abroad.

Schemes for encouraging immigration were initiated as early as 1834, the year in which the first stage of the Abolition of Slavery Act of 1833 came into effect. The first immigrant labourers were Portuguese from the Azores and Madeira and other Europeans recruited in Britain, Germany, France and Malta. By 1841 about 4,500 such immigrants had been attracted to Jamaica, 1,500 to Trinidad and 1,000 to British Guiana.[1]

European migration to the West Indian colonies was seen by both the British and the Colonial governments as serving two purposes beneficial to the planters. On the one hand, it was hoped that these immigrants would provide additional labour for the plantations. On the other, it was envisaged that some of these immigrants could be induced to take up land grants on Crown lands in the interior of some colonies, thereby reducing the availability of such lands to former slaves desirous of finding an alternative to labour on the plantations. In the event, however, the number of European migrants attracted was too small to make an appreciable difference to agriculture.

The first labourers, imported from British-controlled areas in India, arrived in British Guiana in May 1838, where they were allocated to five plantations. However, when the Anti-Slavery Society in Britain exposed the high sickness and mortality rates of those sent to the Bellvue plantation and the bad conditions of employment suffered by Indian labourers imported into the island of Mauritius in the Indian ocean since 1834, it was decided in 1839 not to permit further recruitment of Indian labourers into the West Indian colonies. One reason given was the difficulty of ensuring satisfactory conditions on the long sea voyage.[2]

Early attempts were also made to recruit American 'Negroes' as labourers, some 1,200 of whom came to Trinidad between 1839 and 1842. But this scheme was not successful as wages in the West Indian colonies were low by comparison with wages in America. Efforts to attract labourers to Trinidad from other eastern Caribbean islands were more successful, but the number recruited is not recorded.[3]

After the abolition of the slave trade the British Navy was active in its suppression, boarding ships, other than those flying the US flag, suspected of illegally transporting slaves. In the British West African colony of Sierra Leone a Vice-Admiralty Court was established, empowered to condemn captured slave trading vessels, punish their owners and masters and liberate any enslaved Africans found.

By the 1830s the British government had obtained the, at least nominal, co-operation of Spain, Portugal, France, Brazil and the USA. Mixed commissions had been appointed and assembly points for 'liberated' Africans had been established in Sierra Leone, the island of St Helena off the west coast of southern Africa (declared a British Crown colony in 1834), Havana in the Spanish island of Cuba and Rio de Janeiro and Boa Vista in Brazil.[4]

No arrangements were made to return these 'liberated' Africans to their countries of origin. It would appear that the original British intention in relation to those taken to Sierra Leone was that they should be settled there in the same manner as the Maroons who had been transported to Sierra Leone after the Second Maroon War in Jamaica in 1795.

The Africans were housed until the ship from which they had been taken was condemned. Some, including the children, were then sent to villages near Freetown; other children were placed in local households. Some adults were apprenticed to local tradesmen. Single women were granted rations for three months, by which time they were expected to have found employment or a husband. Many of the men were recruited, voluntarily of forcibly, for military service. By 1837 the whole of the British African Corps and a great part of the West Indian Regiments consisted of 'liberated' Africans recruited in Sierra Leone.[5]

West Indian plantation owners appreciated the potential of Sierra Leone as a source of labourers but initially there was some reluctance on the part of the British government to permit such recruitment. There was opposition from the Governor of Sierra Leone, who feared that this would interfere with plans for the settlement of the colony. Emigration was also opposed by Wesleyan missionaries, who hoped to recruit future missionaries for proselytising work in Africa from those whom they had converted to Christianity.

By 1840 the British government had been persuaded to give permission for recruitment schemes. Initially, emigrants had to have been in the colony for six weeks and to have been allowed 21 days to decide whether or not to leave, but in January 1843, in response to pressure from the plantation lobby in London, the residence requirement was reduced to four weeks and in April 1844 to one week.[6]

At first 'liberated' Africans in Sierra Leone were supported by the British government for up to three months, but after 1844 the period of support was reduced and they had to choose between the alternatives of employment in the West Indies and sustaining themselves by the time the first opportunity to leave the country arose.[7] After 1850 compulsory indenture of Africans captured by the British Navy was authorised for two years.[8]

Of the total number of Africans to enter the West Indies between 1834 and 1867, including free persons recruited from the Kru coast south of Sierra Leone and 'liberated' Africans from St Helena, 8,854 went to Trinidad, 11,391 to Jamaica and 14,060 to British Guiana. A further 5,027 were distributed between Grenada, St Vincent, St Lucia, St Kitts and Dominica.

After 1842 those so transported were bound by contract ('indentured') for one year, after 1850 for two years and later for three years. Though most free Africans were entitled to receive the passage home after the expiration of their indentures, indentured 'liberated' Africans were not entitled to be repatriated to Africa.[9]

The British government approved of the revival of importation of Indian labourers under government control in 1844 and importations recommenced in the following year. Thereafter depressed areas in British India provided the overwhelming majority of indentured labourers imported into the British West Indian colonies.

At about the same time importation of Chinese labourers was under consideration and, in 1851, the recruiting agent of the British Guiana government in India went to China to investigate the possibilities. Between 1852 and 1854, 988 Chinese indentured labourers were imported into Trinidad, 647 into British Guiana and one shipload went to Jamaica. This project was temporarily abandoned, but revived in 1858 when two ships with 761 labourers sailed from China to British Guiana.

In 1859 an Anglo-French force occupied Canton until the following year and this facilitated further recruitment. Between then and 1866, when the scheme was terminated because of Anglo-French disagreement, a further 11,282 Chinese indentured labourers went to British Guiana and 1,557 to Trinidad. Although the Chinese government was opposed to emigration, local officials were prepared to co-operate and one further shipload went to British Guiana in

1878–79. However, many of the Chinese emigrated from British Guiana when their indentures expired, some to other parts of the West Indies.[10]

More than 416,000 indentured labourers were brought from India to the West Indies. Alan Burns gives the following approximate totals of the numbers going to each of the seven British colonies that imported them: British Guiana 239,000, Trinidad 134,000, Jamaica 33,000, St Lucia 4,000, Grenada 3,000, St Vincent 2,700 and St Kitts 300.[11] In the cases of Trinidad and Jamaica these figures are underestimates.

The Indian indentured labourers were shamelessly exploited in conditions little better than had been experienced by the slaves. In Jamaica their indentures bound them for five years and, if renewed for a further five years, entitled them to receive from the government their passage money for a return to India or a cash payment.

The first Indian indentured labourers to come to Jamaica in 1845 were paid one shilling per nine-hour day.[12] In 1913 male indentured labourers in Jamaica were still being paid only one shilling per day and females 9d, when the prevailing rate for male workers was 1s 6d. After ten years men were entitled to one half of their return fare to India and women one third.[13]

There were similar discrepancies between the wages paid to the indentured labourers and the prevailing wage rates in the other colonies. In Trinidad, at the expiration of their indentures, these labourers were entitled to either a part of the cost of the return passage to India or a small parcel of land.

Considerable numbers of indentured labourers did return to India but many decided to accept the land grants or a cash payments in lieu and to settle. Of the 238,960 who went to British Guiana, 75,547 returned to India. Of the 143,939 who went to Trinidad, the majority remained in the colony. Of the 36,548 who went to Jamaica, 15,305 accepted the return passage.[14]

The introduction of indentured labourers in the West Indian colonies in such large numbers, at fixed wage rates substantially below the prevailing wage rates established in the immediate post-emancipation period, was an important strategy employed by the British and colonial governments to depress the level of wages and prevent them from rising. In this way they contributed to maintaining the profitability of the plantations.

CHAPTER 11

Crown Colony Government

As we have seen in Chapter 2, there were frequent changes in the ownership of territory in the Caribbean area prior to the end of the Napoleonic Wars in 1815. During the fighting for Jamaica from 1655 to 1660, the Spanish residents had left voluntarily or been expelled, but by the mid-eighteenth century this had become the exception rather than the rule. In most cases a substantial part of the resident population remained, despite the change of rulers.

When a colony was captured by one European power from another in the course of a war, control of the conquered territory was for some time thereafter exercised by military commanders. But when, as a result of a peace treaty, territory was ceded to the victor and remained under the victor's control for a period of some years, the question of establishing a civil government, and what form this should take, had to be answered. When a colony which had been French was ceded to Britain, the new rulers were Protestant and so were most new arrivals, but most of the former residents who remained were Roman Catholics. This could create a problem which did not arise when the territory acquired had been Dutch, as most of the Dutch settlers were Protestants.

The early English settlers invariably enjoyed the right to elect an Assembly which enacted laws for the internal government of the colony and imposed taxes to provide the necessary revenues. As the economies of these colonies was developed, with the importation of slaves from Africa, the right to vote in elections and be elected was restricted to white residents who possessed certain property-owning or income and tax-paying qualifications.

Following the ceding of Grenada to Britain in 1763 there was an influx of British settlers who, by 1772, numbered 166, but French residents had remained in substantial numbers and these were Roman Catholics.[1] Initially doubts were expressed about whether Catholics should enjoy the same rights as Protestants. This was because the Pope had not recognised the Protestant succession to the throne of England and the loyalty of Catholics to a Protestant monarch was suspect. After 1776 Catholics were enfranchised but were excluded from the Assembly. This was achieved by requiring members to subscribe to a declaration that they did not

54

believe in 'transubstantiation', a declaration which no devout Catholic could make.[2]

The same problem of the presence of predominantly Roman Catholic landowners arose in Dominica, also ceded to Britain by France by the Treaty of Paris in 1763. At first placed under a common government with the other islands ceded by the treaty with its headquarters in Grenada, Dominica became a separate colony in 1770, with its own elected Assembly. The same device was then used to exclude devout Catholics from membership. Before taking their seats, members elected to the Assembly were required to subscribe to the following oath:

> I ... do solemnly and sincerely profess in the presence of Almighty God ... that in the sacrament of the Lord's supper there is not any Transubstantiation of the Elements of Bread and Wine into the Body and Blood of Christ, at or after the consecration thereof by any Person whatsoever and that the Invocation or Adoration of the Virgin Mary or any other Saint and the sacrifice of the Mass as they are used in the church of Rome are superstitious and idolatrous ...[3]

War broke out again between Britain and France in 1788 and in 1789 the French recovered Grenada with assistance from the French residents. During this conflict only one prominent Roman Catholic, La Grenade, was believed to have remained loyal to the British. The not surprising consequence of this was that, when France again ceded Grenada to Britain in 1783, the situation of the resident Roman Catholics became even more difficult.[4]

In 1776 the Spanish monarch had issued a 'cedula' permitting Roman Catholics of whatever origin to settle in the Spanish colonies. In the 1770s the Spanish colony of Trinidad was still sparsely populated and no economic development worth mentioning had taken place. Indeed the island had been regarded as little more than a convenient embarkation point for expeditions searching for El Dorado, the mythical city of gold, in South America.

In 1777 Roume de St Laurent, a French Catholic resident of Grenada, visited Trinidad and was so impressed by the possibilities of settlement there that he proposed a scheme to recruit French settlers, from Grenada in particular and also from other colonies. He argued that, if suitable inducements were offered, there would be a substantial increase in the population, which would increase the island's defence capabilities. Many of the settlers would bring their slaves with them, which would increase the labour supply.

St Laurent's proposal found favour with the Spanish government, which may have been influenced by the possibility that there might be an attempt by Britain to acquire Trinidad. As Spain lacked the manpower to populate the island with Spaniards, a scheme to attract Roman Catholics from elsewhere was a practical alternative. A further 'cedula' was accordingly issued in 1783, specifically designed to attract immigrants to Trinidad. This resulted in an influx of new settlers.

Although initially most of the immigrants were from Grenada, people from other islands followed. As a consequence of the French Revolution and the triumph of the rebellious slaves in Saint Domingue, dispossessed planters with their slaves and other royalists, including royalists from Martinique and Guadeloupe, began to arrive in considerable numbers. These were later followed by both white and coloured immigrants of humbler status, many of whom were republicans. There were also some Irish Catholic immigrants from the British colonies. The 'cedula' of 1783 was the starting point of economic development in Trinidad.[5]

In 1782 the total population of Trinidad had been a mere 2,813, made up of 126 Whites, 295 free Coloureds, 310 slaves and 2,082 Amerindians. By 1789 the total had risen to 18,918, made up of 2,151 Whites, 4,467 free Coloureds, 10,100 slaves and 2,200 Amerindians.[6] Thereafter the population continued to increase rapidly as more and more immigrants arrived. By 1796 there were 159 sugar plantations, in addition to other plantations producing coffee, cotton and cocoa. Even so, only one twentieth of the land estimated to be available for agriculture was under cultivation and the potential for further development was considerable.[7]

In 1797, as we have seen, the British did invade and occupy the island. Military control was replaced in September 1801 by the appointment of Lieutenant-Colonel Thomas Picton as Governor. In October 1802, the government of the colony was placed in the hands of three Commissioners, one of whom was the former Governor. This commission was suspended in the following year and a new man was sent out to act as Governor, though he was not given that title officially until July 1806.[8]

During this initial period of British rule the British government was experiencing difficulty in deciding on the appropriate form of government for its latest acquisitions. In 1803 Britain had, as we have seen, again occupied the French colony of St Lucia, where the same problem of a predominently Roman Catholic plantocracy existed.

Initially it had been assumed that, on becoming British, a colony which had been Spanish or French would acquire the traditional British institutions, as had occurred in the cases of Jamaica and, more recently, Grenada and Dominica. By the beginning of the nineteenth century, however, it had become apparent, in the light of the Grenada experience, that there were religious complications to be considered. There was also, in the case of Trinidad, a racial consideration.

In the older British colonies the majority of the free residents possessing the property or income qualifications to entitle them to enjoy political rights and privileges were white. The free persons of African or partly African descent who possessed property or substantial incomes were in a minority and subject to political, social and and economic disqualifications.

In Trinidad such free persons of African or partly African descent were far more numerous. Under Spanish rule, although they suffered some disadvantages, they enjoyed many rights denied to their counterparts in the older British colonies. They could, for example, be appointed to a number of public offices, hold officers' commissions in the Militia, inherit property devised to them by Whites, purchase property without any limitation as to its value and give evidence in legal proceedings.

Under the centralised Spanish imperial system, colonial legislatures did not exist, and neither white nor non-white residents had a right to elect or be elected to legislative Assemblies. There were however municipal councils known as *Cabildos*, which performed certain local government functions. According to the Trinidad scholar James Millette, although the *Cabildo* had originally been a democratic institution it had by the end of the sixteenth century fallen victim to 'the centralizing tendencies of the Crown ... when its offices, formerly elective, began to be put up for sale by the Spanish monarchs as a means of raising revenue'.

Apart from the *Cabildo*'s officers, its other members tended to be drawn from the higher social strata of colonial society. 'Noblemen, planters, scholars and the like generally gained easy admittance ... [but] shopkeepers and artizans could be admitted only by permission of the Crown.' Members of the *Cabildo* might owe their membership to Royal appointment or be appointed by the Governor, in which case their appointment did not become permanent until purchased from the Crown. But some members were elected:

> In Trinidad at the conquest the Cabildo was oligarchic ... unimpeachable whiteness was an indispensable condition of membership. But even among the whites, membership was restricted to a small group of colonists at the very top of society. This group consisted mainly of the most eminent planters who had either purchased their offices from the Crown or had been elected ... by their social confreres where elections were provided for.[9]

Under the terms of the capitulation the British government had agreed that the residents of Trinidad would not be deprived of any of the rights they had enjoyed under Spanish rule. Lord Liverpool, the British Secretary of State for the Colonies, was therefore faced with the problem of deciding how, in the absence of any corresponding institution in Spanish Trinidad, he was to interpret this if, as in the other British colonies, Trinidadians were now to be granted the right to elect an Assembly.

Liverpool appears to have come to the conclusion that, if Trinidad were to be allowed to elect an Assembly, compliance with the spirit of the capitulation would require that non-white residents who had the necessary property qualifications would have to be given the right to vote and be elected. As he no doubt found this prospect distasteful, and feared that such a concession would stimulate demands from free persons of colour in the older colonies for similar rights, this would have been one of the factors he took into consideration in deciding what form of government he should recommend for Trinidad.

Writing to the Governor of Trinidad, Liverpool explained why the usual form of British colonial constitution would be unsuitable:

> the circumstances of the island of Trinidad are ... different from those of all the West India Colonies ... In all the other West India Islands (with the exception of Dominica which arose out of recent circumstances) the white inhabitants form the great majority of the free people ... and the political rights and privileges of all decriptions have been enjoyed exclusively by them.

> The class of free people of colour in these Colonies ... has grown up gradually. They have thereby in some degree been reconciled to the middle situation which they occupy between the whites and the slaves. But in the Island of Trinidad the free people of colour at this time form a very great majority of the free inhabitants of the Island and the question would arise ... whether in establishing, for the first time, a popular government in that Colony, we shall exclude that class of people from all political rights and privileges.

> Such an exclusion ... would be regarded by them as a grievance and it may be doubted how far it would be consistent with the spirit of the capitulation by which their privileges were to be secured and their situation certainly not deteriorated from that which they enjoyed under the Spanish Government.[10]

Faced with these supposed problems – religious in both Trinidad and St Lucia and racial in Trinidad – the British government had, by 1810, devised a new form of colonial constitution hitherto unknown in the British Empire – a system of direct rule from the metropolis. Under this system, which came to be known as Crown colony government, control was exercised by the appointed Governor without the assistance of an elected Assembly, subject to directions received from the Colonial Office in London. Local legislatures called

'Legislative Councils', presided over by the Governors, consisted initially entirely of officials who took their instructions from him.

The British government had not, however, been confronted by any such problems in connection with the occupation in 1803 of the former Dutch colonies in South America. There the propertied classes were Protestant and free non-Whites (excluding the Amerindians) who owned property or had substantial incomes were in a minority. The planters and merchants had enjoyed a system of internal self-government which bore some similarity to the British system, and that system was retained when these colonies were ceded to Britain in 1814.

An electoral college known as the College of Keizers, was elected for life and this in turn chose five unofficial members who, together with the Governor and four appointed government officials, formed the Court of Policy. This was responsible for legislating except on taxation and the civil list. The Governor had an original and a casting vote. Every year the senior appointed member of this body retired and the Court of Policy chose his successor from persons nominated by the College of Keizers. In addition there was a body known as the Combined Court, consisting of the members of the Court of Policy and six directly elected members called Financial Representatives. The Combined Court was responsible for taxation and the civil list.

The Dutch had merged Essequibo and Demerara under a single government in 1784 and the British carried out a further merger with Berbice in 1831 to create the colony of British Guiana.

CHAPTER 12

Internal Self-Government with a Colour Bar

Unlike the centralised Spanish, Portuguese and French colonisation systems, the original English colonisation system had been a decentralised one. In each colony the English (later British)[1] settlers who owned or rented land were allowed to elect legislatures, enact their own laws and tax themselves to provide the revenues required by the colonial government.

These settlers and their descendants cherished their right to exercise internal self-government and vigorously resisted any attempts by the British government to encroach on their privileges. But it would be wrong to regard the settlers' defence of their traditional rights and privileges as a manifestation of local nationalism. They were regarded and regarded themselves as Englishmen overseas and, if and when they were able to accumulate enough wealth to do so, many of them returned to Britain to become absentee proprietors of the properties they had acquired in the colonies. This was very different from the attitudes of the settlers in the Spanish and Portuguese colonies, who tended to put down permanent roots and to regard themselves as nationals of their countries of adoption.

Initially only white property owners, excluding Jews, were allowed to vote or be elected to the local legislatures. Roman Catholics were barred from election to the Assemblies. Non-Whites and Jews could not hold public office in most, if not all, colonies, and restrictions were placed on the amount of property that non-Whites could acquire.

A statute enacted by the Jamaica Assembly in 1711 provided that:

> no Jew, mulatto, Indian, or negro shall be capable to officiate or be employed to write in or for any of the above offices.

The offices listed included all important public offices – the Judges, the Attorney-General, the Clerk of the Crown, the Clerk in Chancery, the Clerk of the Supreme Court, Justices of the Peace, the Provost-Marshal, Marshals of the inferior courts, the Receiver-General, the Coroner, the Clerk of the Market, Surveyors and many other occupations. Even Constables were included in the proscribed list. The statute further provided that any officer permiting 'such person, so incapacitated, to ... be employed in ... any of the said offices' was to be fined £100 local currency, half the fine to be paid to the informer.[2]

A statute enacted in Jamaica in 1761 provided that after the 1 January 1762:

> no lands, negro, mulatto or other slaves, cattle, stock, money, or other real or personal estate ... shall be given, granted to, or declared to be in trust for the use of, or devised by any white person to any negro whatsoever, or to any mulatto, or other person not being their own issue born in lawful wedlock, and being the issue of a negro, and deemed a mulatto ...

The law provided that if any white person made such a grant, devise, bequest or declaration of trust:

> All lands, slaves, and other real estate so given or ... devised, shall go to, and be for the sole use and benefit of the heir at law ... of such donor, grantor or testator ... and all the personal estate so given ... or bequeathed, shall go to and be for the use and benefit of such person or persons as would have been entitled to the same under the statute of distributions, had such donor, grantor, or testator, died intestate ...

Exempted from these provisions were grants for which 'any full, valuable, and adequate consideration' had been 'really and *bona fide* paid by such negro, Mulatto or other person not born in lawful wedlock' which 'shall not in the whole exceed the value of the sum of two thousand pounds in realty'. The Act also provided that:

> it shall ... be lawful to and for such negro, mulatto, or other person not born in lawful wedlock ... to receive and take any lands, ... slaves, cattle, stock, money, or other estate real or personal ... so that the value ... given, granted, and devised, by all and every of the donors and testators (being white persons) exceed not the sum of two thousand pounds in the whole to any one person, any thing in this act to the contrary notwithstanding.[3]

This meant that a white person could give real or personal property to a non-white person, provided the value did not in total exceed £2,000. These restrictions on the right of non-Whites to acquire real and personal property may or may not have been typical. In Jamaica they remained in force until 1813. Whether similar legislation was enacted in the other colonies, and if so in which colonies, requires further research.

In the late eighteenth century, following the formation of the Abolition Society in England in 1787, there had been increasing exposures of the cruelties of the slave trade and slavery and demands for the abolition of the trade. Such criticisms had been resented by the slave traders and slave owners and repudiated by their representatives.

In the early 1790s the prospect of ending the slave trade seemed favourable. In 1792 the House of Commons debated a Bill, proposed by Wilberforce, for abolition of the trade. It was approved by 230 votes to 85 against, subject to an amendment providing that the abolition should be gradual. When the Bill reached the House of Lords, its passage was delayed by a requirement that the evidence that had been presented to the House of Commons should be repeated in and reconsidered by the Upper House. The move to abolish the trade was however abandoned when its advocates learned of the slave rebellion in Saint Domingue in 1791, which was followed by the outbreak of war with France in 1793.[4]

Typical of the protests of the slave owners was this report, adopted by the Jamaica Assembly in the year 1800:

That ... the legislature of this country has ... fully considered the subject ... the address of the House of the 22nd of December, 1797, to his Majesty ... declared their right, under several acts of parliament, and by several proclamations of his royal ancestors, to the full benefit of obtaining labourers from Africa, and that they never can give up ...

That whatever our enemies in Great Britain may presume to assert to the contrary, it is certain that the legislature of Jamaica has done every thing possible to be done to render the condition of the slaves therein as favourable as is consistent with their reasonable services, and the safety of the white inhabitants ... The legislature of the island is alone competent to determine on such future measures as may be expedient further to contribute to this very salutary object ...

... The being supplied with labourers from Africa ... is a right most sacredly pledged to us, and any attempt to take away or restrict that right, so as to abridge the supply necessary ... must unavoidably defeat the lawful intentions of the inhabitants by their labour and exertions to improve their own fortunes, and thereby ... to contribute to the riches and prosperity of the empire at large.[5]

In 1806 a law enacted in Grenada to prevent the 'too frequent and indiscriminate manumission of slaves' imposed a tax of £100 on manumissions. But unscrupulous slave owners could still avoid an obligation to maintain their 'diseased, blind, aged or disabled slaves' as they could still be manumitted tax-free.[6]

During the first four decades of the nineteenth century, the British government began to exert pressure on the colonial legislatures to support a number of liberal reforms. Although the colonial legislatures regarded such pressures as an unwarranted interference in their internal affairs, they nevertheless considered it prudent to make some compromises.

In 1804 a Bill for the abolition of the slave trade was approved by the House of Commons but held up in the House of Lords until 1807. This Act had forbidden the importation of slaves into any British colony after 1 March 1808. Meanwhile, in September 1805, the British government had used its control of the recently ceded colony of Trinidad and the then militarily occupied but not yet ceded colonies of St Lucia and Demerara to prohibit, by Order in Council, the importation of slaves into these colonies.

In 1812, to prevent illegal importations of slaves, the British government by Order in Council required slave owners in Trinidad to register their slaves. A similar Order relating to St Lucia was made in 1814. These Orders were followed by the threat that the British Parliament would proceed with a Bill, introduced by William Wilberforce in 1815, requiring compulsory registration of slaves in all the colonies. This Bill was withdrawn only when the colonial legislatures reluctantly agreed to enact their own compulsory registration statutes, which they did in the following year.

When Trinidad was ceded to Britain, free men of African and part-African descent had been deemed to be competent witnesses in the law courts. These individuals may have enjoyed a similar status in Grenada and St Lucia. Within the next decade the British government began to suggest that a similar right be conceded to non-Whites in all the colonies.

In Jamaica in 1813 a law was enacted which provided that 'all persons ... of free condition ... who have been baptised, and instructed in the principles of the christian religion shall ... be admitted to give evidence on any trial or suit ... Provided always, that ... such person shall have been baptised six months at least previous ...'[7] Similar legislation was enacted in other colonies which had barred non-Whites from giving evidence.

In Jamaica in 1813, disqualifications prohibiting non-Whites from holding public offices and restricting the value of property that could be acquired from Whites by non-Whites, were also abolished. However, as Southey recorded, the preamble to the Act 'precludes them for ever from holding civil or military rank or in any shape to interfere with the legislation of this island'.[8]

Responding to a petition from free persons of colour, the Jamaica Assembly, in November of that year, resolved:

> that the free people of colour ... have no right or claim whatever to political power, or to interfere in the administration of the

Government as by law established in the Governor, Council and Assembly.[9]

In 1823 the House of Commons adopted a resolution recognising the desirability of abolishing slavery at some unspecified future date. The British government then began to exert pressure on the colonial governments to improve the treatment of slaves, including prohibition of the whipping of females, and to enact other liberal measures.

In 1829 in Jamaica and Dominica, and at about the same time or subsequently in some other colonies, legislation was enacted which gave Roman Catholics the right to be elected to the Assemblies without the necessity of taking an oath that they did not subscribe to the Catholic doctrine of transubstantiation or otherwise repudiating the Catholic faith. In Dominica the first three Roman Catholics were elected to the Assembly in 1832.[10]

In Jamaica suspicions as to the loyalty of Catholics to a Protestant British monarch were strong. The 1829 legislation provided that, before taking their seats in the Assembly, elected Roman Catholics should take an oath declaring that it

> is not an article of my faith ... that princes, excommunicated or deprived by the pope, or any other authority of the see of Rome, may be deposed or murdered by their subjects, or by any other person whatsoever ...

The Act further provided that Roman Catholics were disqualified from holding 'any office or place whatever belonging to any of the public schools within this island'.[11]

In the Crown colonies of Trinidad and St Lucia the British government had, in 1829, placed free non-white British subjects on the same legal basis as Whites.[12] By the late 1820s it had become obvious to a majority of the white planters and merchants, who dominated the colonial Assemblies, that it would be to their advantage to enfranchise free non-white property owners.

When the idea of allowing persons of African descent to vote was first proposed in the Jamaica Assembly by a member in 1823 he had got no support, but when he renewed his proposal in 1829 a majority of the members supported him. The decisive argument that had brought about this change of opinion was that, by removing the racial disqualifications, the Whites would make allies of non-white slave and property owners in opposing the proposed abolition of slavery. In Jamaica and other colonies the legislation enfranchising non-Whites was enacted in 1830.[13] Jews were given the right to vote in 1831.[14]

Racial disqualifications persisted in the Bahamas after they had been abolished elsewhere. In 1833 legislation was enacted which removed the civil disabilities of free non-Whites but not from those born in Africa. The legislation, however, permitted Africans to give evidence in the law courts after six years' residence in the colony on production of a certificate from a clergyman or Justice of the Peace that they were qualified to testify. In 1835 free Africans with seven years' residence became eligible for the first time to serve in the Militia.[15]

When it was acknowledged by the British Parliament in 1823 that the emancipation of the slaves should be its long-term objective, even the abolitionists had not contemplated that this would be achieved at an early date. The scheme proposed by the Society for the Gradual Abolition of Slavery, popularly known as the Anti-Slavery Society, would have taken half a century or more to run its course and that approved by Parliament even longer. The slaves, however, had not been prepared to wait indefinitely for freedom. Rebellions had occurred in Barbados in 1816, in Demerara in 1823 and in Jamaica in 1831–32. These rebellions had made the issue a matter of urgency, resulting in the enactment by Parliament of legislation for the abolition of slavery in 1833. The slave owners had been strongly opposed to this, despite the compensation they received from the British government.

In 1838 another dispute arose when Parliament enacted legislation authorising the Governors of the West Indian colonies to take over the management of the local prisons to facilitate prison reforms. So strong was the opposition in the Jamaica Assembly that they retaliated by refusing to enact any legislation including the legislation required to raise the revenues required for the purposes of paying the salaries of officials and defraying necessary government expenditures.

The British government's answer to this was to introduce a Bill authorising Parliament to legislate for the colony until the legislators saw fit to call off their 'strike'. But the measure was approved with a majority of only five votes, a margin considered unacceptably small in those days. This was one of two reasons which led to the resignation of the British government.

Sir Henry Taylor, a senior Colonial Office official, suggested a radical solution. Referring to the difficulties that the British government had been having with the colonial legislatures, he argued that their intransigence would be even greater in future. This was because, with the recent removal of the racial disqualifications, a majority of their members would soon no longer be white. He therefore suggested that it would be desirable to get rid of the colonial legislatures.[16]

In 1839 the British government decided against proceeding with Taylor's plan, but the idea of persuading the colonial Assemblies to relinquish their powers to the Governors appointed by the

Secretary of State for the Colonies came up again in the 1840s in
private letters from Earl Grey, the Secretary of State, to his kinsman
Sir Charles Grey. The latter was Governor of Barbados from 1841
to 1846 and of Jamaica from 1847 to 1853. In a letter dated 1 June
1847 the Secretary of State wrote:

> From all I can hear it seems certain that before long the negro
> population will obtain a preponderating influence in the Assby,
> & considering their ignorance & the degree to which they are
> under the influence of persons who would not I fear use power
> very discreetly, it seems most important that before this change
> takes place, the authority of the Crown should for the protection
> of the higher classes be somewhat strengthened.

Two months later, in another private letter, he wrote:

> I ... repeat in the strongest manner my opinion that the planters
> are of all persons those who are most deeply interested in giving
> to the Executive Govt of the Colony some power & authority
> independent of the Assby. It is perfectly clear that the Acquisition
> of property by the blacks & the distress of the planters must both
> contribute to throw in a very few years the power of returning
> a majority of the Assby entirely into the hands of the former,
> & I fear that they will not have this power long before the
> influence of the dissenting missionaries & especially the baptists
> leads them to use it to carry measures most injurious to the
> planters and ... the Colony.

But he went on to suggest disguising the reason for the change:

> it would be highly advantageous both to give the negroes a value
> for education & also to avert violent political changes hereafter
> to pass a law rendering ability to read & write a necessary
> qualification for exercising the elective franchise. – I am myself
> strongly of opinion that such a measure would be advisable but
> it is clear that it is one which could only originate with the Assby
> & also that in proposing it the political object ought to be kept
> entirely out of sight and the promotion of education ... alone
> insisted upon.

The Governor, however, failed to persuade the Whites that non-
Whites would soon threaten their dominance of the Assembly.
Perturbed by their lack of foresight, the Secretary of State again
referred to the matter in a letter dated 16 March 1849:

> It appears to me that the Assby is acting in a manner which must
> be as absolutely ruinous in the end to the very parties by whom
> its proceedings are now directed, & I should hope that by
> private communications with some of the leading members

you might be able to make them understand that such is the case.

– Looking to the comparative numbers of the black and white inhabitants of Jamaica, & to the absence of any real impediment to the acquisition of the elective franchise by the former, it seems impossible to doubt that at no very distant period they must acquire a paramount influence in the legislature ...

... therefore if the planters were wise they would use the authority they now possess, not to break down the power of the crown but on the contrary to strengthen it, by restoring to the executive govt some of those functions which properly belong to it but which in Jamaica have been usurped by the Assembly ...[17]

Despite this advice, the Assemblymen refused to relinquish their powers. When a financial crisis, caused by depressed sugar prices, forced Jamaica to apply to Britain for assistance in 1854, they agreed to a constitutional concession in return for a loan of £500,000, but not to any reduction of the legislative functions of the Assembly.[18]

CHAPTER 13

The Morant Bay Rebellion

The 1860s was a decade of great economic distress in the British West Indian colonies. The decline of sugar prices, mainly attributable to the equalisation of the duties on all sugars entering Britain, had caused a reduction of export earnings, employment opportunities and government revenues and expenditures, with consequent adverse effects on living standards.

The increase in social deprivation had been particularly severe in Jamaica where the cultivation of sugar cane on many plantations had been abandoned. This had converted the post-emancipation shortage of labour into a surplus and had caused a reduction of employment opportunities, but the policy of importing indentured labourers had nevertheless been continued.

In January 1865 Dr E.B. Underhill, Secretary of the Baptist Missionary Society, wrote to Edward Cardwell, Secretary of State for the Colonies, reporting these distressing conditions and urging the adoption of remedial measures. The letter was sent to Governor Eyre for his comments. Eyre sent copies to the custodes, judges, magistrates and ministers of religion, no doubt expecting that they would support his belief that Underhill's allegations of distress were exaggerated.

The letter was published in a newspaper and public meetings to discuss it were convened all over the island, some by the custodes, others by the missionaries and other well-known persons. Although a few supported the Governor, the majority approved resolutions agreeing with Dr Underhill's statements.

Richard Hill, a Resident Magistrate in the parish of St Catherine, supported Underhill's report, commenting that the 50 per cent decrease in the number of plantations since the abolition of slavery had created serious unemployment. Based on the findings of their missionaries in many parts of the island, the Baptists too reported severe shortages of employment opportunities, made worse in many districts by the replacement of creole labour by imported indentured labourers. Wages had been reduced, often by as much as 25 per cent.[1]

George William Gordon, popular elected member of the Assembly for the parish of St Thomas in the East, chaired several meetings. At the Morant Bay meeting, as at the Kingston meeting, he criticised legislation enacted by the Assembly as oppressive. Baron Von Ketelhodt, the Custos of St Thomas in the East, was similarly described. At a meeting in Vere, Gordon described Governor Eyre as a 'bad man', who 'sanctions everything done by the higher class to the oppression of the poor negroes'.[2]

Governor Eyre adhered to his opinion that the reports of suffering were exaggerated. When a number of poor people in the parish of St Ann petitioned the Queen, complaining of their poverty, accentuated by a drought, and asking that unused Crown lands be leased to them on favourable terms, Eyre forwarded the petition with a covering letter in which he commented:

> This is the first fruits of Dr. Underhill's letter, which represented the peasantry of Jamaica as being generally in a destitute, starving and naked condition ... and I fear the result of Dr. Underhill's communication and the circulars of the Baptist Missionary Society will have a very prejudicial influence in unsettling the minds of the peasantry.

No doubt influenced by the Governor's scepticism, the response of the British government was unsympathetic. Eyre had the official reply of the Secretary of State printed on 50,000 placards headed 'The Queen's Advice' and posted up all over the island. He also requested ministers of religion to read it aloud in the churches and chapels:

> I request that you will inform the petitioners that their petition had been laid before the Queen, and I have received her Majesty's command to inform them that the prosperity of the labouring classes, as well as all other classes, depends in Jamaica and in other countries on their working for wages, not uncertainly or capriciously, but steadily and continuously, at the times when their labour is wanted, and for so long as it is wanted; that if they would use this industry, and thereby render the plantations productive, they would enable the planters to pay them higher wages for the same hours of work than are received by the best field labourers in this country; and as the cost of the necessities of life is much less in Jamaica than it is here, they would be enabled by adding prudence to industry to lay by an ample provision for seasons of drought and dearth; and they may be assured that it is from their own industry and prudence in availing themselves of the means of prospering that are before them, and not from any such schemes as have been suggested to them, that they must look for improvement in their condition and that her Majesty will regard with interest and satisfaction their advancement through their own merits and efforts.[3]

The insensitivity of the official reply to the St Ann petition, and likewise to similar petitions received from other parishes, indicated a lack of understanding of and sympathy for the sufferings of the poor. It was a situation in which almost any incident could have provided the spark to ignite a social conflagration.

The uprising that did occur took place in St Thomas at the eastern end of the island. It was led by Paul Bogle, a peasant and preacher at an independent Baptist church who was also the local election agent of George William Gordon, the member of the Assembly. It enveloped a much wider area than the name by which it is popularly known, 'the Morant Bay Rebellion', suggests. It is nevertheless surprising that it was not island-wide.

On 7 October, a crowd of some 150 attended a session of the Magistrates' Court in Morant Bay, in support of a man charged with having allowed his horse to trespass on the Middleton plantation. This plantation, belonging to a white owner who was also the Inspector-General of Immigration, had been leased to a farmer who had, in turn, rented parts of it to small farmers. These tenants were currently in dispute with him over the amount of the rents. The man charged, Bogle's cousin, was fined 20 shillings and appealed, with Bogle as his surety.

There was also some disorder at the court in connection with an earlier case, and Bogle may have been involved in frustrating an attempt to arrest a man for contempt of court. The Magistrates thought it imprudent to order further arrests on that day but subsequently issued warrants for the arrest of 28 people, including Bogle.

On Tuesday, 10 October, a party of policemen attempted to arrest Bogle at his home at Stony Gut, a village 4 miles from the town, but were immediately surrounded by a crowd of some 300 men armed with cutlasses and sticks. Some of the policemen had their own handcuffs placed upon them. They reported seeing three gangs of men, armed with sticks, cutlasses and lances, drilling near Bogle's house. One of the policemen subsequently stated that he had been forced to swear on oath: 'So help me God after this day I must cleave from the whites and cleave to the blacks.' He also stated:

> Paul Bogle spoke to the men in a language I did not understand. The men then took an oath, they kissed ... the Bible. Paul Bogle gave each of them a dram of rum and gunpowder which they drank.[4]

That day Bogle sent the Governor a petition containing a warning:

> We, the petitioners of St. Thomas in the East, send to inform your Excellency of the mean advantage that has been taken of

us from time to time, and more especially the present time, when on Saturday, 7th of this month an outrageous assault was committed upon us by the policemen of this parish, by order of the Justices, which occasion an outbreaking for which warrants have been issued against innocent person, of which we are compelled to resist ...

We therefore call upon your Excellency for protection, seeing we are Her Majesty's loyal subjects, which protection if refused to will be compelled to put our shoulders to the wheel, as we have been imposed upon for a period of 27 years with due obeisance to the laws of our Queen and country, and we can no longer endure the same.[5]

On learning from the policemen, who were released that afternoon, that Bogle and his men would be coming to Morant Bay on the following day, the Custos called out the predominently white and brown volunteer Militia to protect the Vestry meeting scheduled to take place on 11 October. On that morning 22 armed militiamen from the Bath company and eight from Morant Bay reported for duty.

Early that afternoon several hundred people, most of whom were peasants or worked or sought part-time work on the plantations of the parish or were landless labourers, converged on the parish capital. The largest contingent was from Stony Gut. Led by Bogle, and armed with cutlasses and sticks, they marched in a regular column, headed by a drum and fife band. Groups of similar composition from other areas also converged on the town.

The first objective of Bogle and his followers was the police station, where they overcame the three policemen on duty and seized the guns, but these turned out to be useless as they had no flints. They then proceeded to the square, marching to the beating of drums and blowing of shells or horns, where they were joined by those who had come from other areas. The crowd numbered about 400.

The focus of the crowd's attention was the Vestry, in session at the Court House under the chairmanship of the Custos and Chief Magistrate, Baron Von Ketelhodt. The atmosphere was tense because of the events which had occurred during the past four days. On being informed of the approach of the marching men the members of the Vestry had come out onto the balcony of the Court House and the militiamen were drawn up in front of the building.

A large crowd of men and women gathered in the square. Ketelhodt attempted to read the Riot Act but was interrupted by a hail of stones and bottles thrown by women in the crowd. Several of the militiamen were injured. The order was then given, either by Ketelhodt or the militia captain, to fire. The Militia discharged their firearms into the crowd. Before they could reload they were charged by the crowd and had to withdraw into the Court House. The doors of the Court House were barricaded and the shooting continued from inside the building. About two hours later a fire was started in the adjoining school house and quickly spread to Court House. Some of those inside jumped out of a back window while other ran down the stairs at the front of the building.

Some of the parish officials were killed and others were wounded. Some escaped and took refuge in a nearby house belonging to a black builder named Charles Price. When darkness fell more were able to escape. In and around the Court House 18 officials and militia men were killed and 31 others injured. Seven members of the crowd were killed and many were wounded.

The rebels appear to have been organised. One of the militiamen, who had been captured trying to escape and beaten, subsequently named individual rebels as captains whom he had seen ordering men to march and to stand guard at various locations in the town. Bogle, recognised as in command, was referred to as 'General Bogle'. The level of discipline and control may explain why, apart from the burned-out buildings in the square, there was little destruction and no looting in Morant Bay.

After the Court House had been destroyed and members of the Vestry and Militia and others who had taken refuge therein had been killed or had escaped, a rebel contingent proceeded to the local prison. They marched in three companies of ten men each, with James Bowie, Craddock and Simmonds as company commanders and Bogle at their head. The crowd at the prison numbered nearly 300. They entered the gaol and freed the 51 prisoners. On Bogle's orders the prison officer was forced to break open a locked chest containing the prisoner' clothes, which were then restored to them.[6]

That the rebellion was basically a class conflict is illustrated by the status of the prominent individuals attacked by the rebels. Ketelhodt and Rev. Herschell, a member of the Vestry, were plantation owners who had had disputes with their labourers over pay. Lieutenant Hall of the Militia was the Collector of Petty Debts at Bath and was targeted by a man from whom he had sought to collect money. Vestryman W.P. Georges was a planter, Francis Bowen a magistrate and planter.

But despite the underlying social realities of the rebellion, class divisions largely coincided with complexion differences and the rebels articulated their protests against oppression and suffering in terms of colour. 'Colour for colour' was a slogan heard on their lips by many witnesses. William Lake, a black man apparently associated with persons who the rebels regarded as their enemies, had a narrow escape. A member of the crowd raised his cutlass to kill him but another man prevented it saying: 'It is your colour; don't kill him. You are not to kill your colour.'

The so-called 'Native Baptists' were closely associated with the rebellion. Their influence was deplored by the white missionaries. A white Methodist missionary reported, in a letter to the Secretaries of his mission written on 23 October 1865, that he had heard a Native Baptist preacher say:

> You're black, and I am black, and you ought to support your own colour. The blacks are seven to one of the others and they ought to have the island.

When Arthur Warmington was captured, he heard members of the crowd cry: 'Kill him, down with the white man.' His life was spared when he pretended to be a doctor who could treat the wounded. Bogle accepted this but, before releasing him, made him swear that he would not dress white people's wounds, otherwise he would kill him.

Most of the Whites captured by the rebels in Morant Bay were killed, including Ketelhodt, Herschell, Walton, Captain Hitchins, Lieutenant Hall, Arthur and Alexander Cooke. But there were exceptions to the basic colour division. George William Gordon, who was not at the Vestry meeting that day, had a white father but he was beloved by the black masses. One of the reasons for their intense hatred of Ketelhodt and Herschell was that they had been responsible for having Gordon temporarily removed from membership of the St Thomas Vestry.

Dr Major, although white and a member of the Vestry, was spared to care for the members of the crowd who had been wounded. But Charles Price, a Black, was beaten to death. He was a political supporter of Ketelhodt and had business relations with Herschell. When a member of the crowd that had captured him said that they had 'orders to kill no Black, only White and Brown', he was overruled by the argument that Price 'has got a black skin and a white heart'.[7]

On the morning of 12 October troops arrived and took control of Morant Bay, but by then the rebellion was spreading to other parts of the parish. During the next few days it extended as far as the parish borders with St Davids to the west and Portland to the north.

At Bath the Chief Magistrate and shop owner William Kirkland, whose shop was attacked, described the rebels who entered the town on the morning of 12 October as 'marching in ranks with flags flying, drum beating, and a horn blowing'. But outside Morant Bay the crowds were less disciplined. A leader of the rebels entering Bath told the people: 'We don't want cloths, we want powder; we do not come here to thieve we come to kill,' but he was unable to persuade those who had taken goods from a shopkeeper to return them. There was also widespread plundering by rebels who attacked the plantations.

In the rural areas the same class basis of the rebellion, articulated in terms of colour, was evident. A white bookkeeper on Blue Mountain plantation was killed. William Miller, the manager of Serge Island, was concealed by a woman employee and was later able to escape, but much of the plantation property was looted. Coley, the adjoining plantation, was also plundered. Fifty armed rebels at Monklands, on the parish border with St Davids, were looking for the owner who had fled to Kingston.

Others targeted by the rebels were Alexander Chisolm, the Overseer at Golden Grove, R.J. Stewart, the overseer at Amity Hall, and S. Shortridge, J. Harrison and Augustus Hire, the attorneys at Golden Grove, Hordley and Amity Hall, respectively. The last three had all had disputes with local people over land and the workers at Amity Hall had long been complaining of low wages.

A woman living on Rhine plantation stated that she heard the rebels singing a song the words of which were:

> Backras' blood we want, Backras' blood we'll have, Backras' blood we are going for, Till there's no more to have.[8]

Bogle arrived at Monklands on Friday, 13 October and appears to have been displeased that his strictures against looting had been ignored, but it is unlikely that he could have done anything to restrain the crowds. Potosi, Holland, Amity Hall, Hordley, Duckenfield, Plaintain Garden River, Winchester, Wheelersfield and Mulatto River plantations were all plundered and extensively damaged. The only great house that was left intact and unlooted was at Golden Grove, where people from Morant Bay had told the crowd that the house was wanted for General Bogle. They did, however, plunder the overseer's house.

On the afternoon of 13 October, some 50 rebels, led by John Pringle Afflick, marched into the small town of Manchioneal, now in Portland but then part of the parish of St Thomas. Armed with cutlasses and sticks they were shouting 'Colour! Colour!' and blowing shells. They were soon joined by several hundred others. As the rebels approached, the white residents fled to Port Antonio. Among them was the Wesleyan missionary Rev. Foote, against whom settlers at Grange Hill had a grievance as he had collected rents from them. Many houses in the town were looted. The rebels took the guns they found in a local gunsmith's shop.

On Saturday, 14 October and Sunday, 15 October, a large number of rebels assembled in Manchioneal with the intention, according to a local goldsmith, of advancing northwards into Portland on the following day. People in Port Antonio, the parish capital, including refugees from St Thomas, were expecting a rebel attack, but this did not materialise. John Ashley Lord, a police inspector who was one of the refugees, believed that this was because they were engaged in pillaging and burning properties. On 16 October, troops arrived and frustrated any possibility of a northward rebel advance.[9]

The forces employed against the rebels were overwhelming. There was never any doubt that the rebellion would be crushed. On the morning of 12 October, 100 black troops of the 1st West India Regiment, under white officers, and 20 men of the Royal Artillery were landed at Morant Bay from HMS *Wolverine*. Also landed from the *Wolverine* were 74 seamen and 31 marines. That afternoon Governor Eyre asked for reinforcements, and General O. Connor, the officer commanding the troops, sent 100 more troops to Morant Bay aboard the gunboat *Onyx*.

The Governor also requested that white troops from the garrison at Newcastle be deployed immediately to march eastwards over the mountains via Mahogany Vale. On the morning of 13 October, martial law was declared over the entire eastern county of Surrey with the exclusion of Kingston. Later that morning Governor Eyre chartered a French ship, which took him that afternoon to Morant Bay, along with Brigadier-General Nelson whom he placed in command of field operations, 50 additional troops and several officers of the Militia. On 15 October, 100 troops were dispatched to march to Manchioneal (see Map 13.1).

On 15 October, Governor Eyre, accompanied by Colonel Alexander Fyffe, a former superintendent of the Maroons in Portland and then Custos of that parish, met some 200 Maroons at Port Antonio who had come to offer their services. They were poorly armed but, when the *Wolverine* arrived four days later, weapons and ammunition were issued to them and arrangements were made for them to be employed under Colonel Fyffe's supervision. They were joined by a further 60 Maroons.

At the commencement of the rebellion Bogle did not know what the attitude of the Maroons would be. About a month before the uprising he and James Bowie had gone to Hayfield, a small Maroon community in the Blue Mountains above Bath, where, according to a Maroon Major, Bogle had discussed various problems with them including the low rate of plantation wages and the high rate of taxes. A Maroon captain said that Bogle had discussed going to Moore Town, the larger Maroon settlement in Portland. He had said that 'he was in fear of the Maroons because they were going to Court to have a battle and he ... wanted to go there and tell them not to interfere with what he wanted to do'.

The Maroons at Hayfield had offered Bogle no encouragement and it seems that he did not visit Moore Town. Richard Fennison

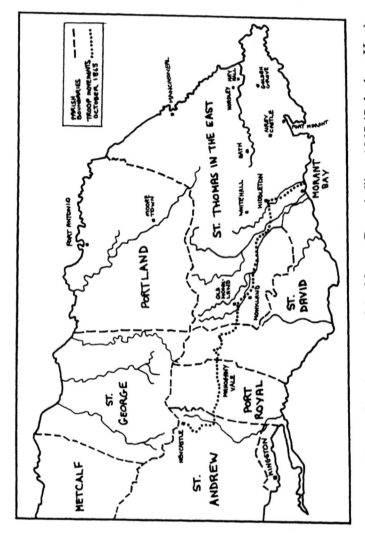

Map 13.1 Eastern Jamaica, scene of the Morant Bay rebellion, 1865 (© Andrew Hart)

who asked Francis Dean, a Moore Town Maroon, if the Maroons would fight against the Whites, was told that they would not entertain such a notion. But if this proclamation rallying their supporters, signed by Bogle, McLaren and others on 17 October, is to be taken at face value, it would appear that they still entertained hopes that the Hayfield Maroons would assist them:

> It is time now for us to help ourselves. Skin for skin, the iron bars is now broken ... the white people send a proclamation to the governor to make war against us ... we all must put our shoulder to the wheels, and pull together.
>
> The Maroons sent ... to us to meet them at Hayfield ... without delay, that they will put us in the way how to act.
>
> Every one of you must leave your house, takes your guns, who don't have guns take your cutlasses ... Come over to Stoney Gut that we might march over to meet the Maroons ...
>
> Blow your shells, roal your drums, house to house, take out every man, march them down to Stoney Gut, any that you find in the way takes them down with their arms; war is at us, my black skin, war is at hand ... Every black man must turn out at once, for the oppression is too great, the white people are now cleaning up they guns for us, which we must prepare to meet them too, Chear men, chear, in heast we looking for you a part of the night or before day break.

This was the last rallying cry of the rebellion. There was never a prospect of Maroon support. On the contrary, there was a skirmish with them at Torrington on 19 October. On 23 October, Maroons captured Bogle and turned him over to the military.[10]

The rebellion was quickly suppressed, but it soon became evident that the real purpose of both the civil and military authorities was to administer indiscriminate punishment to the Blacks for having participated in or given support to the rebellion. Over the ensuing weeks hundreds were summarily convicted at courts martial, which paid absolutely no regard to the rules of evidence or proper procedures, but assumed guilt and ordered execution or flogging.

While they were in custody awaiting trial, Provost-Marshal Ramsay had many of the prisoners flogged without any justification. Others were shot, hanged or flogged without trial, at the whim of military commanders and sometimes ordinary soldiers or Maroons. The victims including some who had not supported the rebellion in any way. There was looting by both soldiers and Maroons and over 1,000 homes were burned down or otherwise demolished.[11]

A man named Fleming, one of the first prisoners to be disposed of, was tried under martial law at Port Morant on 14 October. As pointed out by Ansell Hart:

> Fleming at worst had been guilty of threatening, without injuring anyone. He had not been and was not accused of having been among the rioters in Morant Bay ... he was not taken in arms or in company of any others offering resistance to constituted authority. The offence of which he was charged had been committed, if at all, before the proclamation of martial law; so that his trial by court martial was quite improper.[12]

Eyre personally set the example to be followed. He ordered Fleming's arrest and trial by court martial and assisted at his execution by sending a message to Lieutenant Brand to bring a rope for the hanging. Many of the chief actors in the suppression of the rebellion and its punitive aftermath, including General Nelson who was in charge under martial law, Lieutenant Brand, Militia Captain Lewis and Government Secretary Captain Hunt who presided at many of the subsequent courts martial, and Colonel Fyffe, were all present at Fleming's trial.[13]

Most of the Army officers and officials saw the rebellion in terms of colour. The only Blacks immune from suspicion were soldiers in uniform and the Maroons. Colonel Fyffe thought that almost every black person in the parish was 'by act or connivance an accessory' to a plot to massacre Whites and Coloureds. If some innocent persons suffered, this was unavoidable.[14]

George William Gordon, who represented St Thomas in the East in the Assembly, had long been a harsh critic of the Governor's conduct, in the legislature, in the press and at public meetings. For Eyre the rebellion and the declaration of martial law provided an opportunity to get rid of or silence his most vocal critics and Gordon was his principal target.

On 17 October, Eyre personally secured a warrant for Gordon's arrest. On hearing of the warrant Gordon went to the home of General O'Connor in Kingston to give himself up. While he was there Eyre and Dr Bowerbank, the Custos of Kingston, arrived. They informed Gordon that he was their prisoner. The martial law proclamation did not extend to Kingston and in order to ensure that Gordon would be tried by court martial and not by a civil court, Eyre had him placed on the HMS *Wolverine* and taken into the martial law area at Morant Bay. This was, of course, illegal.

Gordon was tried on two charges:

> First on the charge of high treason against Her Majesty Queen Victoria; Second, with having complicity with certain persons

who were engaged in the rebellion ... at Morant Bay on the 11th day of October 1865.

He was denied legal advice or representation. No credible evidence of his complicity in the rebellion was given. The junior officers who comprised the court martial delivered the judgment that was expected of them:

> The Court ... adjudge the prisoner ... to be hanged by the neck until he be dead, at what time and place the Brigadier General may direct.

General A.A. Nelson readily gave his confirmation:

> I fully concur in the sentence awarded, such being fully borne out by the evidence. The prisoner is to be hung [sic] on Monday next, the 23rd of October 1865.[15]

Bogle, Bowie, McLaren, Bogle's brother Moses and 14 other prominent rebels were also tried by court martial and were hanged on 25 October. According to a military eye-witness, Bogle went calmly and bravely to his death.[16] In 1977, the government of Jamaica awarded the title of National Hero to both George William Gordon and Paul Bogle and a monument to them was erected at Heroes Circle in Kingston. The building in which the legislature meets has been named 'Gordon House' and a postage stamp bears a likeness of Bogle.

CHAPTER 14

The Constitutional Surrenders

Although the Morant Bay Rebellion was suppressed, followed by a brutal and bloody programme of revenge against the black population, the uprising had created fear and alarm among the dominant planter and merchant class. In this atmosphere they were willing to accede to the Governor's proposal that they should surrender the extensive powers of their elected Assembly, previous attempts to reduce which they had tenaciously resisted.

Governor Eyre, long an adherent of the view that the powers exercised by the colonial assemblies should be drastically reduced, seized the opportunity to implement the proposal first advanced by Henry Taylor nearly 25 years earlier. Addressing a joint meeting of the Assembly and the Council on 7 November 1865, Eyre, having reminded his audience of the recent uprising, invited them to draw the conclusion he desired:

> It is necessary to bring these facts before you, in order to convince you how widely spread, and how deeply rooted, the spirit of disaffection is; how daring and determined the intention has been, and still is, to make Jamaica a second Haiti, and how imperative it is upon you, gentlemen, to take such measures as, under God's blessing, may avert such a calamity.

> Those measures may be summed up ... – create a strong government; and then a firm hand to guide and direct ... In order to obtain a strong government, there is but one course open to you, that of abolishing the existing form of constitution ... and establishing one better adapted to the present state and requirements of the colony ...

> I invite you then, gentlemen, to make a great and generous sacrifice for the sake of your country, and in immolating on the altar of patriotism the two branches of the Legislature ... to hand down to posterity a noble example of self-denial and heroism ...

In reply the Governor was assured: 'that the advice and co-operation which you seek of the Legislature ... will not on the part of the Assembly be withheld'. A similar reply was given by the Council. On 9 November a Bill was presented on behalf of the government to alter and amend the political constitution:

Be it enacted ... the present Legislative Council and House of
Assembly shall cease and determine absolutely ... There shall
be constituted ... one single chamber only ... of twenty-one
members to be nominated and appointed for life by her
Majesty ...[1]

It was not long, however, before some of the Assemblymen,
particularly spokesmen for the coloured members but also one Jewish
member, had begun to have second thoughts and to question the
necessity to dispense with elections. There were at that time no black
members of the Assembly and it is probable that most of the
coloured members were thinking in terms of their own middle-class
interests rather than broader considerations of democracy. The
contribution to the debate by Samuel Constantine Burke, a coloured
member, is revealing:

Why should the class to which I belong be deprived of their
right to free expression of opinion? What have they done that
they should be disfranchised? Is it because of the wicked
insurrection by the negroes of St Thomas in the East that a class
of men who have ever been most loyal and conservative – who
have done good service to the state – who have by their honest
industry acquired property equal in proportion to their white
fellow subjects ... who have educated their children so as to fit
them to be good and useful citizens – and who have the greatest
possible interest in maintaining peace and good order in the
community, should be deprived of the right of electing their representatives? I contend that there is no occasion for a Bill like
the present one ...

There was, however, one coloured member, Robert Osborn, who
during the debate, introduced a much broader and, indeed,
prophetic perspective:

It seems to me intended by divine Providence that the wrongs
of Africa are eventually to be vindicated in this hemisphere. Her
people have been forcibly taken from their homes and brought
here by thousands and tens of thousands to be made slaves. They
have been made free by the justice of the British people, and
they are progressing in religion and civilization. We may therefore
make whatever laws we like, but I think they will ultimately be
unavailing.

The elements of our community in whose favour you are making
these exclusive laws are wasting away ... It seems to me that in
years to come ... the government of the colonies will fall into
the hands of the Blacks ... We may strive to prevent it, but I

think our struggle will be in vain. It appears to me to be the decree of an all wise Providence.

There was a cry of 'Sedition'. Then Wellesley Bourke, another coloured member, interjected:

As long as Britain exists this island will never fall into the hands of the negroes to the exclusion of the other classes.

Osborn then continued:

Why it has commenced to fall into their hands already; and therefore this bill has been introduced to hurl them from your Vestry and other Boards, and so prevent their coming here. If it was not so, why seek to destroy a free constitution under which our forefathers and ourselves have lived for over two hundred years? If I be right in my views of the future, the question we ought to discuss is – how are we to prepare these people for self-government – how to elevate them?

I know the subject is unpalatable and that honourable gentlemen become impatient and angry when it is alluded to, but it is a question which must sooner or later force itself upon this or any future legislative body you may succeed in establishing ... The black population must be represented because they form the chief portion of the community. But neither they nor any one else out of this House know anything about your Bill and the injury you contemplate doing them.[2]

While this was not what he intended, Osborn's prediction that eventually control of the government would fall into the hands of a black majority may have had the effect of convincing most of the members, including the propertied coloured members, of the need to surrender the Assembly's extensive existing powers.

As the immediate panic induced by the rebellion receded, even some members of the white majority in the Assembly had begun to show a reluctance to giving up entirely the right to elected representation. This may explain why, although the Bill was approved on the second reading by a majority of 19, the government indicated that amendments would be proposed, at the committee stage, to provide for an elected element.

On 5 December 1865, the Bill, amended to provide for a single-chamber legislature of 24 members, one half to be 'nominated and appointed by Her Majesty ... and the other half ... [to be] elected in this island', was presented by a member of the Executive Committee. The Bill was enacted by the Assembly by a majority of 21 votes to 4 against. Two days later the amended Bill was approved by the Council.[3]

The Colonial Office was however pursuing a plan, which received Eyre's co-operation and may have originated with him, to obtain from the Jamaica Assembly a more comprehensive surrender than envisaged by this legislation. On 12 December, the Assembly, which was still in session, was informed by the same member of the Executive Committee of a message from the Governor:

> that so convinced are her Majesty's Government of the paramount importance of a strong government being at once constituted in Jamaica, that he had been confidentially informed ... there would be no hesitation on the part of Her Majesty's Government, to accept any amount of additional responsibility which circumstances might require.

In view of this:

> The Governor would respectfully invite the Legislature so to amend the act recently passed ... as would leave her Majesty unfettered in determining the character of the future constitution.

Relaying this message to the Assembly, the member gave notice of the government's intention to propose a new Bill. He argued that if the members, when debating the recently enacted Bill, had been aware of the British government's willingness to accept any amount of responsibility which circumstances might require, they would have accepted this offer with open arms. If they were now willing to accept it, their acceptance must be unconditional.

The new Bill proposed repealed all the provisions of the Act recently passed, save and except that providing for the liquidation of the Legislature. It provided that the Queen might create and constitute, and from time to time alter and amend, such form of legislature and administrative machinery as she might consider suitable for Jamaica.

By this stage, except for a final protest from a Jewish member named Alberga, the last flickers of resistance in the Assembly had been estinguished. Even Osborn had given up the struggle. On the first reading, the new Bill was approved by 17 votes to 6, including that of Osborn. In its final version, as approved by the Assembly and the Council on 21 December 1865, the second clause read:

> In place of the Legislature abolished by the first section of the recited act, it shall be lawful for her majesty the Queen to create and constitute a government for this island, in such form, and with such powers as to her Majesty may best seem fitting, and from time to time to alter or amend such government.[4]

By Order in Council a government was then established with a Governor authorised to make laws with the consent of a Legislative Council consisting of official and unofficial members appointed by the Queen. Until otherwise directed the official members were to be the senior military officer in command of the regular troops within the island, the Colonial Secretary, the Attorney-General, the Financial Secretary, the Director of Roads and the Collector of Customs. The unofficial members were to be appointed by the Queen, provided that if at any time they numbered fewer than six, the Governor was authorised to appoint persons to act. The total number of unofficial members was not to exceed six.[5]

The Legislative Council thus created then enacted a law providing that:

> All powers, functions, and duties heretofore ... exercised by the executive committee ... are hereby transferred to, and vested in ... the governor,

and that the Governor's Secretary be replaced by a Colonial Secretary.[6]

That, however, was not the end of this sad story. The counterparts of the Jamaican planters and merchants in all the older British colonies in the Caribbean which had enjoyed similar rights of internal self-government, with the exception of Barbados and the Bahamas, decided to follow the example of their Jamaican counterparts. The British government was only too ready to assist.

The Dominica Assembly surrendered that island's constitution in 1865. In 1866, a similar surrender of powers occurred in Antigua, St Kitts, Nevis, Montserrat and the British Virgin Isles. There were similar surrenders in St Vincent in 1867 and in Grenada and Tobago in 1876. In the Leeward Islands the existing constitutions were amended rather than abolished. The St Kitts and Nevis Assemblies abolished elections entirely, while those of Antigua and Dominica[7] initially retained minorities of elected members. In 1898, however, in return for financial assistance from Britain, they agreed to abolish elections.

Thus it was that the Assemblies in most of the British Caribbean colonies voluntarily surrendered their ancient constitutions. They agreed to accept instead a system of Crown colony government similar to that devised for Trinidad and St Lucia earlier in the century. The white planters and merchants, who by virtue of the restricted franchise had dominated these Assemblies, had been persuaded that the British government would offer greater protection for their property and privileges than they could provide for themselves.

The history of British Honduras in Central America was quite different from that of the other colonies in the Caribbean area. British subjects had established themselves in the Bay of Honduras in the mid-seventeenth century (see Map 14.1). Originally buccaneers, these settlers engaged in the profitable occupation of cutting and exporting logwood used for dye and later mahogany for furniture.

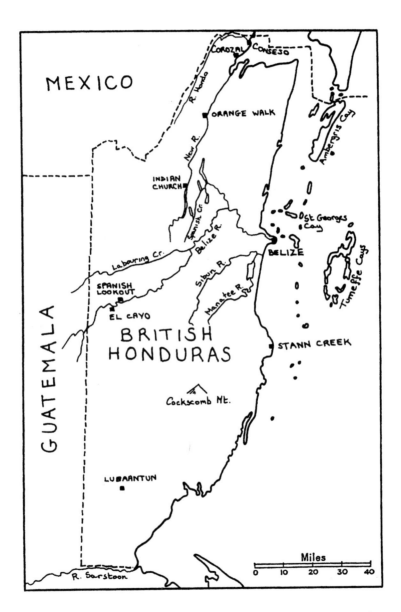

Map 14.1 British Honduras, where trespassers became colonists
(© Andrew Hart)

Some settlers imported African slaves, mainly from Jamaica. As in the island colonies, there had emerged with the passage of time a free brown stratum of mixed African and European descent and smaller numbers of free men and women of purely African origin.

In 1763 a treaty concluded between the Spanish and British governments acknowledged Spain's sovereignty over the territory but permitted the 'Occupation of Cutting, Loading and Carrying away Logwood' by British subjects. In 1765 the settlers established their own machinery for enforcing what were described as 'Customs of the Bay'. This took the form of a public meeting of the white inhabitants. When war with Spain broke out in 1779 the settlers were dispersed and the informal colony was not re-established until after peace was restored in 1783.

The 1783 treaty defined the area in which logging could be carried on and this area was extended by the Convention of London in 1786. But this agreement provided for the evacuation of other British settlements established on the Mosquito Shore and Ruatan island and forbade agricultural or other productive enterprises or the establishment of formal governmental institutions.[8]

In 1765 the settlers were urging the British government to establish some form of government for the territory, but it was not until 1787 that the government appointed a 'Superintendent'. One of his functions was to see that the terms agreed with Spain in the Convention of London were observed by the settlers.

The public meetings continued to function and elect magistrates but, far from being an expression of popular democracy, had become, according to one historian, 'occasional crude gatherings ... dominated by ten or twenty of the richest inhabitants ...'. Although in 1779 there were estimated to be 500 English settlers and 3,000 slaves, only a small minority of the settlers and, needless to say, none of the slaves enjoyed the right to vote. In 1790 it was recorded in the magistrates' minutes that:

> any person entitled to vote at elections for Magistrates for this settlement must be possessed of a fixed Habitation or a Negro Slave or a Mahogany or Logwood work or visible property to the amount of Eighty Pounds Current money of Jamaica and that no person of colour was allowed to vote.[9]

In 1784 the five magistrates were elected by seven residents, in 1786 by 16 electors. In 1787 the number of voters rose to 39. By 1790, when a rough census disclosed that there were 261 Whites, 371 free Coloured or Black and 2,024 slaves, the number of voters was 250. No account was taken of the number of Mayans living in the surrounding countryside.[10]

In 1853 the British government approved a law passed by a public meeting which abolished the public meeting as an institution and established a Legislative Assembly consisting of three nominated and 18 elected members. The right to vote was confined to adult male British subjects who owned real property of an annual value of £7 or were in receipt of an annual salary of not less than £100. Persons elected to the legislature had to own property worth at least £400. Each Assembly was to last for four years unless dissolved earlier by the Superintendent.

Curiously, although the British government had approved the 1853 constitution, British Honduras was not formally declared to be a British colony until 1862. In that year a Lieutenant-Governor was appointed, subordinate to the Governor of Jamaica. In 1871, in the aftermath of the Morant Bay Rebellion in Jamaica and following unrest locally among the Mayan population, the Legislative Assembly agreed to surrender the constitution. This was then replaced, as in most of the other colonies in the Caribbean islands, by Crown colony government. The new Legislative Council consisted of five government officials and four unofficial members nominated by the Crown.[11]

The planters who controlled the Barbados Assembly, the merchants who controlled the Assembly in the Bahamas, and the planters in British Guiana who had been allowed to retain their old Dutch system of government, had been more confident of their ability to control their own disfranchised masses than the ruling classes in the other British colonies in the region. Unlike their more timid counterparts, they retained their ancient constitutions at this time. Not until 1928 did the planters of British Guiana lose their nerve and accept a British model system of Crown colony government.

CHAPTER 15

Imperialism and National Aspirations

The earliest English (British after the Act of Union with Scotland in 1707) colonies were established in the Caribbean. After early expectations of finding gold had been abandoned as unrealistic, the Caribbean islands were seen in Britain as places where Europeans could be settled to grow tropical produce for sale in the home market. The original settlements had not required much of a financial outlay, as land was readily and cheaply available and the crops could be grown by the settlers themselves.

This changed with the development of the more profitable commercial production of sugar. Sugar production required a capital investment in machinery, equipment and slaves. The value of these colonies, as sources of products profitably saleable in Britain, provided the motivation to acquire by warfare colonies previously settled by the French, Spaniards and Dutch.

As sugar and rum were the only manufactured products in the Caribbean colonies, most of these colonies' requirements for manufactured goods were supplied from Britain. The availability of manufactured goods increased rapidly in the last two decades of the eighteenth century and the first half of the nineteenth century with the development of factory production (the so-called 'industrial revolution'), which occurred first in Britain.

However, as the nineteenth century progressed, other countries began to catch up with Britain in industry and manufacturing. This made the earlier acquired colonies more valuable and gave Britain the incentive to expand her empire. In the nineteenth century Britain conquered vast territories and established colonies in Africa. Further expansion occurred when, as a victor in the 1914–18 war, Britain was able to take over the German colonies in Africa.

The reason why colonies had become more valuable was that, by controlling the governments of its colonies, a colonial power could monopolise the market in such colonies for goods manufactured in the metropolis and ensure, by placing discriminatory customs duties on goods imported from commercial rivals, that metropolitan manufacturers were given an advantage over their competitors.

This was the genesis of the system known as 'imperial preference'. Goods from the metropolis were allowed to enter the colonies and exports from the colonies to enter Britain on payment of duties lower than those imposed on goods imported from non-empire sources. Eventually, however, countries forming part of the British Empire demanded that duty preferences allowed on goods manufactured in Britain when they entered the colonies should also be allowed on goods exported from one part of the Empire to another. This was conceded by Britain as part of the 'Ottawa Convention' agreed at a conference in Canada in 1932.

How the British government's control of the colonial governments benefited mainly British manufacturers but also, in some cases, manufacturers in the British Dominions is illustrated by these examples:

1. British motor cars entering Jamaica paid customs duties of 15 per cent while cars from the USA and other foreign countries paid 25 per cent. This was typical of the discriminatory customs duties.

2. In the early 1930s the sale of Japanese canvas shoes commenced in several British Caribbean area colonies at one shilling per pair. Hitherto canvas shoes had retailed in Jamaica at six shillings and 7s 6d per pair. To protect the market for canvas shoes manufactured in the British Empire, in this case in Canada, the Jamaican government was required to impose an additional increase on the duty payable on importation of the Japanese shoes.

When the same discriminatory duty on the Japanese shoes was proposed to the Legislative Council in Grenada in 1932, the members insisted on a more humane solution. They proposed, and the British government had to agree, that in order to keep the price of shoes at a level that more people could afford, instead of the duty on the Japanese shoes being increased the duty on the Empire product should be abolished. In this way the differential required by the British government was introduced in a manner less detrimental to the consumer. It is, however, interesting to note that, in the Secretary of State's memorandum recording his agreement, he took the opportunity of 'pointing out that shoes of the type in question are made just as much in the UK as in Canada'.[1]

Other reasons why it was perceived by the British government that it was desirable to hold other countries in colonial subjection were that a colony provided:

1. a safe place in which investors in the metropolis could invest their capital, where labour was cheap and any labour unrest that occurred could be contained by police, and when necessary military, forces commanded by British officers;

2. the possibility of preventing or discouraging the establishment of industries in the colony which would compete with metropolitan industries;

3. career opportunities for persons in the metropolis who could be sent to the colonies as senior civil servants, managers and supervisers, army and police officers, teachers and ministers of religion;
4. the opportunity to establish naval and military bases, for use in times of conflict with rival imperialist powers.

There are many examples of the use of the armed forces to control labour unrest which, if allowed to continue uncontained, would have adversely affected the profitability of British investments. In addition to the native police forces which were invariably commanded by white officers, there were resident garrisons of British regiments in some colonies. British warships were frequently dispatched to colonies where serious labour unrest occurred or was anticipated, as happened in Trinidad in 1919, St Kitts and St Vincent in 1935, St Lucia in 1936, Trinidad in 1937 and Jamaica in 1938. The resident British regiment was also used to help suppress labour unrest in Jamaica in 1938.[2]

An attempt by a local entrepreneur to establish a cement factory in Jamaica, which would have competed with exports of Portland cement from Britain, was frustrated by the British government in the late 1930s. Not until 1948, when British cement interests decided to participate in the investment, was a licence granted for a cement factory in Jamaica.[3]

In the 1930s and 1940s the Governors and most of the heads of government departments, the officers commanding the troops, the Commissioners of Police and most police officers and many of the clergy and teachers were white, being with few exceptions men sent out from Britain. The few heads of departments who were natives were either white or of very light complexion. When P.W. Gibson, the first black Anglican Bishop of Jamaica, was appointed, this caused considerable surprise.

Some of the factors which made possession of colonies attractive to persons in Britain had the opposite effect in the colonies, encouraging there the development of nationalistic aspirations:

1. One such factor was the imperial policy of reserving most of the top administrative, managerial and supervisory posts for persons sent out from Britain. People educated in the colonies resented this, being aware that these jobs could be performed with equal, sometimes superior, competence by local people. This was a basis for the realisation that, if the colony were to become self-governing, these posts would be filled by natives.
2. Another factor was the imperial policy of using control of the colonial government to place obstacles in the way of industries being established in the colonies which would compete in the local markets with exports from the metropolis. Many local

manufacturers and entrepreneurs responded favourably to the proposition that, if governors sent out from Britain were to be replaced by executive governments comprised of politicians elected locally, such governments would put local interests first, encourage local industrial development and give local industries some protection from the competition of imports.

3. Another policy, which adversely affected and caused dissatis-faction among many local merchants and commission agents, was the fact that, if they imported goods from non-Empire sources, they had to pay higher customs duties thereon than the duties payable on goods imported from Empire sources. This policy, designed to benefit metropolitan exporters, restricted the range of sources from which they could import goods for sale. They too were receptive to the argument that an entirely locally elected government would place the interests of the local consumer above those of British exporters and allow them greater flexibility.

4. The concept of self-government, once properly understood, also became attractive to many workers. Workers who had experienced the use against them at times of labour unrest of armed forces under British control, were able to understand the argument that if there were to be a government controlled by locally elected politicians, it would be more inclined to show sympathy for the workers' cause and less inclined to allow the use of the police and soldiers to prevent strikes from being effective.

It must, however, be pointed out that the development of nationalistic aspirations among the intelligentsia and the business classes preceded its development among the workers. The involvement of the workers in the nationalistic struggle, when it came, transformed colonial nationalism from a mainly middle-class phenomenon into one involving the popular masses, thereby creating some apprehension among the business and professional classes. That it did not do so on a wider scale in the Caribbean colonies may have been attributable to the fact that most of the labour movements of the region were under middle-class leadership.

There is one aspect of the problem of developing nationalistic aspirations which is sometimes overlooked. There were unifying cultural factors, which served to strengthen national opposition to colonialism among the subject peoples of Asia and Africa, which were absent in the West Indian colonies. The peoples of Asia and Africa had intact their languages, religions, institutions and customs which the Europeans were unable to destroy.

By contrast, inhabitants of the West Indian colonies who had been transported as slaves from different parts of Africa had suffered the almost total destruction of their languages, religions and institutions. Even those inhabitants transported later from Asia as indentured labourers, who managed to retain their religions and, for a time, their languages, found themselves subjected to European practices and institutions which undermined their original cultural values.

There were, of course, persons within the colonies who wished to preserve the existing system of external control of the colonial governments:

1. Many white and lighter complexioned natives feared the consequences of a Colonial Governor being replaced by an executive government responsible to an elected legislature, particularly if that legislature were to be elected on a wider franchise. Being a minority of the educated population, they anticipated that their privileged social position and the opportunities they enjoyed of occupying some of the top jobs would be lost to them. Although there were exceptions, there was some relationship between the complexion of individuals and their readiness to support demands for self-government.

2. The largest employers, particularly the sugar manufacturers, were opposed to self-government for two reasons. First, they depended on imperial preferences to enable them to sell their sugar and rum more cheaply in Britain and Canada than their competitors in other sugar-producing countries. Second, being employers of large numbers of workers, they were glad of the assistance they could count on from the armed forces controlled by the British government whenever their employees went on strike to obtain higher wages. There was therefore a relationship between the nature of an industry and the number of workers employed therein and the views of the owners and managers of the industry on the merits or demerits of colonialism and decolonisation.

3. Merchants and commission agents who represented or acted as agents for British manufacturers in a colony were often well satisfied with the existing colonial status of their country.

4. While the majority of workers in the other colonies responded favourably to advocacy of self-government, this was not initially the case, for peculiarly local reasons, in Jamaica. There the demand for self-government, pioneered by the Peoples National Party, was winning working-class support when a rival political party was formed by W.A. Bustamante, the most popular labour leader. In order to counteract the appeal of the PNP's nationalism, Bustamante issued the slogan: 'Self-government means brown man rule.' As the workers were aware that many members of the predominently brown middle classes considered themselves superior to the black masses, this was an effective argument in the 1944 election, despite the introduction at that time of full adult suffrage.[4]

Prior to 1865, the elected Assemblies in the older colonies had resisted all attempts by the British government to reduce their powers of internal self-government. But because the franchise was restricted to those possessing property and income qualifications, these Assemblies had been dominated by white planters and merchants. With few exceptions their members had regarded themselves as Englishmen (or Scots, Welsh or Irish) overseas. Their determination to retain control of the local governments was not therefore a manifestation of Barbadian, Jamaican or any other West Indian nationalism, but was an expression of their resolve to preserve the traditional rights of Englishmen.[5]

By contrast, the demands for modifications in the system of Crown Colony government to provide for greater control by locally elected representatives, heard increasingly in the Caribbean area colonies from the closing decades of the nineteenth century onwards, were the first, albeit hesitant, expressions of a new nationalism. These were the demands or requests not of Englishmen overseas but of people who, for the most part, regarded themselves primarily as Jamaicans, Trinidadians, Grenadians or other permanent residents of the British West Indies.

Slavery, indenture and colonialism had a profoundly damaging mental effect on the inhabitants of the British colonies in the Caribbean area. The prevailing social structure and the education and indoctrination system to which they were subjected caused many, perhaps a majority of, West Indians to have a poor opinion of themselves and a low self-esteem. This was a situation calculated to facilitate and perpetuate external control.

Many generations had observed that those at the top of the social pyramid – the Governor, the Heads of government departments, the most prominent persons in business and society generally, the Bishops and other heads of the established churches with few exceptions – were or looked white. They could see that those at the bottom of the pyramid – the manual workers and cultivators of the soil – were black. Nor could they fail to notice that those on the middle rungs of the social ladder were usually brown in complexion, indicating a partly white ancestry. These were observations from which the inference could easily be drawn that to be white was to be superior, to be black inferior and to be brown or partly white advantageous.

The educational system and the press projected the same idea. European and white North American models were the ideal. Everything African or Asian was portrayed as primitive, backward and unworthy of emulation. The religious denominations too conveyed the same message. God was assumed to be white. The pictures handed out to Sunday school children were of a white Jesus, despite the fact that he had had a Middle Eastern mother!

Some of the indoctrination may have been attributable to a belief on the part of those responsible for the administration of the colonies that the Anglo-Saxons were a superior race with an obligation to 'civilise' the natives. Its main purpose however was to facilitate the task of retaining and governing the colonies. This was clearly explained by R.C. Bodily, an English lawyer and ex-naval commander who had served as a Resident Magistrate in Jamaica for seven years, in an interview published in the magazine *Today's Cinema* in 1932.

Home on leave, Bodily was asked for and gave his views on films shown in the colonies. He deplored 'the bathroom, bedroom and bomb dramas' which, he said, 'belittle the respect of the natives for the whites and ... are in the long run inimical to successful government'. Perceptively he added: 'Our rule exists in the last resort on a carefully nurtured sense of inferiority in the governed. As soon as we lessen that we lessen the security of our laws.'[6]

This processing, designed to induce the black majority in the colonies to believe that they were inferior to white people, had been very successful. Acceptance of Eurocentric standards of value was evident in many ways, including some expressions, still current in the 1930s, in everyday language. 'Good hair' and 'bad hair' were terms often used to describe respectively the straight or wavy hair of white and many partly white persons and the kinky or tightly curled hair of Blacks.

Similarly 'nice colour' or 'good colour' were terms of approval used when the children of parents of different complexions took the complexion of the lighter-skinned parent. A person would sometimes be referred to as 'black but well-mannered'. A person of dark complexion who had a lighter complexioned partner would be said to have 'raised their children's colour'.

The task of overcoming this atmosphere of popular disparagement of blackness had to be confronted by any reform movement dependent, for its ability to influence society, on popular support. The work of the pioneers who first perceived the falsity and challenged the prevailing standards of value was therefore tremendously important. Unless the majority of black people could be inspired to develop racial self-respect, no popular organisation or movement could possibly become effective.

The earliest of the pioneers, whose published works opened the eyes of many educated but misinformed persons, was Edward W. Blyden (1832–1912). Born in St Thomas, US Virgin Islands, he had experienced racism when, in 1850, a theological college in the USA refused to accept him as a student. In that same year he emigrated to Liberia, where his outstanding aptitude for scholarship was recognised. In 1855 he became the editor of the *Liberia Herald*. In 1858 he was ordained in the Presbyterian Church and was appointed principal of Alexander High School in Monrovia. He later resigned from the Presbyterian Church to pursue a broader religious approach, which included Islam.

President of Liberia College from 1880 to 1884, he later returned to the College as Professor of Classics. During a political and diplomatic career of over 30 years he held several posts in the Liberian Government and represented Liberia abroad. He was Liberia's Ambassador to Britain 1880 to 1884 and again in 1892 and Minister Plenipotentiary and Envoy Extraordinary to Britain and France in 1905.

A renowned linguist, Blyden was the author of many books and booklets. These included: *A Vindication of the African Race* (Liberia, 1857), *Africa for the Africans* (Washington, 1872), *Christianity, Islam and the Negro Race* (London, 1887), *West Africa before Europe* (London, 1905), *African Life and Customs* (London, 1908) and *The Negro in Ancient History*, (Washington [?]).[7]

Another pioneer in the task of combating racist concepts of black inferiority was the Trinidadian John Jacob Thomas (1840–89). Although he did not have as much influence on the black intelligentsia internationally as Blyden, Thomas made a significant contribution. Though born in humble circumstances, he was fortunately an early beneficiary of the system of free secular primary education introduced by the Colonial government in Trinidad in 1851. But for this chance circumstance his true potential might never have been realised.

In 1858 Thomas entered the Normal School at Woodbrook where he proved to be an outstanding student, graduating and obtaining his first job as a teacher in 1860. Perhaps it was the fact that many of the children whom he taught and their parents spoke only the local French Creole vernacular that led him to study and master both French and Creole and later also Spanish. In later life he would also teach Greek and Latin.

In a competitive examination for entry into the civil service Thomas topped the list. In 1867 he obtained a job in the Receiver General's Office in the capital Port of Spain, which gave him the opportunity to make use of the public library. In 1869 his first book, *The Theory and Practice of Creole Grammar*, was published in Trinidad. Favourably reviewed in Britain, this book established his reputation as a scholar of outstanding ability.

His promotion in the civil service was rapid and in 1870 he became Secretary to the Board of Education. He was secretary of *The Trinidad Monthly*, the island's first literary magazine, which appeared sporadically in 1871 and 1872. In 1872 he established the Trinidad Athenaeum which promoted discussions and lectures. In 1873 he visited England on leave, where he read a paper 'On Some Peculiarities of the Creole Language', at a meeting of the Philological

Society. Between 1876 and 1879 he translated into English, at the author's request, the first part of P.G. Borde's *Histoire de la Trinidad sous le Gouvernement Espagnol.*

In 1889 *Froudacity: West Indian Fables Explained,* his most important contribution to combating racist stereotyping, was published in London. In it he refuted the denigrations of Blacks by J.A. Froude, Professor of Modern History at Oxford University, in his book *The English in the West Indies,* published in 1888. This important contribution to the combating of racism at the intellectual level was republished by New Beacon Books in 1969. Valuable additions to this edition are a biography of the author by Donald Wood and an introduction by C.L.R. James.[8]

Blyden internationally and Thomas in Trinidad enlightened the then numerically small black intelligentsia. Their successors, Dr Robert Love in Jamaica and Marcus Garvey on a world-wide stage, had a wider awakening and enlightening effect, influencing not only the black intelligentsia but also the popular masses.

Joseph Robert Love (1839–1914) was born, attended school and taught for a while in the Bahamas. In 1866 he went to the USA where, in 1871, he became a deacon in the Episcopalian Church. He served for some years in the southern states, having been ordained as a priest in 1876. He also attended medical school at the University of Buffalo, graduating in 1879. After a spell with the Episcopal diocese in New York State, he joined the Episcopal Mission in Haiti but left in 1882 on falling out with the bishop. He then settled in Jamaica where he remained until his death.

In 1895 Love established and edited the *Jamaica Advocate,* a newspaper he described as 'the literature of political and social freedom'. The Jamaica Union of Teachers adopted it as its organ. An effective public speaker, he gave many lectures. Referring to one of his lectures on Toussaint Louverture, *The Gleaner* newspaper commented:

> he scored a success that assured him a crowded house whenever he chooses to appear again. ... [He] proved himself [a] powerful and eloquent exponent of the rights and wrongs of his down-trodden race.[9]

At public meetings and in his newspaper Love protested against the use of black troops by Britain in its wars in West Africa. In the *Jamaica Advocate* on 23 March 1895 he responded to the British government's praise of West Indian troops serving them in Africa by pointing out that these troops were 'cutting the throats' of their African brothers. In the issue of 23 November 1895 he attacked Britain for waging war against the Ashanti.[10]

Love played a leading part in the popular agitation in 1899 against the decision of Secretary of State Joseph Chamberlain that the seats of four government officials in the Legislative Council, which had been left vacant for some years, should be filled and that all the nominated members allowed by the constitution be appointed, in order to ensure the Governor's majority over the elected members. He was a member of the delegation that went to England to protest against this change. In 1898 Love established the 'Peoples Convention', a forum for discussion of such subjects as popular education, taxation, land distribution, voter registration and citizenship.

In 1889 Love supported the election of Alexander Dixon, the first black man to be elected to the Legislative Council. Years later Marcus Garvey declared: 'much of my early education in race consciousness is from Dr. Love. One cannot read his "Jamaica Advocate" without getting race consciousness.'[11]

Despite the restricted franchise, Love was elected to the Kingston municipality in 1898 and to the Legislative Council in 1906. In his declining years he was a member of the National Club, founded as a political party in 1909 to express Jamaica's national aspirations.

The most famous and influential of all the pioneers was Marcus Moziah Garvey (1887–1940), born in St Ann, Jamaica. A printer by trade, he was an officer of the trade union of printers formed in Kingston in 1907 and an assistant secretary of the National Club in 1910. In 1914 he formed an organisation in Jamaica called the Universal Negro Improvement Association and African Communities League.

In 1916 Garvey emigrated to the USA where he established the Universal Negro Improvement Association. He and the UNIA became world famous. It was easily the largest organisation of black Americans and also established branches in many parts of the Caribbean and Latin America and some African countries. Where other black leaders had influenced thousands Garvey inspired millions, with his message of racial consciousness and racial self-respect. He did more than any other leader to lay the foundations upon which later organisations, relying on the support of the black masses, were able to build.

In 1925 he was imprisoned on a charge of using the US Mails to defraud, in connection with his appeals for funds to establish a shipping line. In 1928 he was deported to Jamaica where he published weekly newspapers, was elected to the Kingston & St Andrew Corporation Council and established the Peoples Political Party to contest the general election in January 1930. However, owing to the restricted franchise, most of the party's candidates were defeated. In 1934 he migrated to Britain where he published *The Black Man*, a monthly magazine which he had started in Jamaica. From there he visited Canada and a number of countries in the Caribbean area to promote the UNIA.

In 1926 Garvey's wife edited and published the first collection of his writings and speeches under the title *The Philosophy and Opinions of Marcus Garvey*, since republished several times. After his death in London in 1940 many books, pamphlets and papers have been written about him and his work. Collections of his Jamaican newspapers, *The Blackman* and *The New Jamaican*, are in the National Library in Kingston. A collection of copies of *The Black Man* magazine has been republished and a comprehensive collection of what he said and wrote and what was said and written about him, in 12 volumes, has been edited by Dr Robert Hill. Ten volumes of the latter collection have already been published.[12]

This selection of Blyden, Thomas, Love and Garvey as outstanding examples of persons who challenged the concept that Blacks are inferior to Whites and performed the task of inspiring black people to acknowledge their racial origins and respect themselves, is not comprehensive. A complete list of such pioneers would include Theophilus Scholes, Sylvester Williams, F.E.M. Hercules, W.E.B. DuBois and many others.

CHAPTER 16

Pioneering Nationalists Organise

The Jamaica Association, formed in 1874, advocated the admission into the Legislative Council (then consisting entirely of government officials) of members to be elected by persons who paid one pound annually in direct taxes and unofficial members to be nominated by the Governor. However, so hesitant was the attitude of the Association that, when it presented a petition signed by 2,447 petitioners in 1876, it omitted the request for the inclusion of elected members in order to obtain the support of certain 'influential gentlemen'.[1]

In 1883 a further petition, signed by 4,677 persons, was drawn up in Jamaica. The signatories included three of the 14 custodes, 34 of the 489 magistrates, seven of the 55 solicitors, eleven of the 207 clergy and 17 'commercial firms of standing'. These would-be reformers, though still modest in their requests, were somewhat more positive. They asked for a Legislative Council consisting of 14 elected members and eight members nominated by the Governor.[2]

With their long experience of colonial administration, British governments were skilled at making concessions which, though not altering the reality of power, were sufficient to divide and diffuse the strength of local dissatisfactions. Sometimes concessions were made in response to petitions. Sometimes, particularly if there had been unrest or widespread dissatisfaction, a Royal Commission was appointed. Sometimes a high-ranking official was sent to a colony or colonies to assess local representations for reform and make recommendations.

In 1884, in response to the recent petition, the Secretary of State for the Colonies agreed to a Legislative Council for Jamaica consisting of the Governor, the officer commanding the British troops in the island, three ex-officio senior civil servants, not exceeding five persons nominated by the British government (who might be either government officials or non-official members) and nine elected members. The right to vote was restricted to males possessing an income of £150 from land or £200 partly from land and partly from an office or business, or £300 arising from an office or business, provided that such voters had paid annually direct taxes or export duties of not less than £10.[3]

99

Although in Grenada the decision to accept Crown colony government had been made as recently as 1876, in 1881 a petition signed by 467 persons, mostly local planters and merchants, requested the Secretary of State to give the taxpayers the right to elect representatives to the Legislative Council.

In 1883, the first demand for the right to be represented, by persons identifying themselves as non-Whites, was articulated. William Galway Donovan, the proprietor and editor of the *Grenada People* newspaper, and 18 others, submitted a memorandum to the West Indies Royal Commission of that year in which they suggested that the denial of the right to elect representatives was due to official racist attitudes:

> We ... draw your attention to the strong feeling which prevades the entire community against the present system of government ... We are thankful for the solicitude which this supposed Crown Government manifests on our behalf; but we beg to assure you that no one can be more solicitous for our well-being than ourselves. We know the people of England entertain very crude notions respecting our condition. Because we are negroes or mulattoes must we be ignorant? Does God give intellectual power and reasoning faculties only to Whites? We cannot submit to be ruled like serfs when we consider ourselves to be free-born Britons. We therefore ask you to make such representations as will secure us a share in the management of our own affairs.

Imprisoned for libel, Donovan on his release declared:

> I shall continue in my journal to advocate the right of the people of Grenada to representative government ... believing as I do that the people of the Colony are qualified to manage through their representatives all local affairs and that until this fundamental right is restored ... neither the prosperity of the colony nor the contentment of the people will be ensured.[4]

In 1886, the franchise in Jamaica was extended to males who had paid a land tax of not less than ten shillings or not less than £1 10s in other taxes. Hitherto the land tax qualification had been £1 10s. In 1906 the franchise was further extended to males earning an annual salary of not less than £50.[5]

In 1887, the British Guiana Political Reform Club was formed. According to H.A. Will, 'Its membership remained narrow and its appeal limited though it was responsible in late 1887 for organising a memorial favouring representative government.' This was signed by 4,647 persons. What the constitutional changes requested were is not clear, but 'representative government' was a term implying at least a majority of elected members in the legislature.

By August 1889, the British Guiana Constitutional Reform Association was founded by R.P. Drysdale, Mayor of Georgetown and a Financial Representative on the Combined Court. In 1890 its candidate Duncan Hudson, a coloured barrister and one of the signatories to the earlier memorial, was defeated by the candidate of the sugar interests by 85 votes to 70 in an election held to choose the Financial Representative for Demerara.

A Franchise Reform bill was introduced in 1890 which provided that, as from 1891, owners of 3 acres and tenants of 6 acres of land might elect eight members of the Court of Policy. But, as the *Berbice Gazette* of 29 November 1890 commented:

> so slight are the amendments proposed to the present constitution that it is hardly worth while making them at all. The number of the Court of Policy, it is true, is to be increased [to 16 – eight officials and eight electives] but the qualification [for membership] being the possession of property of large value, there will be practically no difference in the class of persons eligible for the Legislature, as comparatively few persons unconnected with the planting industry hold property to the value of $7,500.

> This qualification is much too high and there ought also to be, as in the case of Financial Representatives, an income qualification, for the reason that there are in the colony many good and able men who do not own immovable property of any considerable value. The principle of direct representation on a reduced franchise has to a certain extent been recognized, but this concession is worthless without secret voting ...[6]

The number eligible to vote in the general election held in British Guiana in 1892 was a mere 2,046. In the new Combined Court, in which the number of elected members had been increased to 14, 12 of those elected were white. The Court of Policy consisted of five white planters, two white merchants and one coloured barrister. Secret balloting was introduced in 1896 and, after the general election of 1897, the Combined Court consisted of five planters, three merchants, five lawyers and one store manager. It is probable that the lawyers and the store manager were coloured.[7]

The Trinidad Workingmen's Association, formed in 1897, performed the functions of both a trade union seeking wage increases for the workers and a political pressure group. Giving evidence before the West India Royal Commission in that year, its President Walter Mills:

> informed the Commission that the Association had plans to press for a reduction of taxes, especially on foodstuffs and agricultural impliments used by the labouring people. They wanted better transport facilities, the setting up of minor industries, the

introduction of Savings Banks and the further opening of Crown Lands. In addition, the Association was strongly opposed to state-aided immigration which ... increased the competition for the 'starvation wages paid on sugar estates'. He argued ... [that labourers should be granted] five-acre blocks of land and free plants.

Stressing the need for constitutional changes, Mills stated:

we shall always suffer these injustices as long as we have not the right of sending our representatives to the Legislative Council because the sugar interests predominate there and the Government heads of departments generally keep friends with them because they know their power.

In 1899 the British government abolished the Borough Council which, though elected by the ratepayers comprising a small minority of the city's population, had been responsible for local government affairs in Port of Spain. It was replaced by a board of appointed commissioners. In 1906 the TWA, then under the presidency of Alfred Richards who, like his predecessor, was a small pharmacy owner, petitioned the Secretary of State for the Colonies for:

A purely elective Municipal Council for the city of Port of Spain and some measure of reform of the Legislative Council on a representative principle.[8]

Replying in his newspaper, the *Jamaica Advocate*, to a recent statement by British Prime Minister Joseph Chamberlain that 'as the dominant race, if we admitted equality with inferior races, we would lose the power which gave us our dominance', Dr Robert Love wrote:

It is with this principle that they vex the Africans with 'punitive expeditions', and destroy the Indians with famine and oppression ... But Englishmen will wake up some day to find they are making a great mistake ... The subject races will not always be governed by that spirit. They were not always thus governed. The Indian will some day repel the assumption, the African will do the same thing, the Egyptian and Burmese, etc., will vindicate their individuality, and will prove that temporary dominance is not evidence of constitutional superiority.[9]

Love did not refer specifically to West Indians in this prophetic list of those who would repudiate English domination.

The National Club, the first political organisation in the twentieth century to express Jamaica's nationalistic aspirations, was launched by the barrister S.A.G. (Sandy) Cox in March 1909. Its manifesto recorded that 'the system of Crown Government which obtains in Jamaica today has ceased to be paternal' and declared that:

> Each member pledges himself to do all he can to secure self government for this island. Its founders expressed their intention to correct abuses by the Government and to put themselves in communication with those Trade Unions in England, (and if possible to affiliate with them) as also Labour members of Parliament.[10]

Cox was elected to the Legislative Council in a by-election in 1909 where he joined his sitting National Club co-founder Alexander Dixon. On 1 July 1910, the newspaper *Our Own*, edited by Cox, began publication. In its issue of 15 August 1910, announcing the National Club's campaign for the next general election, the paper declared: 'we desire a greater measure of self government within the empire'. In the issue of 15 October 1910, listing numerous grievances, the editor wrote:

> We are dissatisfied with the system of Government which obtains, because it places a great deal of power in the hands of one man, who is known as the Governor ... when we get a really good, accomplished, just and honourable gentleman, it is a system that works like a charm. But ... [it is] a system that can be made extremely oppressive ... The Governor, Sir Sidney Olivier, is responsible for ... this scandalous state of affairs ...

> We ... cannot in future take the risk of having another such Governor ... We therefore say, you must give us a better form of government whereby those of us who are deeply interested in the welfare of the people may be able to take a larger share in the government of our own people ... [We are] showing to the English people that they are governing us in a manner distasteful to us and not calculated to give us the maximum of benefit, and that if given a trial we could do better than they are doing.[11]

Answering a complaint from a reader that membership of the National Club was confined to persons born in Jamaica and that 'Your attempt to treat Englishmen in Jamaica as foreigners and enemies of the country is wrong', Cox replied:

> We invite white men ... to join with us in resisting wrong; although we do not invite them to join with us in getting a greater measure of self-government within the empire, because we feel that they are not in sympathy with our aspirations in that direction.[12]

In the general election of 1911 Cox, Dickson and another National Club candidate were elected. Not surprisingly, Cox aroused the opposition of officials and local conservatives and was constantly under attack from the editors of the principal newspapers – the *Daily Gleaner* and the *Telegraph & Guardian*. In 1911 he lost his seat in the legislature when it was determined by the Court that he did not possess the required qualification of residence in his constituency.

In 1912 Cox emigrated to the USA where, in Boston, he was admitted to practise as an Attorney-at-Law. After his departure, the National Club ceased to function but was revived by Dickson for a short period in 1914. Cox died in Boston in 1922.

In 1917 the Grenada Representative Association was formed. Its membership included both a radical wing led by the journalist William Galway Donovan, which advocated a completely elected legislature, and more conservative reformers such as the planter D.S. DeFreitas who advocated only limited elected representation. The young journalist T.A. Marryshow was a member of the Association.

In 1919 the Association reached a compromise decision that they would advocate a legislature with an equal number of elected and non-elected members and the inclusion of elected members on the Governor's Executive Council. They agreed that the qualifications for voting should be the same as those for elections to the existing District Boards. However, these details were not spelled out in its petition to the Secretary of State in 1920, which asked for an end to Crown colony government.[13]

Representative Government Associations were also formed in St Kitts, Dominica, St Lucia and St Vincent. These associations made similar representations for the addition of elected members to their Legislative Councils.

For the first time in the region women were enfranchised in 1919, but only in Jamaica. Their qualifications for voting were however higher than for men. They had to have attained the age of 25 years as against 21 for men, and to be literate, which was not required of men. Their land tax qualification was two pounds as against ten shillings for men.[14]

In 1921 the British government appointed E.F.L. Wood to review constitutional government in the British West Indies. He visited these colonies from December 1921 to February 1922, making a study of their existing constitutions and receiving representations. In his report he recorded that, apart from Barbados and British Guiana (where the constitutions had not been surrendered or amended following the Morant Bay Rebellion of 1865), the only colony in which there were elected members in the legislature was Jamaica.

Prior to Wood's appointment the British government had agreed to the admission of an elected element to the Legislative Council of Grenada in response to the petition mentioned above. They had also agreed to an elected element in Dominica in response to a resolution approved by the Legislative Council. These decisions had not yet been implemented.

In March 1922, following Wood's departure, the Legislative Council of Jamaica petitioned the Crown, observing the customary level of humility:

> We approach ... with a feeling of respectful confidence ... asking Your Majesty to take into consideration our earnest desire to be invested with a larger measure of political rights by an extension of the privileges of the representatives of the people, in granting to them greater authority and responsibility in connection with a levying and appropriation of our revenues, and a larger share in the initiation and framing of our domestic legislation ...

> We pray ... to direct Your Majesty's attention to the composition of the Executive Council of the island on which the popular section of the Legislative Council is entirely unrepresented, and on which as a consequence the representatives of the people have no recognised voice, and therefore no direct means of offering advice or contributing opinions on matters affecting general legislation, and on the fiscal and financial policy of the government.[15]

In 1925, on Wood's recommendation, Dominica was transferred from the federal colony of the Leeward Islands to the Windward Islands, which were separate colonies sharing the same Governor. Minorities of elected members were introduced in the Legislative Councils of all the colonies which had not had elected members, except British Honduras and the remaining Leeward Islands (which were not allowed minorities of elected members until 1936).

The constitution recommended by Wood for the islands of Trinidad and Tobago, which had been amalgamated in 1889, provided for a Legislative Council consisting of the Governor, with an original and casting vote; twelve government officials; six unofficial persons nominated by the Governor; and seven elected members (one for Tobago and six for Trinidad). As regards the qualifications to be required for voting in elections and for persons standing for election, Wood recorded the proposals made to him but made no recommendations. He suggested that these matters be considered by a locally appointed commission.[16]

Wood's constitutional recommendations were accepted by the British government and introduced in 1925. The constitution introduced in Trinidad and Tobago provided that candidates for election were required to be male and literate in English, to own real estate worth not less than TT$12,000 or to have an annual income exclusively from land of not less than TT$960 or from other sources of TT$1,920. The right to vote was restricted to males over 21 years of age and females over 30 who owned property of a rateable value of TT$60 in a borough or TT$48 elsewhere, or who paid a rental of TT$60 or rent and board combined of TT$300, or who paid annual land taxes of TT$2.40 or were in receipt of an annual salary of TT$300.[17]

As regards the British Guiana constitution Wood had commented:

> I do not think that at present there is any ground for suggesting any material changes. The loans of this Colony have, with a few very small exceptions, been floated locally. If the Colony ... sought to obtain ... a large loan in London through the Crown Agents, the question of the constitution must inevitably be raised, but so long as the Colony is able to finance its current expenditure and to obtain money on loan without assistance from the Crown Agents, it would be a mistake to raise ... the question of revising the constitution which ... is regarded with pride by so many of the inhabitants ...

> I do not anticipate that there would be the same feeling in regard to some changes in the constitution, if such were on examination found to be necessary to attract the necessary capital ... It is quite obvious that the Colony cannot be adequately developed unless outside assistance in capital and direction is obtained, but until the source and nature of this assistance is made clear, it would seem both unwise and unnecessary to disturb the 'status quo'.[18]

However, an election took place in 1926 which brought about a change in the thinking of the local planters and merchants and the Colonial Office. The election resulted in several seats being won by the Popular Party, led by Nelson Cannon, a white man, and the popular coloured journalist A.R.F. Webber, which the plantation owners considered to be threat to their interests.

British Guiana's financial difficulties, a budget deficit having occurred in every year but one since 1921, provided the excuse for the British government to send in Parliamentary Commissioners to report on the colony's economic condition and recommend steps that might be taken to promote development. The Commissioners' report criticised the existing constitution in terms which indicated their preference for Crown colony government though they left settlement of the details for further consideration.

Snell, one of the Parliamentary Commissioners, had said that he 'could not help feeling ... alarm that ... the white people in the colony were more and more disinclined to take their part in the responsibility of government'. But it was the changing composition of the electorate rather than 'disinclination' that reduced the number of the white people likely to be elected.

The Constitutional Commission subsequently appointed had only one member, E.G. Woolford, who was a native of the colony. It recommended the replacement of the Combined Court and the Court of Policy by a Legislative Council consisting of the Governor, ten Government officials, five nominated unofficial members and 14 elected members, the Governor having the power to approve a measure defeated in the Legislative Council if he considered it necessary 'in the interest of public order, public faith or other first essentials of good government'. Only Woolford refused to sign the report. The British Parliament enacted these recommended changes in the British Guiana Act, 1928. Thus did British Guiana become a Crown colony.[19]

Meanwhile, in 1924, a physician named Duncan O'Neale, who had become a Socialist under the influence of the Fabian Society in Britain, had returned to Barbados. In October 1924 he formed the Democratic League, the first Barbadian political party. At that time voters in Barbados were required either to have an income of not less than £50 or to own land with a rental value of not less than £5 per year. Despite this restricted franchise the Democratic League's candidate C.A. (Chrissie) Braithwaite won a seat in the Assembly in a by-election in December 1924. In 1930 another Democratic League candidate was elected and in 1932 O'Neale won a seat.[20]

In 1928 Marcus Garvey was released from prison in the USA and deported to Jamaica, where branches of his Universal Negro Improvement Association were already established. Soon after his arrival he commenced publication of The Blackman newspaper and formed the Peoples Political Party. His first pronouncements on the constitution were not critical of its limitations but of the failure of the electorate to make good use of the existing franchise:

The British Government has given us a Constitution which bestows semi-representative privileges and places enormous power in the hands of the ten shilling voter. A small minority only of the mass of the people has to some extent made use of this power in circumstances which conclusively prove that they are hardly conscious of the vast power entrusted to them for the direct purpose of selecting, for their own representatives on the Government, persons who know and understand them ...

Let the ten shilling voter realize that their representatives are not their masters. On the contrary they are their servants ... Let the voter begin to cultivate the spirit of independent thought and consider how his vote will influence [not] himself alone but his children.[21]

A subsequent editorial commenced by blaming the 'classes' for surrendering the pre-1865 constitution, went on to castigate the 'coloured' and ended up suggesting that the existing constitution could be used effectively by a united body of elected members:

We have in the columns of 'The Blackman' shown ... that this colony enjoyed full representation during a period of two hundred years, when its inhabitants were less fitted than they are today to appreciate such representation; that it was a wicked intent and hate of the so-called classes that deprived us of the Legislative distinction that we enjoyed; that this loss issued in disunion of the black and coloured elements of the population ... resulting in disintegration instead of progress and in this process the COLOURED man has played the part of a sneak and hypocrite, is treacherous to the black man, cringes to the white element ... and is an impediment to progress.

This state of things must change. And it is a fully Representative Government that will change it. We have a well defined and articulate Constitution which postulates this very important improvement. Let us organise this system. ... The Government act as a Party under the leadership of the Colonial Secretary who takes directions from the Governor ... The Elected Members must, therefore, constitute themselves into a Party ...[22]

Garvey's manifesto for the election held in January 1930 contained the following demand for constitutional reform:

Representation in the Imperial Parliament or a larger modicum of self government for Jamaica.[23]

With only 10 per cent of the adult population eligible to vote, it is not surprising that most PPP candidates, including Garvey, were rejected by the voters. However, in expressing his disappointment with the results after the election, Garvey did not mention the restricted franchise. In *The Blackman* on 30 January he commented editorially:

We have seen how low down in the scale of political intelligence we are. We have constantly begged you to think for yourselves, but it seems to us that your brains just won't function. The common people of Jamaica will sell their mother for a morsel of bread and a drink of rum ...

Subsequently however, in the *The Blackman* of 23 August 1930, Garvey advocated full adult suffrage.

In the 1930s the constitutional position in the British West Indies was that Crown colony government prevailed in all the colonies except Barbados and the Bahamas. In those two colonies the restricted franchise ensured that political control remained in the hands of planters and merchants in the former and merchants in the latter.

Although there were elected members in the legislatures of the Crown colonies, these members were chosen by less than 10 per cent of the adult populations. The numbers of electors and the percentages they comprised of their respective populations are shown in Table 16.1.

Table 16.1 Number of Electors, 1930s

Colony	Number of Electors	Percentage of Population
Antigua	1,048	3.06
Barbados	6,359	3.30
British Guiana	9,578	2.84
British Honduras	1,156	2.00
Dominica	1,248	2.46
Grenada (1921)		3.25
Jamaica	61,621	5.25
Montserrat	260	1.90
St Kitts-Nevis	1,628	2.30
St Lucia	1,509	2.18
St Vincent	1,598	2.78
Trinidad and Tobago	30,911	6.64
The Bahamas	13,146	21.97[24]

CHAPTER 17

Labour Unrest and Organisation, 1875–1933

Prior to 1871, organisations formed by workers to obtain increases of wages or improvements of their working conditions were also illegal in Britain as combinations in restraint of trade. In 1871 trade unions were made lawful there by statute. A further law enacted in 1875 legalised peaceful picketing of an employer's premises by workers engaged in an industrial dispute and gave trade unions and their members immunity from actions for tort or breach of contract by employers whose business was adversely affected by a strike. This British legislation was not, however, applicable in any part of the Empire outside of Britain.[1]

In Jamaica the legislation forbidding strikes, enacted in 1839 and 1841, was strengthened by the Protection of Property Law in 1905. This made it a criminal offence for anyone under a contract of service for the supply of water or light or the conveying of passengers or freight by railway, tramway or coach to 'break his contract of service, knowing or having reasonable cause to believe that the probable consequence of his so doing ... will be to deprive the inhabitants ...'. For breaches of this law offenders could be fined not more than £20 or imprisoned, with or without hard labour, for not exceeding three months.[2]

Nevertheless, despite their illegality, strikes took place and workers' organisations were formed. The earliest strikes of plantation workers in Jamaica and British Guiana have already been mentioned. Indian indentured workers clashed with the police in British Guiana in the 1870s. In 1884 the Immigration Report stated that there had been only five minor stoppages of work but a period of militancy soon followed.

There were 31 'strikes and disturbances' in British Guiana in 1886, 15 in 1887 and 42 in 1888. There was widespread dissatisfaction among plantation workers in the 1890s and five strikers were killed and 59 wounded by the police in a strike at Non Pareil in 1896. Further strikes of plantation workers occurred in 1903, 1904 and 1905. In 1905 and 1906 there were strikes of waterfront workers in the capital Georgetown.[3]

It would appear that the first organisations formed by working people were benevolent societies, providing their members with sickness and death benefits, and organisations with social objectives which in some cases included improvement of occupational skills. Organisations which limited their objectives in this way would not have been illegal.

The Bakers Association formed in British Guiana in 1888 and the Patriotic Club and Mechanics Union formed in 1890 by the carpenter E.A. Trotz and others, were probably organisations of this type. In 1897 Trotz presented a petition, signed by 200 carpenters, masons, engineers, bricklayers, builders, porters and carters to the West India Royal Commission of that year. The petitioners complained of decreased employment opportunities but do not appear to have claimed to represent an organisation.[4]

The first organisation to represent workers in respect of claims for wage increases in Trinidad was the Trinidad Workingmen's Association, formed in 1897. It functioned as both a political pressure group and a trade union. It sought, but was refused, affiliation with the recently formed British Labour Party. Its first president was the pharmacist Walter Mills. He was succeeded by another pharmacist, Alfred Richards, in 1906. The Secretary then was Adrien Hilarion, a tailor. The TWA sought to organise both skilled artisans and unskilled labourers.[5]

The 'Jamaica Union of Teachers' had been formed in Jamaica on 30 March 1894 to unite:

> by means of local associations, school teachers throughout the island, in order to provide a machinery by which teachers may give expression to their opinions when occasion requires, and may take action in any matter affecting their interests.[6]

It brought together several existing local associations of elementary school teachers which were professional associations rather than trade unions and initially the Jamaica Union of Teachers would appear to have been no more than that. Approved by the Governor, its first two presidents were principals of the Mico Teachers Training College. Later, under the leadership of two of its founders, the teachers J.A. Mason and W.F. Bailey, it began to concern itself with teachers' wages and working conditions.[7]

The first trade unions of manual workers in Jamaica were organised by artisans. In 1898 the Carpenters, Bricklayers and Painters Union, popularly known as the Artizans Union, was formed with E.L. McKenzie as President and S.A. Phillips, soon succeeded by W.E. Hinchcliffe, as Secretary. In 1901 McKenzie assisted with the formation of a Tailors and Shoemakers Union.

In 1907 two more trade unions of skilled workers were formed in Jamaica, by printers and cigar makers. The printers' organisation was a 'local' of the International Typographers Union affiliated to the American Federation of Labour. It was organised in Chapters or branches for pressmen, compositors and bookbinders, each with their own officers. Its only overall officer was the Organiser. The young Marcus Garvey, later to become internationally famous, was Vice-President of the Compositors' chapter. The Cigar Makers Union was organised by A. Bain Alves, a cigar maker, and was also affiliated to the American Federation of Labor (AFL). Both these unions called their members out on unsuccessful strikes in 1908, as a result of which they ceased to function.[8]

Hinchcliffe was subsequently a member of the Jamaica Trades and Labour Union, which was also affiliated to the AFL as Local No. 12575. In an interview with a newspaper he later attributed its decline in 1909 to the fact that its most 'zealous' members had 'through circumstances had to emigrate, some to Haiti, and some to Colon. Others to Port Limon ...'.[9]

In 1909, S.A.G. (Sandy) Cox, a progressive member of the Legislative Council who was president of the National Club, Jamaica's first organisation in the nature of a popular political party, asked the Governor to introduce legislation legalising trade unions. The Governor, Sidney Olivier, the well-known Fabian Socialist, referred the request to the Colonial Office where it was placed before the Secretary of State with the following memorandum by a senior civil servant:

> This movement is apparently being engineered by the 'American Federation of Labor' and if it is successful, will mean that any unions formed in Jamaica will be controlled by the American organisation, thus leading to a further development of the Americanisation of Jamaica, which we are trying to hinder in other directions. Setting aside any questions of its merits as a matter between employer and employed, I think it is on this ground a dangerous movement which we should not help forward if we can avoid it.

This cunning civil servant then went on to point out that if Mr Cox were reminded that he could raise the matter himself in the legislature, the proposal would be killed there if he did so as it would 'probably be objectionable [to the majority of members] on other grounds'. The Secretary of State accepted this advice.[10]

There is no evidence that any of the organisers or members of these early illegal trade unions were prosecuted. This may have been because the governments wished to avoid the adverse publicity that would have followed the disclosure that what was perfectly lawful in Britain was illegal in the colonies. This may also explain why the manager of the Gleaner Company in Jamaica, who had no difficulty in breaking the strike of his employees in 1908, gave as his reason for refusing to recognise the printers' union not the fact that it was illegal, but that it was affiliated to an American rather than a British trade union.

In British Guiana, in the period from 1908 to 1913, not a single year passed without strikes taking place. In 1908 match factory workers at Vreed-en-Hoop were on strike for a week and there were strikes of sugar workers at Plantations Friends and Wales on West Bank Demerara, at Marionville on Leguan Island in the Essequibo and at La Bonne Intention on East Coast Demerara. In 1909 workers were on strike on Plantations Wales and Leonora, West Coast Demerara, and Peters Hall, East Bank Demerara. In 1910, 1911 and 1912 strikes occurred on West Bank Demerara at Friends, Lusignan, Uitvlugt, on East Bank Demerara at Diamond and on West Coast Berbice at Blairmont. But despite the militancy of these workers no organisation was formed.[11]

The first wave of working-class protest and organisation in the English-speaking Caribbean area had ceased to flow before the First World War commenced. By 1910 all the organisations in this first batch of trade unions in Jamaica had ceased to exist and by 1914 the Trinidad Workingmen's Association had become inactive. No trade unions had appeared in the other colonies.

The atmosphere in the early years of the war was not conducive to organised expressions of working-class protest. However, the rising cost of living and wartime deprivations, combined with reports of racial discrimination suffered overseas by West Indians who had enlisted to serve the Empire, brought about a change of attitude as the War progressed. By the end of 1916 the first signs of unrest were evident.

In British Guiana on 7 December 1916 a petition signed by 585 workers, calling for wage increases and a reduction of the working day from 11.5 to 10 hours, was presented to the legislature. The reply came from the Chamber of Commerce. After suggesting that only a minority of workers were dissatisfied and that the grievances alleged were exaggerated, the Chamber met with representatives of the petitioners at the beginning of 1917 and offered new rates and hours of work. The waterfront workers rejected this offer and, on 6 January, came out on strike. Strikes by Georgetown Railway workers and the Sea Wall Defence workers at Lusignan and Clonbrook commenced on 10 January.

By 20 January these strikes had all ended, the workers other than those on the Sea Wall having been awarded modest improvements. The Governor was, however, apprehensive. Writing to the Colonial Office on 31 January he warned: 'In view of the undoubted increase of prices due to the war. I fear the labour unrest in the Colony cannot yet be regarded as at an end.'[12]

In Trinidad in February 1917 there was a strike of oilfield workers at Fyzabad and Point Fortin, but the strikers were intimidated into returning to work. In the same month workers employed to the asphalt company at the pitch lake struck work. In the course of the strike there a serious fire and troops were called in to assist the police. Five of the strike leaders were arrested, two were sent to prison for two years and one for one year, all with hard labour.

At about this time the TWA was revived under the leadership of the stevedore James Braithwaite and a progressive commission agent Sidney DeBourg and in March 1917 it took the decision to support the workers' strikes. In May the TWA negotiated an increase of pay for the asphalt workers of 33.3 per cent, a reduction of the working day by one hour and allocation to the workers of vegetable plots.[13]

In St Lucia in February 1917, the Administrator reported to the Colonial Office that there had been several strikes, that the merchants had increased the wages of the striking coal carriers by 15 per cent and that stevedores had obtained on average increases of 25 per cent. He recommended that wages of public employees be increased.[14]

The veteran journalist Jos N. France, a contemporary of these events, reported that in 1917 workers in St Kitts attempted to form a trade union but, conscious of the fact that trade unions were illegal, did not dare to go beyond what was permitted under the Friendly Societies legislation. In that year the St Kitts–Nevis Benevolent Association was formed by J.A. Nathan and J. Mathew Sebastian. Nathan, a small shopkeeper, had become familiar with trade unionism during a period of residence in the USA. Sebastian started a newspaper, *The Union Messenger*, which was published by the Association in 1921.[15]

In 1917, 1918 and 1919, there was an eruption of strikes in Jamaica. In Kingston, in 1917, there was a strike of ice factory workers and several strikers were sent to prison. In October of that year the cigar makers again went on strike, this time successfully, and formed another Cigar Makers Union under Bain Alves' leadership. In Kingston the Fire Brigade workers struck in April. Between April and June 1918, there were strikes by longshoremen on the Kingston wharves and coal heavers at the Palisadoes Coaling Station. Bain Alves assisted longshoremen, coal heavers, hotel workers and other categories of workers to form separate unions, which were then grouped together under his presidency in a Jamaican Federation of Labour.[16]

There was also unrest in 1918 among Jamaican agricultural workers. There was a strike at Amity Hall in Vere which, on 1 July, closed down the factory. Workers were shot and killed on 3 July when they attempted to prevent the boilers from being restarted. Another strike took place at Caymanas in St Catherine and there were strikes at Golden Grove in St Thomas and at Annotto Bay in St Mary. These events and other disturbances led the government to appoint a Conciliation Board.[17]

Following a successful strike in 1918, the workers at the Jamaica Government Railway, on 17 September 1919, formed the Workingmen's Co-operative Association. They chose that name because they had taken legal advice and been warned that trade unions were illegal. But the organisation was, in the words of Percy Aiken, one of the strike leaders, 'a union under cover'. The WCA nevertheless negotiated increased wages and improved working conditions. At the same time as the railway strike some policemen also went on strike; their grievances were quickly settled.

In the early 1920s the railway manager succeeded in destroying the Workingmen's Co-operative Association by transferring leading members to out-stations well away from the Kingston workshops, where the main strength of the organisation lay, and harrassing others until, in desperation, they left the service. When the railway drivers came out on strike in 1923 there was no organisation to represent them. By the mid-1920s, as the tide of the post-war militancy ebbed, all the unions affiliated to the Jamaican Federation of Labour had also ceased to function.[18]

In British Guiana, towards the end of 1917, Hubert Critchlow, a stevedore who had been one of the organisers of the waterfront workers' strike in Georgetown in 1906, organised a campaign for increased wages, using the traditional method of a petition. In October this petition was presented to the Chamber of Commerce. In negotiations with the petitioners' representatives in December the Chamber agreed to a wage increase of 10 per cent. Emerging publicly at this time as the recognised leader of the workers, Critchlow immediately organised a campaign to collect signatures for a petition calling for adoption of an eight-hour working day. As this campaign gathered momentum, the employers decided that Critchlow must be stopped and he was barred from further employment on the waterfront. This made him more popular than ever and in December 1918 he led a massive demonstration to Government House. The Governor received a delegation from the demonstrators and accepted the idea of the formation of a trade union. On 11 January 1919, the British Guiana Labour Union was formally launched, with Critchlow as General Secretary.[19]

At the war's end West Indian soldiers serving overseas were repatriated, disillusioned by the racial discrimination they had experienced. The inadequate arrangements made for their re-establishment in civilian life added to their discontent. This added to the general atmosphere of unrest.

In March 1918 there was a strike in Antigua, resulting from an attempt to reduce the rate paid for cutting cane. The workers were aware that higher rates were paid to workers in St Croix in the nearby US Virgin Islands. Cane fields were burned and some planters were attacked. When tension spread to the capital St John, police fired on an allegedly riotous crowd, killing two.[20]

In mid-November 1919 the Trinidad Workingmen's Association put forward demands for wage increases on behalf of the waterfront workers of Port of Spain. The shipping agents refused to negotiate, describing these demands as 'a piece of impudence on the part of those who had no authority from the men to make such representations'. On 15 November, the waterfront workers struck work. Public sympathy for the strikers was overwhelming and there was massive support for a march through the streets of the city on 1 December, which brought all business to a standstill.

Such was the mood of militancy that the government adopted a conciliatary attitude and arranged negotiations. At a single sitting the TWA representatives obtained wage increases of 25 per cent and the strike was called off on 3 December. Meanwhile, however, the Governor had telegraphed for armed assistance.

Two British warships arrived in Trinidad on 6 December. The government then abandoned its policy of conciliation. Several leaders of the TWA, including Braithwaite and Phillips, were arrested and sent to prison; Howard Bishop was fined. Nearly 100 of the strikers and other members of the TWA were prosecuted, many being sent to prison. But the TWA's membership, which had risen to 3,000 during the strike, stood at 6,000 at the end of the year. At mid-January a membership of 10,000 was claimed.[21]

The result of this post-war working class militancy led to the enactment of legisation making trade unions lawful in Jamaica on 25 October 1919 and in British Guiana in June 1921. Even so, this legislation differed from the trade union enabling legislation in Britain in that in did not legalise peaceful picketing of employers' premises, nor did the Jamaica legislation give trade unionists immunity from liability for tort and breach of contract in industrial disputes.[22]

In the colony of Trinidad & Tobago there was no legalisation of trade unions at this time. Instead a series of repressive statutes were enacted:

- The Habitual Idlers Ordinance of 1918, designed to discourage indentured labourers whose terms of indenture had expired from leaving the plantations, provided that any male, who could not prove that he had worked for four hours per day during the preceding three days, could be sent to a labour camp or be contracted out by the government to private employers.

- The Strikes and Lockouts Ordinance, enacted in January 1920, was a temporary measure which prohibited strikes and provided for arbitration to settle disputes between employers and employees. When this Ordinance expired in June 1920 it was replaced by the Industrial Court Ordinance (No. 26 of 1920) which achieved the same purpose on a permanent basis.
- The Seditious Acts and Publications Ordinance (No. 10 of 1920), in addition to banning a number of publications, created the criminal offence of 'disaffection' against the King, the Government of Trinidad and Tobago or any other British possession and the colony's Executive and Legislative Councils. Offenders could be sentenced to imprisonment for up to two years and/or fined up to £1,000.[23]

Why did official policy in Trinidad & Tobago differ so sharply from that in Jamaica and British Guiana? A possible explanation may have been that, as Trinidad was then the British Empire's principal source of oil and the British Navy had in 1910 gone over to oil instead of coal burning, it may have been decided that liberalisation of the labour laws there would have been inappropriate. Alternatively, the explanation may have had to do with the personal characteristics of the respective Governors and the British policy of trusting the judgement of the man on the spot. Further research on this matter is required to determine the reason for this difference in the official approach.

In Jamaica all the unions formed in the immediate post-war period had depended on employees at their respective workplaces to run them, none of them having developed to the point of being able to employ independent union officials. This was a point of weakness. Although the unions were now lawful, they were often resented by managements as an infringement of their authority.

In Trinidad, in the late 1920s, there had been a similar decline in the membership of the Trinidad Workingmen's Association, but partly for a different reason. In or about 1923 the TWA had installed Captain Arthur Cipriani as its President. Cipriani, a Trinidadian of Corsican descent, had been able to obtain an officer's commission because he was white. But, unlike the other West Indian officers, he had been concerned about the racial discrimination suffered by the black soldiers and had fearlessly championed their cause. When he returned to Trinidad after the war, his reputation had preceded him and he was very popular.

Under Cipriani's leadership the membership of the TWA had for a time rapidly increased. The new constitution granted to Trinidad and Tobago in 1925 had provided for a minority of members in the legislature elected on a restricted franchise, and

Cipriani and two other TWA candidates had won three of the main island's six elected seats. Cipriani had then requested legislation making trade unions lawful but, when this request was refused, had decided that, until trade unions were made lawful, the TWA should not engage in trade union activities. This decision caused a decline in working-class support for the organisation.[24]

Legislation making trade unions lawful was enacted in 1932, modelled on the Jamaican legislation. Cipriani then requested amendments to the law to allow picketing and give trade unions the same immunities as in England. When the Colonial Office rejected this request, he insisted that the TWA continue to refrain from trade union activities. There was opposition to this in the TWA, but his wishes prevailed.[25] In 1934 he had the name of the organisation changed to the Trinidad Labour Party.

In Grenada legislation was introduced in 1933 making trade unions lawful, with the same limitations in respect of picketing and immunities from civil liability for damages in actions for tort or breach of contract. As had happened in Trinidad and Tobago, representations by T.A. Marryshow to have these defects in the legislation rectified were unsuccessful.[26]

There were expressions of dissatisfaction among the black intelligentsia in Barbados in the immediate post-war years, articulated by the journalist C.W. Wickham, but there was little working-class unrest. It was not until the return to the island of Dr Duncan O'Neale in 1924 that workers' demands for improvements found organised expression.

When, in 1927, the longshoremen in Bridgetown went on strike, O'Neale had agreed to represent them. The employers, however, refused to recognise the Workingmen's Association which he had formed to represent the workers.[27]

No trade unions were formed in the 1920s in any of the other colonies in the English-speaking Caribbean area. In Jamaica there was a further attempt to organise the workers led by S.M. DeLeon, from 1929 to 1931. This was assisted by two leftist organisations in the USA – the Trade Union Unity League and the Negro Labour Congress. The latter organisation sent its 'field organiser', the Suriname-born Communist Otto Huiswood, to assist in this work.

Marcus Garvey co-operated with DeLeon, appointing him Secretary of a committee which met at the headquarters of his Universal Negro Improvement Association 'to pave the way for labour unions'. DeLeon accompanied him on a delegation to the Governor in 1930 to request the introduction of a minimum wage of four shillings a day.[28]

By 1931, this renewed effort to organise the workers in Jamaica had failed. In the early 1930s, the only trade union organising manual workers that was still in existence in the British colonies in the Caribbean area was the British Guiana Labour Union. The first two waves of labour unrest and organisation had no doubt provided the workers with valuable experience. But it was not until a further wave of working-class unrest and militancy had swept across the region in the middle and late 1930s that the foundations were laid for permanent trade union movements.

CHAPTER 18

Labour Rebellions, 1934–37

In the 1930s a wave of labour unrest, the third such wave since the turn of the century but much wider than those preceding it, surged across the Caribbean. The fact that this unrest was regional indicates the extent to which similarly distressing economic conditions in all the British colonies in the Caribbean area had created a situation in which any labour/employer or social conflict could set off a major social upheaval.

The earliest manifestations of social unrest were in Belize City, British Honduras, where an organisation called the Unemployed Brigade was formed which, in February 1934, organised a march of unemployed workers. In that same year there was a demonstration by some 400–500 unemployed workers in Port of Spain, Trinidad, and there were strikes in the sugar industry. In May and October there were strikes in Jamaica of workers at the out-ports of Falmouth and Oracabessa and of banana carriers at a wharf in Kingston.

The popular leader who emerged in British Honduras at this time was Antonio Soberanis Gomez, a barber who had travelled in Latin America and the USA and had recently returned to the colony. He formed the Labourers and Unemployed Association which demanded work and a minimum wage, spoke at numerous protest meetings in Belize City and was arrested when a major riot occurred there. Later in 1934 he organised a strike for higher pay in Stann Creek in the south of the country. In Trinidad the demonstration of the unemployed led to the appointment of an official committee of enquiry.[1]

In British Guiana in September 1934 there was a strike at Plantation Leonora on West Coast Demerara, followed by a strike on Plantation Uitvlugt during which 2,000 strikers converged on the factory to prevent milling operations restarting. No sooner had work resumed than strikes occurred on two other Booker Brothers plantations – De Kinderen and Tuschen. Another strike occurred on Plantation Leonora in September 1935, and there were strikes at Plantations Vryheids Lust, La Bonne Intention, Enmore, Lusignan, Ogle and Farm.[2]

In January 1935 workers on the Shadwell plantation in St Kitts refused to accept work cutting canes at 8d per ton, a rate which workers had accepted under protest during the previous year's crop. News of their refusal spread rapidly around the island and workers on other plantations also refused to cut cane at that rate. Workers at the island's sugar factory, whose wages had been reduced by 1d in the shilling in 1930 and subsequently by a further 1d, also came out on strike.

On the following day the striking workers marched round the island, encouraging workers on all the plantations to refuse to accept the rates offered and the stoppage developed into a general strike. At Buckley's plantation, when 300 workers carrying sticks entered the estate yard and refused to leave, the manager fired his gun into the crowd injuring several of them. Stones were thrown, but whether before or after the shooting was never established.

A party of armed police arrived but the workers refused to disperse, demanding that the manager be arrested. At about 6 p.m., by which time the crowd had swelled to 400–500, a military contingent arrived. The Riot Act was read and the armed men fired into the crowd killing three and injuring eight others.

Next day a British warship arrived and marines were landed. Thirty-nine strikers were arrested and prosecuted. Strike leaders John Palmer and Simeon Prince were imprisoned for five years, Albert Sutton and James Liburd for three years, Thomas Fergus for two years and six months and Thomas Saddler for two years. All these sentences were with hard labour. For several weeks thereafter marines and police patrolled the island. Many arrests were made, an atmosphere of intimidation prevailed and most workers returned to work.[3]

In St Vincent, also in 1935, there was evidence of smouldering discontent. In October there was dissatisfaction with tax increases on items of popular consumption and a decision to maintain a high tariff on locally consumed sugar to subsidise sugar producers at the consumers' expense. This led to a protest demonstration.

On 21 October, the Legislative Council, presided over by the Governor of the Windward Islands who had his headquarters in Grenada, was in session. A crowd gathered outside the drugstore of George McIntosh, a popular member of the Kingstown Town Council. They demanded that he make their grievances known to the Governor. McIntosh wrote a letter to the Governor requesting an interview, which was delivered by hand. He informed the crowd that the Governor had agreed to receive a deputation at 5 p.m.

Knowing that the Governor usually left the island to return to Grenada before that time, the crowd became suspicious that he intended to leave without redressing their grievances. Some of them forced their way into the Council building and there were shouts of 'We can't stand any more duties on food and clothing', 'We have no work' and 'We are hungry'. Such was the alarm created that the Legislative Council session was adjourned.

As the Governor and officials emerged and tried to restore calm, the Attorney-General, who had prepared the new taxation measures, was assaulted and the Governor was pushed and struck. Panes of glass of several of the windows of the building were broken and the motor cars of a number of officials were damaged. Members of the crowd then broke into the nearby prison and released the prisoners. The business of F.A. Corea, a member of the Legislative Council and the island's largest merchant and plantation owner, was ransacked.

A large force of armed police arrived and the Governor personally took command of their operations. The Riot Act was read and the crowd at Corea's store was fired on; one was killed and others injured. As news of these events spread, rioting broke out in Georgetown, 22 miles to the south of Kingstown, and at Chateaubelair, the same distance to the north. Telephone wires were cut and several bridges were destroyed.

At midnight on 21 October, a British warship arrived. 'Volunteers' were also brought in from other islands. On 22 October, a state of emergency was declared. Though the uprising in the capital was suppressed that day, disorders in other areas continued for the next two days. Strong popular resistance was encountered at Byera's Hill, Camden Park and Stubbs. In these districts demands for land and for increased wages were made. The state of emergency was continued for three weeks.

In Kingstown the leaders who emerged were Sherriff Lewis, called 'Selassie', and Bertha Mutt, 'Mother Selassie'. These nicknames reflected popular identification with the people of Ethiopia in Africa, currently being invaded by Italy. But attention was soon concentrated on George McIntosh who, despite his appeals for observance of law and order, was prosecuted for treason. He was acquitted and emerged as the popular leader.[4]

At the end of 1935 there was a strike of coal loaders in St Lucia. Early in 1936 a British warship arrived in response to the Governor's request. Marines were landed and patrolled the streets of Castries and for several nights the ship's searchlights illuminated the town. Intimidated, the strikers returned to work and the unrest subsided.[5]

In mid-1935 the Jamaica Trades and Labour Union was formed. A.G.S. Coombs, its president, had been a soldier and a policeman but had left the police force after coming to blows with a white officer. He described himself as 'a peasant of low birth, and very limited education, and a very poor man'. A natural rebel, he had no theoretical motivation. H.C. Buchanan, its secretary, was a master brick mason and Jamaica's first active Marxist.[6]

In Jamaica, in June 1936, the report of an official Unemployment Commission referred to acute unemployment in the country parishes. The report stated that in the city, 'The classes suffering the greatest hardships are the artizans and those educated and trained to become clerks, shop assistants, etc.'[7]

In British Guiana in 1937, the Man Power Citizens Association, formed in 1936 and led by the jeweller Ayube Edun, was registered as a trade union. It organised sugar workers, who had always shown great militancy but had not previously had an organisation to represent them. In 1938 seven other trade unions were organised. Six of these new unions – the British Guiana Seamens Union, the Transport Workers Union, the Post Office Workers Union, the Subordinate Government Employees Association and the British Guiana Clerks Association – were separate industrial unions serving the workers in specific industries or occupations. The seventh was the British Guiana Congress of General Workers.[8]

In Trinidad in the mid-1930s there was unrest among the workers. Oilfield workers' wages, averaging 91.5 cents per day in 1936, were lower than in 1920, while the purchasing power of the dollar in the early months of 1937 was 70 per cent of what it had been in 1929. On the sugar and cocoa plantations wages were even lower, averaging at best 40 cents per day for male workers.[9]

The dividends of the foreign oil companies, on the other hand, were remarkably high. In 1934–35 Apex Oilfields (Trinidad) Ltd's total dividends amounted to 35 per cent and in 1937 the company declared a dividend of 45 per cent. For the year ending 30 June 1936, Trinidad Leaseholds Ltd's total dividends amounted to 25 per cent and in 1937 to 30 per cent.[10]

Uriah Butler, who had been an enlisted soldier during the First World War, had migrated to Trinidad from Grenada and become an oil worker but had been forced to retire prematurely due to injury and had became a Baptist preacher. He came into prominence in 1935 as leader of a hunger march to the capital of dismissed employees of Apex Oilfields Ltd. Granted an audience with the Governor, he had pleaded the cause of the dismissed workers. An associate of the leftist barrister A. Cola Reinzi in the Trinidad Workingmen's Association, he too had rejected the increasing conservatism of its leader, Captain Arthur Cipriani.[11]

Butler was involved in planning a strike of oilfield workers which commenced at midnight on 18–19 June 1937 at Forest Reserve and Fyzabad (see Map 18.1). The oil companies' representatives rejected the Governor's advice to negotiate. Instead, they called for Butler's arrest and the prohibition of meetings in the oil-producing counties. On 19 June, police and paramilitary forces were rushed to the area and a warrant was issued for Butler's arrest.

When the police attempted to arrest Butler while he was addressing a meeting, the crowd rescued him. In the ensuing riot a much-hated police corporal was drenched with oil and burned alive. Telephone lines between Fyzabad and San Fernando were cut. Police

Map 18.1 Trinidad, scene of the labour rebellion of 1937 (© Andrew Hart)

reinforcements were stoned when they arrived. Members of the crowd were shot and killed, as was a police sub-inspector.[12]

By the morning of 21 June the workers employed by United British Oilfields at Point Fortin were on strike and barriers had been erected across the road to prevent access to the refinery. What had commenced as an oilfield workers' strike had spread to the sugar industry with a strike at the Usine St Madeleine plantation and an island-wide strike was developing.

In San Fernando, the principal town in the south, angry, frustrated crowds rioted, closing all businesses, cutting telephone wires and smashing the windows of business premises. A battalion of the Light Infantry Volunteers, which had been rushed to the area, repulsed an attack on the telephone exchange in which two members of the crowd were killed and eight were wounded. The Governor telegraphed for further assistance.

On the morning of 22 June, crowds halted work on Waterloo, Wyaby and Woodford Lodge plantations. At Woodford Lodge one man in the crowd was killed and two were wounded. That morning the unrest spread to Port of Spain, the capital in the north of the island. Demonstrators marched through the city closing businesses. Police opened fire to repulse an attack on a train carrying arms to the south. That day the disturbances spread to

Tabaquite and Rio Claro, where five were killed and 20 wounded when crowds were fired on by the police.

On 23 June, workers on the Caroni sugar plantation struck work, as did workers on O'Meara, Carapo, Esperanza, La Reunion, San Raphael and Golden Grove plantations in the area around Arima. Workers also came out on strike on the government-owned St Augustine estate. In the city, waterfront workers, street cleaners employed by the municipality and employees of the Public Works Department were on strike. By 26 June, the strikes had spread to Mayaro, halting work on Beaumont, St Anns and Lagoon Doux plantations.

That day two British warships, HMS *Ajax* and HMS *Exeter*, arrived with marines. There were numerous arrests of striking oil and sugar workers and rioters, and these arrests continued to take place over the next few weeks. The *Port of Spain Gazette*, on 26 June, reported that the industrial unrest had assumed island-wide proportions and was still spreading. On 27 June, bus drivers at Arima and Tuna Puna struck work, as did labourers at Caigual and Fishing Pond and on Non Pareil and St Lawrence plantations. By 29 June, workers employed by the Manzanilla Road Board were on strike.

Butler, who had been in hiding since the attempt to arrest him at Fyzabad had been frustrated by the workers, wrote to Reinzi requesting him to represent the arrested oilfield workers in court, he being one of the few lawyers, if not the only lawyer, willing to do so.[13] By the first week of July Reinzi had assumed a more important role than that of legal representative of the striking workers.

Reinzi became the leader of a group of oilfield workers – Ralph Mentor, F.J. Rojas, Macdonald Moses and Simeon Blades – who were determined to ensure that the spontaneous labour rebellion would be channelled into the permanent form of an organised trade union movement. Meanwhile Cipriani, President of the Trinidad Labour Party, totally discredited himself in the eyes of the workers by denouncing the strikes and by his opposition to the formation of trade unions unless the law was first amended to allow for picketing and immunity from actions for breach of contract.

Contrary to allegations by the employers that the strikes and demonstrations had been in pursuance of a communist plot, the labour rebellion in June 1937 had been a spontaneous outburst of popular frustration and dissatisfaction. There had been no preconceived strike plan and certainly no conception of the possibility of a working class seizure of control of the state.

The overwhelming armed force at the disposal of the government made it inevitable that the unrest would eventually be contained. On 6 July the *Trinidad Guardian* announced with satisfaction that the strikes had ended and 'only their ghost remains to be laid'. The employers were not inclined to make concessions and demanded that the government suppress the unrest with a firm hand and restore the state of affairs that had previously existed.

Had the government followed the course recommended by the employers, it is possible that the social upheaval that had occurred would have proved to have all been in vain. However the Governor, Sir Murchison Fletcher, and the Acting Colonial Secretary Howard Nankivell, while approving the use of force to suppress the disorders, adopted a conciliatory and sympathetic approach to the workers' demands for improvements in their living conditions.

In a letter to an official in the Colonial Office shortly after the labour rebellion, Fletcher wrote:

> the roots of this colony-wide unrest go very deep. Labour has lived in conditions of extreme poverty and squalor, and the colour line has kept employer and employed at a long arm's length apart ... The recent troubles have supplied the colony with a purge it sorely needed.

In an address to the colony's Legisative Council he expressed concern about the level of wages and the poverty and malnutrition he had witnessed, and stated his conviction that the employers were financially capable of improving labour conditions. Referring sympathetically to the representations made to him before the outbreak by Butler, he said: 'The white employer class in Trinidad would find in tact and sympathy a shield far more sure than any forest of bayonets to be planted here.'

Nankivell reminded the Legislative Council that in 1936 a Wages Advisory Board had been presented with data as to the hardships endured by the workers but had felt unable to recommend any comprehensive remedy for the situation. He pointed out that since then the cost of living had risen, industry had prospered and government revenues had increased. Even more outspoken than the Governor, Nankivell added:

> In the past we have had to salve our consciences with humbug and we have had to satisfy labour with platitudes. Those days have gone by ... An industry has no right to pay dividends at all until it pays a fair wage to labour and gives the labourer decent conditions.[14]

The government set up a Mediation Committee, under the chairmanship of Nankivell, to hear the workers' grievances. It approved of the steps taken to organise trade unions and recognised the Oilfield Workers Trade Union, the formation of which was announced on 25 July 1937.[15] Official recognition gave the union the status to appear before the official Commission of Inquiry subsequently appointed by the British government and was no doubt a decisive factor in the subsequent decision of the employers to recognise the union as the workers' representative.

Employers in both the oil industry and the sugar industry and the big employers generally were infuriated by the sympathetic attitude towards the workers' grievances displayed by the two principal colonial officials. Both the powerful Petroleum Association, representing employers in the mainly foreign-owned oil industry, and the Chamber of Commerce protested.

The big employers, though displeased with Governor Fletcher, were even more apprehensive about the Acting Colonial Secretary and urged his replacement as chairman of the Mediation Committee. The Governor too appears to have thought that Nankivell was not displaying sufficient impartiality and in October 1937 made this confidential report to the Secretary of State:

> From the start, Nankivell has shown a bias towards labour. Employers believe that he is a Communist in league with Reinzi and they will have no contact with him. In connection with government labour and social services he is doing useful work, but position is most awkward.[16]

So strong was the oil barons' influence with the Colonial Office that they secured the removal of both the Governor and the Acting Colonial Secretary from the scene. Fletcher, though an experienced official who had previously served as Governor in a number of other colonies, was forced into early retirement. Nankivell was transferred to another colony.[17]

In 1936, the Amalgamated Building & Woodworkers Union had been formed. Out of the labour rebellion of 1937 there emerged, in addition to the Oilfield Workers Trade Union, a number of other trade unions. These were the All Trinidad Sugar Estates and Factory Workers Union, led by the oilfields mechanic Macdonald Moses, the Public Works & Public Service Workers Trade Union led by Rupert Gittens who had recently returned from residence in France, the Seamen & Waterfront Workers Trade Union led by Simeon Alexander and the Federated Workers Trade Union led by the Accountant Quintin O'Connor.

With the exception of the Federated Workers Trade Union, all these unions were organised on the industrial unionism principle, being designed to serve the workers in their particular industry or occupation. The FWTU, based in Port of Spain, was a general workers union with members in several different industries.

Soon after the Trinidad labour rebellion, a social upheaval occurred in Barbados. Clement Payne, born in Trinidad of Barbadian parents, had gone to Barbados at the end of March 1937. Soon after his arrival he had begun to speak at public meetings.

But when, in or about May 1937, he announced his intention to start a trade union, he was denied the hireage of a meeting hall. He then took his advocacy of the need for the workers to be organised to the streets of the capital. As the attendances at his meetings grew, Payne acquired a number of supporters.

Discovering that he had declared on entering the island that he had been born in Barbados, the Governor had him prosecuted for wilfully making a false declaration. Payne asked the lawyer Grantley Adams to defend him, but could not afford his fee. Defending himself, he explained that his parents were Barbadians and that he had thought he had been born in Barbados. Found guilty, he was fined £10 or three months' imprisonment with hard labour if the fine was not paid. His supporters made a collection and paid Adams to argue his appeal.

Released on bail, Payne, the following day, led a march to Government House and requested an audience with the Governor to protest against his conviction. He and several of his followers were arrested. Refused bail, he was kept in custody until his appeal was heard on 26 July. A crowd estimated at about 5,000 assembled outside the Court House and the Appeal Court quashed his conviction. He was then arrested on a Deportation Order and smuggled onto a ship which was about to leave for Trinidad.

When, on the night of 27 July, it was discovered that Payne had been secretly deported, there was widespread popular resentment. Several street lamps and motor car windows were smashed and large protest meetings were held at Lower Green and Golden Square. On 28 July, widespread rioting broke out in Bridgetown. Police patrols were forced to flee under a hail of stones. Business was brought to a standstill in the capital. There was some looting and street lamps and more car windows were smashed.

During the next two days the rioting spread outside the capital. In a rural area a sweet potato field was raided by hungry people. A strike of lightermen which had started on 28 July was hurriedly settled. By the time the police had regained control on the third day after after the outbreak had commenced, the tally of those they had killed was 14, with 47 wounded.

Vicious sentences were imposed on Payne's principal supporters. Olrick Grant and Mortimer Skeete were sentenced to ten years' imprisonment, Israel Lovell and Darnley Alleyne to five years and Fitz A. Chase to nine months. Chase was found guilty when the judge decided that what he was reported to have said – 'Tonight will be a funny day' – was a veiled incitement to the crowd to riot.[18]

CHAPTER 19

Labour Rebellion in Jamaica, 1938: the West India Royal Commission, 1938–39

At the end of December 1937 most of the workers on Serge Island Estate in St Thomas in eastern Jamaica refused to start harvesting the sugar cane crop at the rates being offered (see Map 19.1). On 4 January 1938, the sergeant in charge of the police, who had been rushed to the area, reported that some 400–500 workers had forced those who had started to cut cane to stop work. Sixty-three strikers were arrested and, on 13 January, their trials commenced in the Resident Magistrates' Court. Three were sentenced to one month's imprisonment with hard labour; others were fined.

In the first week of May 1938 there was a strike and disturbances at the new central factory being constructed by the West Indies Sugar Company at Frome in Westmoreland, at the western end of the island. Four workers were shot and killed by the police and scores were wounded. Numerous arrests followed and 109 workers were brought to trial in batches commencing on 13 May. Many were convicted and imprisoned, the sentences ranging from 30 days' to one year's imprisonment.

In the third week of May waterfront workers in Kingston came out on strike. The level of dissatisfaction was reaching a critical point and on 23 May an explosion of strikes and demonstrations erupted in the capital. The arrest next day of William Alexander Bustamante, a well-known public figure, and his associate St William Grant, sparked off an island-wide labour rebellion.

Bustamante was a complex, charismatic character. A moneylender, he was nevertheless public-spirited and concerned about the poverty and distress of the majority of the workers. He expressed his feelings at public meetings from platforms provided by St William Grant and other street orators and in letters to British politicians. For a time in 1936 and 1937 he had associated himself as an officer with the Jamaica Workers and Tradesmen's Union but, unable to obtain much publicity in that role, had severed his relations with Coombs and offered himself instead in the role of a mediator between employers and employees.

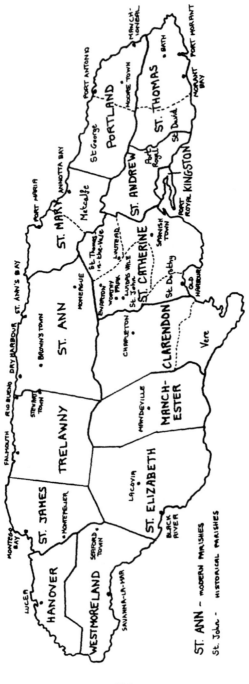

Map 19.1 Jamaica, scene of the labour rebellion of 1938 (© Andrew Hart)

The waterfront workers accepted his offer to mediate, but their employers rejected it. There was, they said, no need for anyone to intervene between them and their employees. By ordering his arrest, the Governor, who regarded him as an irresponsible agitator, provoked strikes all over the island. The workers refused to return to work unless Bustamante was freed. Only his release after a week in custody and the dropping of all charges against him made the settlement of the strikes possible. The intransigence of the employers, the high-handedness of the Governor and the militancy of the workers combined to catapult Bustamante into the role of the island's principal labour leader.

During the week that Bustamante was in custody it was suggested to the waterfront workers, by a political group called the National Reform Association, that they should form a trade union to represent them in negotiations with the Shipping Association. The strike leader, W.A. Williams, replied that they would form a union only if Mr Bustamante was freed and agreed to be its President. To satisfy the workers on this point Bustamante's solicitor had to give Williams a letter, stating that he had conferred with Bustamante and that he was willing to be the union's President. On his release on 28 May, at a monster meeting at a Kingston wharf, Bustamante announced the formation of a 'maritime union'.

After the announcement of the formation of this union and the establishment of a union office in Kingston, many other categories of workers also wanted to be unionised. Bustamante then announced that he intended to form five trade unions, a number he later increased to seven. The telephone at the union office was listed in the name 'Bustamante Maritime Union' and an advertisement was placed in the press which stated: 'Look out for the name Bustamante on all his Unions.'[1]

Over the next few weeks thousands of workers flocked to the union office to enrol as members and pay their dues. As the workers enrolled there was never any real attempt to group them into separate organisations. By the time that registration under the Trade Union Law was effected on 23 January 1939, any idea of seven separate unions had been abandoned and a single union, the Bustamante Industrial Trade Union, was registered.[2]

The trade union movement that emerged in Jamaica out of the 1938 labour rebellion was quite different in structure from that which had developed in Trinidad and was developing in British Guiana. The form of the BITU was unique. It was not established in the traditional way by workers meeting and resolving to form an organisation. It was done from the top downwards. From the start it was made clear that the union belonged to its leader.

The registered rules of the BITU provided that Bustamante would be president for life, would be responsible for appointing its governing body and would be in charge of the union's funds. The organisation of the BITU in the parishes outside of Kingston was rapid. Bustamante selected the branch secretaries and drove through the island installing them in branch offices in all the principal towns.

For the great majority of workers at that time this was an acceptable arrangement. They were not concerned with constitutional niceties but with practical results. Bustamante had emerged as the man who had challenged the establishment and championed the workers' cause. Their militant determination to better their conditions was a response to his leadership.

All over the island there was direct action. Workers went on strike and then a telephone call was put through to the union office to send someone to come and negotiate a settlement. Sometimes these calls were made by the workers' representatives but sometimes they were made by the employers. Many months were to pass before wage negotiations would settle down into a more orthodox pattern.

Except in the parish of St James in western Jamaica, where for some time Coombs retained his stronghold, the members of the branches of the Jamaica Workers & Tradesmen's Union transferred their allegiance to the BITU. The small union of transport workers in Kingston, which had been organised by Ken Hill, merged with the BITU and Hill was appointed to be one of its vice-presidents. Another development in 1938 was that the building trades workers, who had been members of the JWTU, hived off by agreement to form a Builders & Allied Trades Union.

The Jamaica United Clerks Association led by the barrister politician E.E.A. Campbell and the accountant F.A. Glasspole, which organised shop assistants in some Kingston stores, endeavoured to maintain a separate existence but many shop assistants joined the BITU. The only employees' organisations with which Bustamante was prepared to allow the BITU to coexist, without attempting to destroy them and absorb their members, were the Jamaica Union of Teachers and the Civil Service Association.

The wave of labour rebellions that had swept across the region from the mid-1930s prompted the British government to resort to a time-honoured technique for diffusing dissatisfaction – the appointment of a commission of enquiry. It is probable that they were also aware that, in the light of the conditions likely to be revealed, some reforms would be unavoidable.

The West India Royal Commission was appointed on 5 August 1938. Its chairman was Lord Moyne, a Conservative who would later be appointed Secretary of State for the Colonies. Among its members were two people whose presence was no doubt designed to lend it credence in the eyes of the disaffected popular masses of

the region – Sir Walter Citrine, General Secretary of the British
Trade Union Congress, and Morgan Jones, a Labour Member of
Parliament. The Commission took evidence from interested parties
in London and then visited all the British colonies in the Caribbean
area, taking evidence from a wide variety of witnesses.[3]

The Commission's Report was presented to the British
Government on 21 December 1939, shortly after the
commencement of the Second World War. It revealed such extreme
poverty, poor housing, malnutrition, unemployment and illiteracy
that the War Cabinet decided not to publish it. Their fear was that
the German propaganda machine would make effective use of it
to the discredit of the British Empire.[4]

In the mid-1930s, except where enabling legislation had been
introduced as in Jamaica in 1919, British Guiana in 1921, the
Leeward Islands in 1931, Trinidad and Tobago in 1932 and
Grenada and St Lucia in 1933, it was still a criminal offence for
workers to combine for strike action or to form a trade union. In
no British colony was there legislation allowing picketing of an
employer's premises. Only in British Guiana had trade unionists
been given immunity from actions by employers for loss suffered
as a result of breach of contract by going on strike.

Commenting on the situation of trade unions in the colonies the
Commissioners had reported:

> we were unable to discover that any real effort had been made
> until quite recent times to assist their formation and development.
> One explanation of this may be that the influence of powerful
> vested interests has stood in the way; whatever may have been
> the cause, the fact is that even today the obstacles to the
> successful working of trade unions have not been removed by
> legislation in most of the West Indian Colonies ... It is not
> surprising that, when confronted by such legal obstacles, the
> formation of trade unions in the West Indies has been slow.[5]

The Commissioners recommended the enactment of legislation
by colonial legislatures which would bring trade union rights into
line with the rights of British trade unions, and the establishment
of government Labour Departments where they did not exist.
West Indian governments were urged to consider establishing
schemes of Workmen's Compensation and the 'larger colonies' were
advised to examine the possibility of unemployment insurance.[6]
As a consequence of these recommendations trade union enabling
legislation was enacted or appropriately amended in all these
Crown colonies.

In 1939 Soberanis and R.T. Meighan organised the British
Honduras Workers & Tradesmen's Union and the first trade union
was formed in St Lucia. The Antigua Trades & Labour Union was

formed in 1939 and held its first annual conference in February 1940. Also in 1940 the St Kitts–Nevis Trades & Labour Union, with Sebastian as president, was established. The St Vincent Workingmen's Co-operative Association, led by McIntosh, did not at this time register as a trade union but, as W. Arthur Lewis recorded in 1939, it 'represents the workers in all negotiations'. In 1941, the Barbados Workers Union was registered.[7]

In February 1939, with no prior preparation or notice, Bustamante called a general strike in Jamaica. His reason for doing so was that he claimed he had been insulted by a member of the Jamaica Workers & Tradesmen's Union in Montego Bay and that the United Fruit Company, to whom the man was employed, had refused to dismiss him. While some workers responded, many were confused as to what the issue at stake was and ignored the call. In this tense situation the Legislative Council agreed to grant the Governor emergency powers and it was widely believed that he intended to arrest Bustamante.

Norman Manley, the island's most eminent barrister and President of the recently formed Peoples National Party, then intervened and persuaded the Governor that the arrest of Bustamante would cause considerable unrest. He assured the Governor that, with the agreement of Bustamante and Coombs, he would convene a Trade Union Advisory Council to which existing trade unions would affiliate and which would seek to settle any jurisdictional disputes that arose. This was agreed and Bustamante cancelled his strike call. A few months later however, after the danger that he would be arrested had passed, Bustamante withdrew the BITU from the TUAC.

The TUAC then renamed itself the Trade Union Council and became the co-ordinating body for those trade unions in Jamaica that remained in affiliation and other trade unions that were subsequently formed and affiliated. Similar Trade Union Councils had been formed earlier by the trade unions in Trinidad and British Guiana.

Thus it was that, out of the labour rebellions that occurred in the 1930s, and following the legalisation of trade unions in those colonies in which they had formerly been illegal, the foundations of the modern trade union movements in the colonies of the English-speaking Caribbean area were laid.

CHAPTER 20

Towards Decolonisation

In the first quarter of the twentieth century Britain was still a major colonial power with an extensive empire. British colonies included India (with Pakistan), Burma, Malaysia, Singapore, Cyprus, Hong Kong, Egypt and other large territories in Africa and the colonies in the Caribbean, Central and South America.

As a result of the wave of working-class unrest that flowed across the region in the 1930s, culminating in the labour rebellion in Jamaica in 1938, the British government appointed the West India Royal Commission. Initially its terms of reference excluded consideration of proposals for constitutional reform. It was appointed:

> To investigate social and economic conditions in Barbados, British Guiana, British Honduras, Jamaica, the Leeward Islands, Trinidad and Tobago, and the Windward Islands, and matters connected therewith, and to make recommendations.[1]

As this limitation had led to criticisms, the Secretary of State made a tactical retreat on the eve of the Commission arriving in the West indies. In what purported to be an explanatory telegram to the Officer Administering the Government of Jamaica, the Commission's first port of call, he advised:

> Commission may also wish to hear evidence about the Jamaica constitution and organisation of local government so far as may be necessary to elucidate social and economic problems.[2]

No objections were raised to similar evidence being received in the other colonies.

At that time it is unlikely that the British government had intended to concede meaningful advances towards self-government in these colonies. Nor did the West India Royal Commission recommend any substantial constitutional changes. Its response to representations made for constitutional advancement was:

> We do not support either of the extreme proposals put before us for the grant of immediate and complete self-government based on universal suffrage, or for a wide increase of the authority of Governors which would convert the existing system into a virtual autocracy; the one because it would render impossible the financial control necessary if, as we consider to be inevitable,

substantial assistance is to be afforded by His Majesty's
Government through the West Indian Welfare Fund and
otherwise; the other because it would be politically a retrograde
step ... At the present stage, we attach more importance to the
truly representative character of Legislative Councils than to any
drastic change in their functions.[3]

But despite this acknowledgement that it would be desirable,
without substantially increasing their powers, to make the legislatures
'truly representative', the recommendations on franchise extension
were less than positive. The Commissioners were divided on the
question of if and when full adult suffrage should be introduced
and even left open the issue of whether women should as voters
be placed on equal terms with men:

> That in order to secure that the elected element in Legislative
> Councils shall be as truly representative as possible, the object
> of policy should be the introduction of universal adult suffrage.
> Some of us hold that this should be introduced forthwith,
> others that it should be reached by gradual stages and to this
> end recommend the appointment of local committees to
> consider the extension of the franchise both for local and for
> central government. Such committees should keep in close
> touch with their counterparts in other West Indian Colonies,
> and should consider carefully whether, as is strongly desirable,
> their recommendations would assure substantial equality as
> between the sexes.

On the issue of the qualifications for membership of the
legislatures, the recommendation was:

> That in all West Indian Colonies a careful examination should
> be made at an early date of the possibility of reducing substantially
> the margin between the qualifications for registration as a voter
> and those for membership of the Legislative Council, the latter
> being in many cases unnecessarily high.[4]

In Trinidad and Tobago in 1941, nine government officials
were withdrawn from the Legislative Council and the elected
members were increased from seven to nine. Thus the Legislative
Council consisted of the Governor with an original and casting vote,
three Government officials, six nominated and nine elected
members. But the Governor was given the power to certify measures
not approved by the Council when he considered this in the
interests of good government, a power he had not previously had.
The number of elected members in the Governor's advisory
Executive Council was increased to two and the franchise was
slightly extended.[5]

At the end of 1941, Japan had inflicted defeats on British troops in Malaya and Burma, and by mid-May 1942 the supposedly impregnable fortress of Singapore had been surrendered. These defeats had seriously damaged Britain's prestige in the eyes of the subject peoples. At the same time Britain had become increasingly dependent on the USA, both militarily and financially. In these circumstances Britain was by 1942 less able to resist colonial demands for self-government and insistent American advice that she make constitutional concessions to her colonies.

The British Prime Minister, Winston Churchill, nevertheless remained defiant. In a radio broadcast on 10 November 1942 he declared:

> Let me make this clear in case there should be any mistake about it. We mean to hold our own. I have not become the King's First Minister in order to preside over the liquidation of the British Empire. For that task, if ever it were prescribed, someone else would have to be found ...[6]

Churchill's broadcast was revealing for two reasons. It indicated his resolve, but was also an acknowledgement that the idea, sacrosanct for centuries, that Britain had a right to subjugate other peoples and keep them in subjection was being increasingly widely disputed. Britain's right to the ownership of other countries was not only being challenged by the subject peoples of the Empire but was also being questioned by pragmatists, liberals and leftists in Britain and by Communists in all countries. It was also being questioned, however politely, by the government of the USA, Britain's ally, which wished to obtain access to Britain's colonies on terms of equality for American exporters and investors.

In Churchill's War Cabinet there were those who recognised the necessity for Britain to grant reforms and the impossibility of telling the Americans to mind their own business. This had been acknowledged by the dispatch to the USA, at the US President's request and two weeks before Churchill's broadcast, of Sir William Gater, a Permanent Under-Secretary, to discuss American concerns about the Caribbean colonies. Reporting Gater's reception by President Roosevelt the The Times, on 27 October 1942, gave this account of what the President had said to the British diplomat. He was interested in

> an extension of the franchise, in compulsory education, and in an attempt to make the islands self-sustaining ... He hoped for a new economic social system ... a big improvement on present conditions ... Asked if it would require some form of political unity, he replied 'certainly not', but it would require more self government.[7]

The first indication of the British government's acceptance of the necessity to make meaningful concessions to Caribbean demands came in negotiations concerning the constitution of Jamaica in 1943. If indeed there had been any disposition to adhere to the inadequate constitutional changes proposed in 1941 by the then Secretary of State Lord Moyne, and rejected by all sections of opinion, subsequent events had made this imposible.

Agreement had been reached between the Elected Members Association, the Peoples National Party and the Federation of Citizens Associations on demands for a new constitution and a memorandum embodying their joint proposals had been forwarded to the Secretary of State on 5 November 1942. Later that month Sir William Battershill, a Deputy Permanent Under-Secretary of State in the Colonial Office, advised that:

> Such is the internal political condition of Jamaica that I doubt whether the position can be held there much longer without some serious trouble, if we proceed as we are doing.

On the other hand, he continued:

> If we proceed vigorously towards a new constitution we shall proclaim our good faith to the world, and to the American world in particular; we shall be able to assess the actual strength of the P.N.P.; we shall to some extent avoid the perpetual references to Jamaica in both Houses of Parliament, references which are so disturbing to good government in that island; and we shall at least appear to give some constitutional advance willingly instead of having it dragged out of us as has so often been the case in other constitutional advances elsewhere.[8]

On 10 February 1943, the British government's offer of a new constitution providing for full adult suffrage, representative government in internal affairs and semi-responsible participation in executive government was communicated to the Governor. On 14 May the Legislative Council agreed to accept the offer. The principal features of the new constitution were:

1. a House of Representatives wholly elected on the basis of full adult suffrage;
2. a nominated second chamber (Legislative Council) with delaying powers only;
3. an Executive Council consisting of the Governor and ten members, five of whom would be chosen by the elected legislature.[9]

The new constitution, embodied in an Order in Council, was proclaimed on 27 October and the first general election on the basis of full adult suffrage was held thereunder on 14 December 1944.

In Trinidad and Tobago the the number of elected members on the Governor's advisory Executive Council was further increased to four in 1944, while the number of nominated members was decreased from three to one. The advisory Executive Council would then have consisted of the Governor, three *ex officio* members, one nominated unofficial member and four elected members, but even then the Governor was not obliged to take its advice. In 1945 full adult suffrage was introduced.[10]

CHAPTER 21

Formation of Nationalist Political Parties in the 1930s, 1940s and 1950

Parallel with the wave of labour unrest and organisation flowing across the English-speaking Caribbean area in the 1930s, there was an upsurge of nationalistic political aspirations. This was most evident in Jamaica, Barbados, British Guiana and British Honduras where, in the late 1930s, 1940s and 1950 the foundations were laid for modern and lasting political parties, but not to the same extent at that time, for peculiarly local reasons, in Trinidad.

As has been mentioned in Chapter 17, the Trinidad Workingmen's Association had for many years performed both political and trade union functions but, under Cipriani's influence, had discontinued its trade union activities because of the refusal of the British government to permit the legalisation of trade unions. Even after trade unions became lawful in 1932, Cipriani had insisted that the TWA continue to refrain from trade union activities because of inadequacies in the legislation. In 1934, the TWA had confirmed this policy by changing its name to the Trinidad Labour Party.

Cipriani had had great faith in the British Labour Party and the Labour government that was in office from 1929 to 1931, but had been sadly disappointed. As Bridget Brereton records:

> Cipriani's disillusionment – and that of TWA members – was ... great when the Labour Government ... failed to change colonial policy along the lines of Labour pledges and programmes. None of the benefits that Cipriani had anticipated from a Labour government materialised, and in 1931 the Labour Colonial Secretary explicitly rejected constitutional change for Trinidad on the grounds that the colony was not ready for further advance towards self-government ...[1]

When the labour rebellion broke out in Trinidad in 1937, Cipriani had discredited himself and damaged the credibility of the Trinidad Labour Party by denouncing the strikes and demonstrations that were taking place. This had occurred at a time that the momentum for political organisation was developing in Jamaica and Barbados. It had an adverse effect on the prospects of political development in Trinidad which lasted for nearly a decade.

Several political parties were formed in the 1940s and early 1950s, including the West Indian National Party, the Caribbean Socialist Party and the West Indian Independence Party, but none of these was able to obtain much popular support or advance the movement for constitutional reform. Not until the entry into politics of Dr Eric Williams in 1956 and the formation of the Peoples National Movement was there a political party in Trinidad capable of mobilising mass support for constitutional advancement.

In 1936 a group of Jamaicans in New York, led by W. Adolphe Roberts, W.A. Domingo, Jaime O'Meally and Rev. Ethelred Brown, formed the Jamaica Progressive League, the main purpose of which was to promote the idea of self-government for Jamaica. That same year the accountant O.T. Fairclough, the newspaper reporter Frank Hill and the teacher and writer, originally from England, H.P. Jacobs commenced publication of the news magazine *Public Opinion*. This journal provided a forum for discussion of progressive ideas including proposals of self-government and the need for a political party.

In 1937, the newspaper reporter Ken Hill, Frank Hill's brother, formed the National Reform Association, an organisation with a vaguely nationalistic programme. At or about the time of the labour rebellion of May 1938, Norman Manley became convinced of the need for a political party and agreed to take the initiative in its formation. The Peoples National Party was launched at a public meeting in Kingston on 18 September 1938, at which the principal speakers were Manley and Sir Stafford Cripps, a prominent leader on the left of the British Labour Party who happened to be in the island on holiday.[2] The National Reform Association was dissolved to make way for the party.

At a conference of representatives of its local 'groups' held in 1939 the PNP approved a programme which included advocacy of constitutional reform:

> The Party advocates and will work to achieve the claim of this country to a representative form of government ... The system advocated is ... a parliamentary democracy on the lines which obtain in the other self-governing units of the British Commonwealth ...

> The Party advocates ... the right of all persons of full age ... to vote as a condition precedent to a representative form of government.[3]

In July 1943, five months after the British government had confirmed its approval of local demands for a new constitution based on full adult suffrage, Bustamante announced the formation of the Jamaica Labour Party.[4] Bustamante initially campaigned against the PNP's demand for self-government. This was to counteract the popular support that the PNP was obtaining through its advocacy of self-government. The argument Bustamante advanced was that self-government would mean 'brown man rule'. This widely publicised statement was designed to exploit the resentment justifiably felt by the black masses towards the brown middle classes, many of whom displayed a contemptuous attitude towards them. Because several prominent members of the PNP were of brown middle-class status, this argument was effective in the campaign for the first election held under full adult suffrage in 1944.

In that election Bustamante's Jamaica Labour Party won an overwhelming victory, winning 22 seats as against the PNP's five in the 32-member House of Representatives. The Jamaica Democratic Party, a party formed by a group of businessmen and led by the merchant Abe Issa, won no seats though they did succeed in ensuring the defeat of Manley by a JLP candidate in a constituency with a large middle-class element. It is, however, interesting to note that most of the big planters did not support the JDP, preferring Bustamante to the socialist PNP and confident that they would be able to do business with him.[5]

Although the PNP lost the election in 1944 and was again, but more narrowly, defeated by the JLP in 1949, it had continued to gain support among the workers and and small farmers. Bustamante's opportunistic opposition to self-government in 1944 had for some years isolated a majority of the workers and small farmers from the national movement, thereby considerably weakening its impact. But the understanding among the black masses of the meaning of self-government continued to increase and, sensing this, Bustamante had abandoned his opposition to it by the end of the decade.

His transition to support for self-government was, however, uneven. His first concession was in July 1947 when he said, in the House of Representatives: 'We are ripe to have a constitution that will give us the proper authority ... to administer the affairs of the people for the good of the people, particularly ... the majority.' In March 1949, on the eve of the general election, he backtracked, declaring in the House that: 'We are not fit yet for complete self-government. It is a financial impossibility and there is not enough law and order ... for complete self-government.' But in 1950, following his party's victory in the general election, he proposed a motion in the House asking it to declare itself in favour of self-government and prepare a constitution providing for it at an early date.[6] During the 1949 election campaign he did not, as in 1944, campaigned against it.

In Barbados the barrister Grantley Adams, who had long been an opponent of Duncan O'Neale and the Democratic League and had been editor of the planters' paper the *Agricultural Reporter*, was elected to the Assembly in 1934. After his election, and possibly, among other things, because of his support for a proposal for the extension of the franchise in 1936, he fell increasingly into disfavour with the planter–merchant elite. In October 1938, Adams joined C.A. Braithwaite and others in launching the Barbados Progressive League, an organisation which engaged in both advocacy of political reforms and representation of workers in their disputes with employers. By the middle of the following year he had gained control of the organisation, ousting his more radical colleagues from the leadership. In the general election of 1940, five of the League's candidates were successful.

In October 1941 the League separated its trade union and political functions, the former being thereafter conducted by the Barbados Workers Union, a separate organisation established at that time. The League continued to conduct its political activities and subsequently changed its name to the Barbados Labour Party. Adams held the office of President in both organisations. Meanwhile the planters, intent on resisting change, had formed a political party called the Electors Association.

Dissatisfied with Adams leadership, a section of the Progressive League under the leadership of W.A. Crawford, broke away in 1941, and Crawford later formed the West Indian National Congress Party. In 1941 Crawford was elected to the Assembly in a by-election. In 1943 a proposal for the extension of the franchise was debated in the Assembly and the income qualification for voters was reduced from £50 to £25.[7] In the 1944 general election the Progressive League/Labour Party won seven seats, the Congress Party eight seats, the Electors Association eight seats and one independent candidate was successful. Both Adams and Crawford were appointed to the Governor's Executive Council.

Later, three Congress Party members of the Assembly transferred their allegiance to the Labour Party and Crawford resigned from the Executive Council. Adams, who enjoyed the support of the Governor and the Colonial Office, and who the Electors Association preferred to his more radical rival Crawford, was then in a dominant position. In 1944 women were given the vote. In 1950 property and income requirements for both voters and members of the Assembly were removed and full adult suffrage was introduced. In the 1951 general election the Labour Party won 16 seats, the Electors Association four seats and the Congress Party two seats. In 1954 a semi-cabinet system was introduced.[8]

In 1943, the young dentist Cheddi Jagan returned from the USA to British Guiana with his American-born wife, Janet. In 1944, assisted by the trade unionists Jocelyn Hubbard and Ashton Chase, they formed the Political Action Committee. Its main objective was to prepare the ground for the formation of a political party. In the general election of 1947 Cheddi Jagan was elected to the Legislative Council. Several of the successful candidates had contested the election as candidates of a 'Labour Party' and Jagan joined their ranks. But this was only a group of leaders, not a real party.

In 1950, the Jagans and their PAC colleagues, with the assistance of the young lawyer L.F.S. Burnham recently returned from Britain, launched the Peoples Progressive Party. The PPP won a decisive victory in the general election of 1953, the first to be held under full adult suffrage. 133 days later British armed forces invaded, the constitution was suspended and Cheddi Jagan and others were were imprisoned. The British government alleged that it had acted to forestall a plan to establish a Communist state.[9]

In 1955, Burnham broke away from the party to found a rival organisation with the same name. Constitutional government was restored in 1957 and in the ensuing election the PPP led by Jagan again won a majority of seats in the legislature. Burnham then renamed his party the Peoples National Congress. Both parties, however, advocated political independence. Internal self-government was conceded in 1961 and the PPP won the election held in that year, but was soon faced with a determined campaign of destabilisation in which the American CIA played a decisive role. Proportional representation, introduced in 1964, facilitated the coming to office of a coalition government headed by Burnham. This development, recorded by Cheddi Jagan in *The West on Trial*, is outside the scope of this study.[10]

In January 1950, a 'Peoples Committee' was formed in British Honduras with George Price as Secretary, John Smith as President and Clifford Betson, President of the General Workers Union, as a member. This committee, though initially formed to protest against the use by the Governor of his reserve powers to devalue the dollar, condemned 'colonial exploitation' and advocated self-government. On 29 September 1950, this committee was dissolved when the Peoples United Party was launched. Its officers were George Price, secretary, John Smith, leader, Leigh Richardson, chairman, and Philip Goldson, assistant secretary.[11]

During the late 1940s, 1950s and 1960s political parties advocating self-government, or self-government through federation, were formed in most of the other colonies.

CHAPTER 22

Onwards to Independence

Weakened by the Second World War, faced with the nationalistic demands of the subject peoples in many parts of the Empire and pressure from the US government to decolonise, and having decided to concede a new constitution to Jamaica, Britain had to consider what was to be done with the colonies in the Caribbean area. This was the context in which a policy emerged which included, on the one hand, creation of a federation of colonies and, on the other, constitutional concessions to individual colonies, and ultimately the policy of complete decolonisation.

The idea of a federation of the British West Indian colonies had been under discussion for more than a decade in the eastern Caribbean islands, where it had been advocated by labour and progressive organisations. It was believed by popular leaders in these colonies that, although the British government was unwilling to grant self-government to individual colonies, a federation of the British colonies in the area would be a political entity to which, if the demand for it was sufficiently strong, 'dominion status' might be conceded. From the British government's point of view, the attraction of the idea of a federation was that it would make administrative economies possible and overall control easier to maintain.

On 14 March 1945 the Secretary of State for the Colonies wrote to the Governors of the Caribbean area colonies proposing a conference of representatives of their legislatures to consider establishing a West Indian Federation. When this proposal was discussed in the colonial legislatures, all colonies except British Guiana and British Honduras expressed their willingness to participate in a federation.

In his despatch the Secretary of State had said:

> It will ... be generally agreed that under modern conditions it has become more difficult for very small units ... to maintain full and complete independence in all aspects of government. Nor do existing tendencies make it appear ... likely that such independence would be easier for these small communities in the future ... I consider it important, therefore, that the more immediate purpose of developing self-governing institutions in the individual British Caribbean Colonies should keep in view

the larger project of their political federation, as being the end
to which ... policy should be directed.[1]

A memorandum from an official in the Colonial Office,
summarising the replies, made the same point:

> it is ... impossible in the modern world for most of the present
> Colonies in the area to reach full self government on their own,
> e.g. it is ludicrous to think of, say, Barbados or British Honduras,
> with their populations of 200,000 and 60,000 respectively,
> standing on their own feet in international discussions ...[2]

In July 1945, the founding conference of the Caribbean Labour
Congress, attended by representatives of trade unions and progressive
political organisations, was held in Barbados. There the Peoples
National Party and the Trade Union Council of Jamaica were for
the first time associated organisationally with their counterparts in
the eastern Caribbean and Guyana. At its annual conference in 1944
the PNP had accepted the idea of a West Indian Federation and
its participation in the founding of the Caribbean Labour Congress
was a natural consequence of this.

The conference demanded the establishment of a federation
with dominion status of all these colonies, including British Guiana
and British Honduras. 'Dominion status' was then the term usually
used to describe political independence of member states of the
British Commonwealth. The conference further demanded that,
simultaneouly with the formation of the federation, each unit be
granted internal responsible government and be related to the
Federal Government not the Colonial Office.[3]

The British Secretary of State convened a conference of representatives of the colonial legislatures that had accepted his proposal,
which was held in Montego Bay, Jamaica in September 1947. Also
in attendance were observers from British Guiana, British Honduras
and the Caribbean Commission, a body that had grown out of the
wartime Anglo-American Caribbean Commission. At Montego Bay
the following resolutions were approved:

> That this conference, recognising the desirability of a political
> federation of the British Caribbean territories, accepts the
> principle of a federation in which each constituent unit retains
> complete control over all matters except those specifically
> assigned to the federal government.

> That this conference believes that an increasing measure of
> responsibility should be extended to the several units of the British
> Caribbean territories, whose political development must be
> pursued as an aim in itself, without prejudice and in no way
> subordinate to progress towards federation.[4]

Arising out of the Montego Bay conference a standing committee of representatives of the colonial legislatures concerned and the British government was set up, which met many times over the next few years to discuss the structure of the proposed federation. Under the guidance of the Colonial Office a federal constitution was devised which had little in common with the type of federal structure advocated by the Caribbean Labour Congress. Not only did it exclude British Guiana and British Honduras, but the units retained their existing colonial constitutions and their control by the Colonial Office. The Federal government itself was not given 'dominion status' though there was a promise that, after five years, another conference would be convened to consider further constitutional advancement.[5]

In 1948 the Trinidad and Tobago Legislative Council was allowed to appoint a committee of members and others to recommend a new constitution. This committee was dominated by the conservative-nominated member Sir Lennox O'Reilly and the former radical turned conservative elected member Albert Gomes. The report it submitted was approved by the Legislative Council despite the opposition of seven of the nine elected members of the Legislative Council.

The constitution proposed provided for: a Legislative Council with 18 members to be elected on full adult suffrage, six members to be nominated by a Governor appointed by the British government, three government officials and a Speaker also to be appointed by the Governor; an Executive Council with seven elected and three nominated members chosen from the Legislative Council and three government officials, over which the Governor would preside with a casting vote and reserve powers of veto and certification as in the Jamaica constitution. Although the Committee, by a majority of one, had advocated that all adults should have the right to vote, 16 members of the Committee had voted against this and put in a minority recommendation that voters should be required to possess property or income qualifications.

Disagreeing with the majority report, Dr Patrick Solomon, an elected member, wrote a minority report which called for:

1. A fully elected single chamber Legislature of 25 members elected on the basis of adult suffrage ...
2. Representation to be on a population basis ...
3. A speaker to be elected by and from the House and removable on a vote of no confidence [and] to have a casting vote only.
4. An Executive of at least nine members elected by the Legislature ... to be the principal instrument of policy, and the Governor to be obliged to act on its advice in all internal matters

... although the Executive cannot expect to control foreign policy, it ought ... to be consulted on external affairs ...

5. The members of the Executive to have full ministerial responsibility for specific Departments of State, the Executive or Cabinet to be collectively responsible to the Legislature by which it should be removable on a vote of no confidence.
6. The Prime Minister to allocate portfolios ...
7. ... the Prime Minister to be empowered to create new ministries.
8. The Prime Minister to preside at all Cabinet meetings.[6]

Soon after the official delegation had left for London to present the majority report, Dr Solomon and another elected member followed to lobby the Colonial Office and Labour Members of Parliament in support of the minority report. The constitution proposed in the majority report was no advance on, and in some respects less advanced than, the existing constitutions of Barbados and Jamaica. For this reason it was seen by progressive opinion, both in Trinidad and in the region as a whole, as a retrograde step.

It was important at that time to grasp the opportunity to demand a constitution for Trinidad and Tobago which would be an advance in the direction of self-government on the constitution conceded to Jamaica four years earlier. The Caribbean Labour Congress therefore responded to representations from Trinidad by convening a conference in Port of Spain on 4 July 1948 to address the issue. This was attended by representatives of all the political organisations and trade unions in Trinidad and several other community organisations. The conference unanimously supported the recommendations of the minority report and forwarded a petition in support of them to the Secretary of State for the Colonies.[7]

A new constitution for Trinidad and Tobago was introduced in April 1950. Though this was a marginal improvement on what had been asked for in the majority report, in the main it followed the recommendations of that report. Thus it was that in Jamaica in 1944 and Trinidad and Tobago in 1950 the slow process of making constitutional concessions in the Caribbean area colonies had commenced.

It seems improbable that, prior to 1948, the intention of the British government had been to concede to even the larger colonies in the region more ultimate freedom than internal self-government. But such was the flow of the international tide of events, particularly after India and Burma had achieved independence in 1947, that it would have been difficult if not impossible for Britain to halt the process of decolonisation part-way.

In 1950 the right to vote was conceded to all adults by the Barbados Assembly. This had been dependent on the local Assembly not the British government, as Barbados, unlike most of the other colonies in the region, had not surrendered its ancient internally self-governing constitution in the panic that had gripped their ruling elites following the events in Jamaica in 1865.

In 1951 new constitutions were conceded to British Honduras and Dominica which provided for full adult suffrage, for majorities of elected members in the Legislative Councils and for minorities of elected members in the Executive Councils. In 1953 a new constitution based on full adult suffrage was conceded to British Guiana, although the process was reversed 133 days later when British troops invaded and the constitution was suspended. Constitutional government was restored there in 1957.

The Leeward Islands Federation was dissolved in 1956, Antigua and Barbuda, St Kitts–Nevis, Montserrat and the British Virgin Islands becoming separate colonies so that they could enter the proposed West Indian Federation as separate units on its formation in 1958.

In May 1960, Bustamante, aware of the widespread popular suspicions in Jamaica of the wisdom of the island remaining in the West Indian Federation, declared his opposition to Jamaica's continued membership. To reassure the public, Manley then announced the decision of his Cabinet that when the form of a new federal constitution, to be settled in the forthcoming negotiations, had been decided, the question of whether it would be acceptable to Jamaica would be determined in a referendum.

Some years previously, though he may not have had a referendum in mind at the time, Manley had declared:

> When the time comes for the constitution to be reviewed, Jamaica will withdraw from the federation unless the type of federation devised and the constitution is so changed as to suit the special circumstances of the West Indies and the unit territories themselves.

He had also said:

> We are in for the first five years of federation and at the end of that time we'll make up our minds when we'll go and where we'll go.[8]

Apparently well informed of popular sentiment in Jamaica, the Colonial Office had in April 1961 drafted a memorandum for submission to the Cabinet Colonial Policy Committee which illustrates a growing sentiment that Britain should rid itself of its responsibilities in the Caribbean area:

> The Caribbean is an area of the world where there are no vital United Kingdom interests and few strategic considerations, and where our fundamental aim in the area since 1945 has been

political disengagement. This being so our principal objective following secession by Jamaica must be to avoid any situation which results in our being left with any of the present federated territories on our hands for which we can see no obvious future except as colonies.[9]

In May 1961 a conference of representatives of the federal government and the unit governments was held in London in an attempt to reach agreement on a form of dominion status for the Federation, but the conference ended in failure. The Trinidad and Tobago delegation stated that it was unwilling to accept the proposed distribution of powers between the unit governments and the federal government. In September 1961 Jamaica decided, in a referendum, not to remain in the Federation. When this occurred the British government agreed that the Federation could not continue. It was accordingly dissolved in 1962.

The separate colonies had meanwhile continued to operate under their existing constitutions. A federation of some of the eastern islands was attempted but soon abandoned. Thereafter each colony pursued its separate negotiations for constitutional advancement. In the Leeward and Windward Islands there were constitutional amendments in the late 1950s and 1960. These made provision for majorities of elected members, elected on full adult suffrage, in the Legislative Councils.

Control of their executive governments continued to be exercised by the Governors appointed by the British government but, from 1960, provision was made for minorities of elected members in several colonies to be admitted to the Executive Councils and be designated 'Ministers', with some responsibility for particular departments of government. Similar arrangements were made in British Honduras by constitutional amendments in 1960 and 1963.

In 1959 full internal self-government was conceded to Jamaica, followed by similar concessions to Trinidad and Tobago and British Guiana in 1961. In 1962 Jamaica and Trinidad and Tobago became fully independent. Barbados and Guyana (formerly British Guiana) became independent in 1966 and the Bahamas in 1973.

The main colonies in the region having obtained their independence, the British government reached the conclusion that there was nothing to be gained by holding on to the remainder. Starting with Grenada in 1974, independence was conceded to those of the remaining colonies requesting it. The last to be granted independence were St Kitts–Nevis and Belize (formerly British Honduras) in 1981. All that then remained in the Caribbean area of the once proud British Empire were the tiny islands of Montserrat, the British Virgins and Anguilla.

On becoming independent, Trinidad and Tobago in 1962 and Guyana in 1966 retained their allegiance to the British monarch, represented locally by Governor-Generals. Guyana, however, became a republic with a titular president in 1969 and Trinidad and Tobago did likewise in 1976. At the time that Dominica obtained independence in 1978 it became a similar type of republic, adopting the name 'Commonwealth of Dominica' to distinguish itself from the Dominican Republic. In 1980 the Guyana constitution was amended to provide for an executive instead of a titular president.

All the other former colonies have retained the British monarch with local Governor-Generals as their head of state. In Jamaica it has been agreed by all political parties that the island should become a republic. At the ceremony to swear in the new government after the election in December 1997, the prime minister announced that this would be the last occasion on which members of a Jamaican government would swear an oath of loyalty to the British monarchy.

Notes

Chapter 1

1. A.M. Josephy, *The Indian Heritage of America*, Penguin Books, Harmondsworth, 1975, p. 278.
2. Lennox Honychurch, *The Dominica Story*, Macmillan, London, 1995, contains an interesting speculation on the origins of Amerindian colonisation of the Caribbean islands and an excellent bibliography of archaeological works on the subject.
3. Irving Rouse, 'Archeology in Lowland South America and the Caribbean', in *American Antiquity*, Vol. XXVII (1961), pp. 56–62, and *The Tainos: Rise and Decline of the People who Greeted Columbus*, Yale University Press, New Haven, 1992; Josephy, *The Indian Heritage of America*.
4. V.W. Von Hagen, *World of the Maya*, Mentor Books, London, 1960, p. 36; Luis A. Rodriguez Garcia, 'Esbozo histórico', Web Site (Internet), Universidad Interamericana de Puerto Rico; J.S. Tyndale Biscoe, *The Jamaican Arawak*, Jamaica Historical Review, Kingston, 1962, p. 6 and Plate 1.
5. *Dictionary of World History*, Nelson, London, 1973, p. 1509; C.R. Boxer, *The Portuguese Seaborne Empire 1415–1825*, Pelican Books, Harmondsworth, 1973, p. 85.
6. Alan Burns, *History of the British West Indies*, Allen & Unwin, London, 1954, pp. 179–80 (citing *Calendar of State Papers 1574–1660*, p. 23), and pp. 173, 214.
7. Thomas Southey, *Chronological History of the West Indies* (3 vols), London 1827, new impression Frank Cass, London, 1968, Vol. 1, p. 94; Burns, *History of the British West Indies*, pp. 321, 329.

Chapter 2

1. Information on the wars between the European powers in the seventeenth, eighteenth and early nineteenth centuries and the changing ownership of their colonies is to be found in Bryan Edwards, *History, Civil and Commercial of the British Colonies in the West Indies*, London, 1793; Thomas Southey,

Chronological History of the West Indies; Alan Burns, *History of the British West Indies*, London, 1954; Thomas Coke, *A History of the West Indies*, Liverpool, 1808; R. Pares, *War and Trade in the West Indies, 1739–63*, Oxford, 1936; W.L. Burn, *The British West Indies*, London, 1951; J.H. Parry, *Trade and Dominion: European Overseas Empires in the 18th Century*, London, 1974; Henri Bangou, *La Guadeloupe 1492–1848*, Editions du Centre, Paris, 1962; C.L.R. James, *The Black Jacobins*, (2nd edn), New York, 1963; O. Nigel Boland, *Colonialism and Resistance in Belize*, Cubola Productions, Belize, 1988.

Chapter 3

1. Richard Ligon, *A True and Exact History of the Island of Barbados 1647–1650*, 2nd edn, London, 1763; Henri Bangou, *La Guadeloupe*, p. 79; Southey, *Chronological History*, Vol. 1, pp. 284–5.
2. G.W. Bridges, *The Annals of Jamaica* (2 vols), John Murray, London, 1828, reprinted Frank Cass, London, 1968, Vol. 1, pp. 258–60; Southey, *Chronological History*, Vol. 2, pp. 96–7.
3. An 'indenture' was a form of contract, originally written in duplicate on a single sheet of parchment. The separation of the two parts was done by severing them along an indented line so that they could subsequently be fitted together if it was necessary to prove that one was a true copy of the other. This term for a contract survived long after the practice had fallen into disuse, hence the term 'indenture of conveyance', used in English legal jargon until quite recently.
4. In the famous *Domesday Book*, a census allegedly ordered by William the Conqueror in 1066 though assigned a later date (1189) by some authorities, one twelfth of the population was classified as slaves. Slavery was, however, being replaced by feudal serfdom, which the Normans introduced.
5. R. Hart, *Slaves Who Abolished Slavery* (2 vols), University of the West Indies, Kingston, 1980 and 1985, Vol. 1, pp. 108–9, quoting extracts from *The History of Jamaica* by Edward Long, the planter historian.
6. These statistics have been gleaned from several sources including Southey, *Chronological History of the West Indies*.
7. Noel Deerr, *The History of Sugar* (2 vols), Chapman & Hall, London, 1949, Vol. 2, p. 332; Edward Long, *The History of Jamaica*, (2 vols), London, 1774. Such capital investments were far beyond the means of small farmers. A hogshead contained 16–17 cwt, a puncheon 72–120 gallons.

8. Howard Johnson, *The Bahamas in Slavery and Freedom*, Ian Randle Publishers, Kingston, 1991, pp. 3 and 12.
9. Johnson, *The Bahamas in Slavery and Freedom*, p. 70, citing D. Eltis, 'The Traffic in Slaves between the British West Indian Colonies 1807–1833', in *Economic History Review*, Vol. 25 (1972) p. 58 and D. Gail-Saunders, *Slavery in the Bahamas 1648–1838*, Nassau, 1985, p. 80.

Chapter 4

1. Quoted in Eric Williams, 'The Golden Age of the Slave System in Britain', in *Journal of Negro History*, Vol. 25, No. 1 (January 1940).
2. W.W. Claridge, *A History of the Gold Coast and Ashanti*, John Murray, London, 1915, 2nd edn, Frank Cass, London, 1964, p. 173; D.P. Mannix, *Black Cargoes*, Viking Press, New York, 1962, p. 123.
3. John Newton, *Thoughts upon the African Slave Trade*, London, 1788, reprinted in B. Martin and M. Spurell, eds, *Journal of a Slave Trader*, Epworth Press, London, 1962.
4. *Parliamentary Papers, 1790–1791*, Vol. 92.
5. Hilary Beckles, *Natural Rebels: A Social History of Enslaved Black Women in Barbados*, Zed Books, London, 1989, pp. 11–15.
6. Beckles, *Natural Rebels*, pp. 31–3.
7. B.W. Higman, *Slave Population and Economy in Jamaica 1807–1834*, Cambridge University Press, Cambridge, 1976, pp. 71–2, 197–8.
8. By contrast, there was a natural increase in the slave populations of the North American colonies. Was this perhaps due to the exploitation of labour having been less intense on cotton plantations than on sugar plantations? Or were transportation costs to the American mainland greater, a factor making the exhaustion and replacement of slaves less economic than their preservation?
9. Long, *History of Jamaica*, Vol. 2, p. 427.
10. Higman, *Slave Population and Economy in Jamaica 1807–1834*, pp. 121–2, citing *Parliamentary Papers, 1832* (127), Lords Vol. 1, p. 578 and Vol. 2, p. 833, and *Parliamentary Papers, 1832* (721), p. 43.
11. W.J. Gardner, *The History of Jamaica*, 1st edn, London, 1873, new edn, Unwin, London, 1909, pp. 244–5; Statement No. 93, printed 9 March 1838 by order of the House of Commons.

Chapter 5

1. Hart, *Slaves Who Abolished Slavery*, Vol. 1, p. 90, citing letters from Alex Moir to Mrs M. Goulburn, 10 April and 15 May 1802, in the Goulburn Papers, Surrey Record Office.

2. Hilary Beckles, *Black Rebellion in Barbados*, Antilles Publications, Bridgetown, 1984, pp. 34–8, citing Minutes of Council, June 1657, Lucas MSS, Reel 1, f.365 and PRO: CO 1/35 f.23 – Governor Atkins to Williamson, 3 October 1675.

3. Hart, *Slaves Who Abolished Slavery*, Vol. 2, pp. 5–6, citing *Calendar of State Papers*, 1663, p. 122, and an extract from the Journal of William Beeston in *Interesting Trades Relating to the Island of Jamaica*, Lewis, Luman & Jones, St Jago de la Vega, 1800.

4. Hart, *Slaves Who Abolished Slavery*, Vol. 2, pp. 13–14, citing Br. Museum Ad. Ms.12431; *Calendar of State Papers* (Colonial Series – America & the West Indies) 1675, No. 690, 1676, Nos. 793 & 822, 1685–88, No. 445; PRO: CO 133/5 f.87 – Molesworth to Lords of Trade.

5. Burns, *History of the British West Indies*, p. 349, citing *Calendar of State Papers*, 1865–8, Nos. 1175, 1189 and 1193.

6. These and the other rebellions, conspiracies and guerrilla warfare in Jamaica, mentioned below, are recorded in more detail in Hart, *Slaves Who Abolished Slavery*, Vol. 2, with references to the primary sources.

7. Beckles, *Black Rebellion in Barbados*, pp. 30–8 and 44–6; Burns, *History of the British West Indies*, p. 196, citing *Calendar of State Papers*, 1693–6, No. 31. Burns does not record the fate of the Irish conspirators.

8. Southey, *Chronological History*, Vol. 2, pp. 258 and 264; Burns, *History of the British West Indies*, pp. 460 and 462, citing *Calendar of State Papers*, 1726–8, No. 1 and 1733, No. 446.

9. Robert Moore, 'Slave Rebellions in Guyana', University of Guyana, unpublished; C. Northcott, *Slavery's Martyr*, Epworth, London, 1976.

10. Alan Burns, *History of the British West Indies*, pp. 507 (citing K.S. Wise, *Historical Sketches of Tobago*, 1934–38, Vol. 1 pp. 91, 106–7), 509.

11. O. Nigel Boland, *Colonialism and Resistance in Belize*, Cubola Productions, Belize, 1988, pp. 21–2, quoting from PRO: CO 137/62 – Joseph Maud to W.H. Lyttleton, Governor of Jamaica, 7 October 1765 and CO 137/63 – Memorial of Allan Auld to Lord Hillsborough, July 1768.

12. Boland, *Colonialism and Resistance in Belize*, pp. 22–3, citing Admiralty reports in J.A. Burdon, *Archives of British Honduras* (3 vols), Sifton Praed, London, 1935.
13. Southey, *Chronological History of the West Indies*, Vol. 2, p. 425.
14. Honychurch, *The Dominica Story*, pp. 94–7, citing L.A. Roberts, *The Nègres Marrons of Dominica*, Notes, Roseau Public Library, Dominica and PRO:CO 71/10 – Orde dispatches, February–July 1786.
15. Honychurch, *The Dominica Story*, p. 103.
16. George Brizan, *Grenada, Island of Conflict*, Zed Books, London, 1984, pp. 59–77, citing Minutes of the Legislative Body of Grenada 1792–97, and *Narrative of the Revolt and Insurrection of the French Inhabitants of Grenada* by an eye witness, George Turnbull, Edinburgh, 9 November 1795.
17. William Young, *An Account of the Black Charaibs in the Island of St Vincent's*, 1795, reprinted by Frank Cass, London, 1971; Burns, *History of the British West Indies*, pp. 570–2. Known as the Garifuna, their descendants today comprise 6.6 per cent of the population of Belize. On attaining independence in 1981, the former colony of British Honduras changed its name to Belize.
18. Hart, *Slaves Who Abolished Slavery*, Vol. 2, contains a detailed account of these events, with references to the primary sources.

Chapter 6

1. James, *The Black Jacobins*; R. Korngold, *Citizen Toussaint*; David Nicholls, *From Dessalines to Duvalier*, Macmillan, London, 1979.
2. Thomas Clarkson, *The History of the Abolition of the African Slave Trade* (2 vols), Longman, 1808, Vol. 1, pp. 282ff.
3. Hart, *Slaves Who Abolished Slavery*, Vol. 1, pp. 195–201.
4. *Parliamentary Debates* (2nd series), IX, pp. 265ff.
5. *Parliamentary Debates* (2nd series) IX, pp. 285–6.
6. Abolition of Slavery Act, 1833.

Chapter 7

1. Honychurch, *The Dominica Story*, pp. 111–13, citing papers in connection with the defence of Governor A. Cochrane Johnstone and letters relating, London, 1805.
2. Bridges, *The Annals of Jamaica*, Vol. 2, p. 289.

3. Johnson, *The Bahamas in Slavery and Freedom*, p. 35, citing PRO: CO 23/63 – Governor Cameron to Secretary of State Bathurst, 24 January 1816.

4. Honychurch, *The Dominica Story*, pp. 116–19, citing PRO: CO 71/51.

5. Beckles, *Black Rebellion in Barbados*, Antilles Publications, Bridgetown, p. 87, citing *Remarks on the Insurrection in Barbados and the Bill for the Registration of Slaves*, London, 1816, f.7.

6. Beckles, *Black Rebellion in Barbados*, pp. 86–114.

7. C. Northcott, *Slavery's Martyr*, Epworth, London, 1976.

8. Hart, *Slaves Who Abolished Slavery*, Vol. 2, pp. 244–336.

9. Henry Bleby, *Death Struggles of Slavery* (3rd edn), London, 1868, pp. 25–30 and 110–17.

10. The Abolition of Slavery Act, 1833.

11. Bleby, *Death Struggles of Slavery*, p. 118.

12. Bernard Martin Senior, *Jamaica as it was and as it may be Comprising ... An Authentic Narrative of the Negro Insurrection ... by a Retired Military Officer*, London, 1835, p. 293.

Chapter 8

1. D. Robotham, *The Notorious Riot: The Socio-Economic and Political Bases of Paul Bogle's Revolt*, University of the West Indies, 1984, p. 32, citing Jamaica Assembly 19, 18/15/18/9, 71.

2. Robotham, p. 31, citing House of Commons 14, 600–99.

3. V.T. Daly, *A Short History of the Guyanese People*, Macmillan, London, 1975, p. 173.

4. Bridget Brereton, *A History of Modern Trinidad 1783–1962*, Heinemann, Port of Spain and London, 1981, pp. 88–9.

5. O. Nigel Boland, 'Labour Control and Resistance in Belize in the Century after 1838', in *Slavery & Abolition*, Vol. 7, No. 2 (September 1986), p. 179, citing Lord Normandy to Supt. Macdonald, 22 April 1839, Supt. Stevenson to Governor Barkly, 30 July 1855, and Governor Longden to Governor Grant, 6 March 1868, in Belize Archives 15, 48 and 98 respectively, Belmopan, Belize. The territory was not declared to be a British colony until 1862.

6. Noel Deerr, *The History of Sugar*, Vol. 1, pp. 176, 198–9, and Vol. 2, pp. 530–1.

7. Thomas Holt, *The Problem of Freedom*, Johns Hopkins University Press, Baltimore and London, 1992, p. 131, citing K.M. Butler, 'Slave Compensation and Property, Jamaica and Barbados 1823–1843' (PhD thesis, Johns Hopkins University, 1986).

8. G. Eisner, *Jamaica 1830–1930, a Study in Economic Growth*, Manchester, Manchester University Press, 1961; Holt, *The Problem of Freedom*, p. 144.
9. Sidney Olivier, *Jamaica, the Blessed Isle*, London, 1936; Also *Jamaica Almanac*, 1845 for the increased number of holdings of from 5 to 10 acres – over 19,000 in ten years.
10. Brereton, *A History of Modern Trinidad*, p. 89.
11. Janet Momsen, 'Land Settlement as an Imposed Solution', in J. Besson and J. Momsen, eds, *Land and Development in the Caribbean*, Macmillan, London, 1987, p. 46.

Chapter 9

1. Holt, *The Problem of Freedom*, p. 68; Swivin Wilmot, 'Politics and Labour Conflicts in Jamaica 1838–1865', in *Caribbean Political Economy*, K. Levitt and M. Witter, eds, Ian Randle Publishers, Kingston, 1996, p. 110.
2. Hilary Beckles, *A History of Barbados*, Cambridge University Press, Cambridge, 1990, pp. 109–10. One of the changes in the 1840 re-enactment was that a worker who had worked for five consecutive days was deemed to have agreed to a hiring of one month rather than one year. This law remained in force until repealed in 1937.
3. *Statutes and Laws of the Island of Jamaica, 1 Victoria to 10 Victoria – AD 1837 to 1847*, Govt. Printing Establishment, 79 Duke Street, Kingston, 1889, reprinted by the Govt. Printing Office in 1912 in *Laws of Jamaica, 1839* as Chapter XXX. Whether there were similar statutes in other colonies requires further research, but combinations were unlawful at common law.
4. *Statutes and Laws of the Island of Jamaica*, 5 Victoria, Cap 43. This Act, still in force a century later, was reprinted in the *Revised Laws of Jamaica* (1938 edn) as *The Masters and Servants Law, Cap. 387*. The section quoted (section 3) was repealed by Law 27 of 1940 and what remained of the law was repealed by Law 31 of 1974.
5. Wilmot in 'Politics and Labour Conflicts', pp. 110–11, citing the *Falmouth Post*, 15 and 29 August, and the *Morning Journal*, 5, 11, 19 and 24 September 1938.
6. Wilmot in 'Politics and Labour Conflicts', pp. 113–14, citing the *Royal Gazette and Jamaica Standard*, 25 September and 8 October 1841.
7. Bridget Brereton, *A History of Modern Trinidad*, pp. 78–9, no primary source cited.

8. Walter Rodney, *History of the Guyanese Working People 1881–1905*, Johns Hopkins University Press, Baltimore, 1981, pp. 32–3.
9. *Falmouth Post*, Vol. 1, No. 4, 28 January 1845.
10. Brereton, *History of Modern Trinidad*, p. 79.
11. Sidney Olivier, *Jamaica: the Blessed Island*, London, 1936.
12. *Falmouth Post*, 19 January 1864.

Chapter 10

1. K.O. Laurence, *Immigration into the West Indies in the 19th Century*, Caribbean Universities Press & Ginn & Co., Kingston, 1971, p. 12. The only source cited by this author is his own PhD thesis at Cambridge University, 1958.
2. Laurence, *Immigration into the West Indies*, pp. 10–11, citing I.M. Cumpton, *Indians Overseas in British Territories 1834–1854*, London, 1953, pp. 15–35. Laurence says this was a Colonial Office decision, but Burns, *History of the British West Indies*, p. 663, says recruitment of Indian labourers was prohibited from 1839 to 1844 by the Colonial government of India.
3. Laurence, *Immigration into the West Indies*, p. 12.
4. Maureen Warner-Lewis, *Guinea's Other Suns*, The Majority Press, Dover, Mass., 1991, pp. 10–11.
5. Warner-Lewis, *Guinea's Other Suns*, p. 11, citing J. Asiegbu, *Slavery and the Politics of Liberation*, Longman, London, 1969, and R.R. Kuczynski, *Demographic Survey of the British Colonial Empire*, 1948.
6. Warner-Lewis, *Guinea's Other Suns*, pp. 11–12, citing K.O. Laurence, 'Immigration into Trinidad and British Guiana 1834–1871', University of Cambridge PhD thesis, 1958.
7. Laurence, *Immigration into the West Indies*, p. 14.
8. Warner-Lewis, *Guinea's Other Suns*, p. 12, citing Laurence 'Immigration into Trinidad and British Guiana', pp. 179–3.
9. Laurence, *Immigration into the West Indies*, pp. 13–16.
10. Laurence, *Immigration into the West Indies*, pp. 9, 21, and 36–9.
11. Burns, *History of the British West Indies*, p. 663.
12. Douglas Hall, *Free Jamaica: 1838–1865*, Caribbean Universities Press, London, p. 54, citing PRO: CO 137/284 – Elgin to Stanley, 21 May 1845, No. 49; CO 137/315 – memorandum by Sir John Parkinson; and CO 137/288 – Elgin to Gladstone, 4 February 1846, No. 27 (enclosures).
13. R. Hart, *The Origin & Development of the People of Jamaica*, T.U.C. Education Dept, Kingston, 1952, pp. 15–16, citing

Rev. Ethelred Brown, in *Journal of Negro History*, New York, October 1919.

14. Daly, *A Short History of the Guyanese People*, pp. 183 and 224; Brereton, *A History of Modern Trinidad*, pp. 103 and 109.

Chapter 11

1. James Millette, *Society and Politics in Colonial Trinidad*, Zed Books, London, 1985, pp. 9–10, citing L.J. Ragatz, *The Fall of the Planter Class in the British Caribbean 1763–1833*, Century Publishers, New York, 1928, pp. 115ff.

2. Millette, *Society and Politics in Colonial Trinidad*, pp. 9–10, citing *Cambridge History of the British Empire* (8 vols), Cambridge, 1929–59, Vol. 2, pp. 150–2. Transubstantiation was the doctrine that the bread and wine administered by the priest at communion was transformed into the actual flesh and blood of Jesus. According to D.S. DaBreo, *From the Beginning: A History of Grenada*, Grenada, 1973, p. 40, it was later decided that not more than two Catholics could be elected to the Assembly, but no reference for this statement is given.

3. Honychurch, *The Dominica Story*, pp. 61–2, citing T. Atwood, *The History of the Island of Dominica*, Johnson, London, 1791 and Bryan Edwards, *The History, Civil and Commercial of the British Colonies in the West Indies*, London, 1793.

4. The monument to La Grenade is still in place.

5. Millette, *Society and Politics in Colonial Trinidad*, pp. 9–14. Concerning St Laurent's part in these events, Millette cites F.P. Renault, 'L'Odysée d'un Colonial sous l'Ancien Régime: Phillippe-Rose Roume de St. Laurent', in *Revue de L'Histoire des Colonies Françaises*, Vol. 9, 1920, pp. 327–48.

6. Millette, *Society and Politics in Colonial Trinidad*, p. 7, citing Claude Hollis, *A Brief History of Trinidad under the Spanish Crown*, Trinidad, 1941, p. 81, and L.M. Fraser, *History of Trinidad* (2 vols), Trinidad, 1891, Vol. 1, p. 289.

7. Millette, *Society and Politics*, p. 19, citing J.J. Dauxion Lavaysse, *A Statistical, Commercial and Political Description of Venezuela, Trinidad, Margarita and Tobago*, London, 1820, p. 332.

8. Millette, *Society and Politics*, p. 212, citing PRO: CO295/14 – Windham to Hislop (draft), 3 July 1806.

9. Millette, *Society and Politics*, pp. 38–9, citing J.H. Parry, 'The Sale of Public Office in the Spanish Indies under the Hapsburgs', in *Ibero Americana*, No. 37 (1953), and W.W. Pierson, 'Some Reflections on the Cabildo as an Institution'

in *Hispanic American Historical Review*, Vol. V, No. 4, (1922) pp. 584–5.

10. Lord Liverpool, Secretary of State, to Governor of Trinidad, 27 November 1810, quoted in Eric Williams, *History of the People of Trinidad & Tobago*, Andre Deutsch, London, 1962, pp. 69–72.

Chapter 12

1. The original colonies were referred to as 'plantations' of the English monarch, but after the Act of Union with Scotland in 1707 they became British rather than English colonies.

2. *The Laws of Jamaica*, A.A. Aikman, St Jago de la Vega, 1792, Vol. 1, pp. 111–12 – Public Acts 1711, 10 Ann Chap. 4.

3. *The Laws of Jamaica*, Aikman, Vol. 2 (1760–92), p. 23 – 1761, Chap. 8.

4. R. Blackburn, *The Overthrow of Colonial Slavery 1776–1848*, Verso, London, 1988, p. 146, citing R. Anstey, *The Atlantic Slave Trade and British Abolition*, London, 1975, pp. 286–320.

5. Quoted in Southey, *Chronological History*, Vol. 3, pp. 169–74.

6. Southey, *Chronological History*, Vol. 3, pp. 360–1.

7. Southey, *Chronological History*, Vol. 3, p. 520.

8. Southey, *Chronological History*, Vol.3, p. 521.

9. G. Heuman, *Between Black and White*, Clio Press, Oxford, 1981, p. 28, citing *Postscript to the Royal Gazette*, 13–20, November 1813.

10. Honychurch, *The Dominica Story*, p. 174.

11. *The Laws of Jamaica 1829–1830*, St Jago de la Vega, A. Aikman Jr., 1830, Chap. 12, 19 December 1829.

12. Heuman, *Between Black and White*, p. 41, citing C.H. Wesley, 'The Emancipation of the Free Coloured Population in the British Empire', in *Journal of Negro History*, Vol. 19 (April 1934) p. 159, where reference is made to an Order relating to St Lucia dated 15 January 1829 and a similar Order two months later relating to Trinidad.

13. *Laws of Jamaica 1829–1830*, St Jago de la Vega, Aikman Jr., 1830 – 59 George III, Chap. 29, 13 February 1830 and *Laws of Jamaica 1830–1836*, Chap. 17, 21 December 1830.

14. *Laws of Jamaica 1824–1826*, Chap. XXVII (disallowed) and *Laws of Jamaica*, 2 William IV, Chap. 2 (November 1831).

15. Johnson, *The Bahamas in Slavery and Freedom*, pp. 39–40, citing 'An Act to relieve His Majesty's Free Coloured and Black Subjects of the Bahama Islands from all Civil Disabilities', 4 William IV, Chap. 1.

16. Heuman, *Between Black and White*, pp. 110–11, citing PRO: Cardwell Papers CO 30/48/7/44 – Memorandum by Henry Taylor, 19 January 1839; Henry Taylor, *Autobiography of Henry Taylor, 1800–1875* (3 vols), London, 1885, Vol. 1, pp. 248–9.

17. The letters from Earl Grey to Sir Charles Edward Grey were made available to the author by Mrs B.D. Renison, a descendant of Sir Charles. The letters from Sir Charles to Earl Grey were obtained from the Department of Palaeography & Diplomatic of the University of Durham, where they are on deposit. Copies of the entire correspondence have been deposited in the National Library of the Institute of Jamaica and the Library of the University of the West Indies, Mona Campus, Jamaica.

18. The reform agreed to was the creation of an Executive Committee to which the Governor, who would preside, would appoint one member of the nominated, but planter-dominated, Council and two or three members of the elected Assembly. Financial measures would be initiated by the Executive Committee, but approval of legislation which such measures required would remain with the Assembly.

Chapter 13

1. G. Heuman, *The Killing Time: The Morant Bay Rebellion in Jamaica*, Macmillan, London, 1994, p. 46, citing PRO: CO 137/391 – Eyre to Cardwell, 6 May 1865, and Report of the Baptist Union, 1 May 1865.

2. Heuman, *The Killing Time*, pp. 57–9.

3. Ansell Hart, *The Life of George William Gordon*, Kingston, Institute of Jamaica, n.d. [1972], pp. 44–51 and 61–7, quoting Underhill to Cardwell, 5 January and Cardwell to Eyre, 14 June 1865. According to Heuman, *The Killing Time*, p. 54, the official reply was drafted by Henry Taylor.

4. Heuman, *The Killing Time*, pp. 3–6.

5. Hart, *The Life of George William Gordon*, p. 75.

6. Heuman, *The Killing Time*, pp. 3–14, citing the report of the trial of Bogle and others for felonious riot in the papers of the Special Commission of Enquiry, 1866, and other sources.

7. Heuman, *The Killing Time*, pp. 4, 9 and 85.

8. Heuman, *The Killing Time*, p. 22.

9. Heuman, *The Killing Time*, pp. 17–28.

10. Heuman, *The Killing Time*, p. 91, citing PRO: 884/2, Confidential Print No.2 – Papers Relating to the Insurrection

in Jamaica, Printed for the Use of the Cabinet, December 1865, p. 23.

11. Hart, *The Life of George William Gordon*, p. 91, citing Lord Olivier, *The Myth of Governor Eyre*; Heuman, *The Killing Time*, pp. 113–43.
12. Hart, *The Life of George William Gordon*, p. 87.
13. Hart, *The Life of George William Gordon*, pp. 86–7, quoting Lord Olivier, *The Myth of Governor Eyre*, Hogarth Press, London, 1933.
14. Heuman, *The Killing Time*, pp. 132–3, citing Jamaica Royal Commission, p. 896 – evidence of Fyffe.
15. Hart, *The Life of George William Gordon*, citing the official report of the trial in the report of the Jamaica Royal Commission and the verbatim report of the trial by A.W.H. Lake, special correspondent of the *Colonial Standard*, a Kingston newspaper.
16. Heuman, *The Killing Time*, pp. 87–91 and 139.

Chapter 14

1. Hart, *The Life of George William Gordon*, pp. 114–19.
2. Hart, *The Life of George William Gordon*, pp. 120–3.
3. *Laws of Jamaica* (1865), Cap. XI – 'An act to alter and amend the political constitution ...'.
4. Hart, *The Life of George William Gordon*, pp. 124–6; *The Laws of Jamaica (1865)*, Cap. XXIV, 'An act to amend an act passed in the present session ...'.
5. Order of the Queen in Council for providing for the Government of ... Jamaica ... made 11 June 1886.
6. Law No. 8 of 1866 – A Law for making Alterations in the Law consequent on the Constitution of the Legislative Council ....
7. Dominica was then one of the Leeward Islands. It was transferred to the Windward group of colonies in 1940.
8. Boland, *Colonialism and Resistance in Belize*, pp. 16–26 quoting PRO: CO 123/1 – 'The Definitive Treaty of Peace' 1763, and citing the Treaty of Versailles in 1783 and the Convention of London of 1786.
9. Boland, *Colonialism and Resistance in Belize*.
10. Boland, *Colonialism and Resistance in Belize*, p. 35, citing PRO: CO 123/15.
11. Assad Shoman, *Party Politics in Belize*, Cubola Productions, Belize, p. 16; *West Indies and Caribbean Year Book, 1969*, Chapel River Press, Andover, pp. 124–5.

Chapter 15

1. PRO: CO 321/349 File 95103 – Memorandum from Secretary of State, 14 November 1932.

2. Brereton, *A History of Modern Trinidad*, p. 163; B. Samaroo, 'The Trinidad Disturbances 1917–20', and K. Singh, 'The June 1937 Disturbances in Trinidad', in R. Thomas, ed., *The Trinidad Labour Riots of 1937*, pp. 37, 66–7; R. Hart, 'Origin & Development of the Working Class in the English-Speaking Caribbean Area', in M. Cross and G. Heuman, eds, *Labour in the Caribbean*, Macmillan, London, 1988, pp. 67 and 69; O. Nigel Boland, *On the March: Labour Rebellions in the British Caribbean 1934–39*, Ian Randle Publishers, Kingston, 1995, pp. 61, 72, 79, 91, 93 and 151; Hart, *Rise and Organise*, Karia Press, London, 1989, pp. 50, 68, 72, 86, 88 and 92.

3. R. Hart, *Towards Decolonisation*, Canoe Press, University of the West Indies, Kingston, 1998, Chap. 14.

4. Hart, *Towards Decolonisation*, Chap. 26.

5. R. Hart, 'Jamaica and Self-Determination 1660–1970' in *Race*, Vol. XIII, No. 3 (1972).

6. *Today's Cinema*, 10 October 1932, reprinted in *Daily Gleaner*, Kingston, 3 November 1932 and reproduced in Charles F. Tomlinson, *The Case of the Rainbow Book*, Black River, Jamaica, 1935, a pamphlet containing the correspondence between Tomlinson and L.R. D'Orsay.

7. 'Edward Wilmot Blyden – A Biographical Outline', compiled by Jennifer Ryan for a Caribbean Radio Network series on his life; *E.W. Blyden: Select Bibliography*, courtesy E-C. R. Blyden, both available on the Internet.

8. Biographical Note by Donald Wood in the republication of J.J. Thomas, *Froudacity: West Indian Fables Explained*, London, New Beacon Books, 1969, pp. 9–21.

9. Robert Hill, ed., *The Marcus Garvey and Universal Negro Improvement Association Papers* (12 Vols), University of California Press, Los Angeles and London, 1983 ff. Vol. 1, Appendix 1, pp. 532–6 quoting *Daily Gleaner* editorial, 12 October 1898.

10. Information about the public meetings was given to the author in 1942–43 by W.A. Domingo, who had attended such meetings in Kingston. For these references to items in the *Jamaica Advocate* the author is indebted to Dr Joy Lumsden and Dr Rupert Lewis.

11. Hill, *The Marcus Garvey ... Papers*, Vol. 1, pp. 534–5, citing *Daily Gleaner*, 17 February 1930; *Daily Gleaner*, 10 February 1930.

12. Amy Jacques Garvey, ed., *The Philosophy and Opinions of Marcus Garvey*, New York, 1926; *The Blackman: A Monthly Magazine of Negro Thought and Opinion*, compiled by Robert Hill, Kraus-Thomson, New York, 1975; Hill, *The Marcus Garvey ... Papers*; Rupert Lewis, *Marcus Garvey: Anti-Colonial Champion*, Karia Press, London, 1987; E.D. Cronon, *Black Moses*, University of Wisconsin Press, 1968; R. Hart 'The Life and Resurrection of Marcus Garvey', in *Race*, Vol. IX (2), 1967. There are many others.

Chapter 16

1. H.A. Will, *Constitutional Change in the British West Indies 1880–1903*, Clarendon Press, Oxford, 1970, p. 4.
2. *Petition from the Inhabitants of Jamaica ... together with the Reply of Her Majesty's Government ...*, Eyre & Spottiswoode, London, 1884, presented to both Houses of Parliament by command of Her Majesty, February 1884.
3. Order in Council, 19 May 1884, 21/3 (300) Jamaica Archives, Ref: Order in Council 1884 1B/5 CSO. In 1895, in response to a further petition, the number of elected members was increased to 14 but at the same time the number of *ex officio* members was increased to five and authority was given to the Governor to appoint up to ten nominated members (P.C. 2/261 Order in Council 3 October 1895).
4. Brizan, *Grenada*, pp. 208–9, citing Report of the Royal Commission, Part II, p. 58, and the *St. Georges Chronicle and Grenada Gazette*, 9 May 1885.
5. *Laws of Jamaica*: Law 22 of 1886 and Law 20 of 1906.
6. F.R. Augier and S. Gordon, *Sources of West Indian History*, Longmans, London, 1962, pp. 123–4.
7. H.A. Will, *Constitutional Change in the British West Indies*, pp. 147–9.
8. B. Samaroo, 'The Trinidad Workingmen's Association and the Origins of Popular Protest in a Crown Colony', in *Social and Economic Studies*, Vol. 21, No. 2 (June 1972), p. 207; Brereton, *A History of Modern Trinidad*, pp. 147–51.
9. Lewis, *Marcus Garvey: Anti-Colonial Champion*, pp. 32–3, citing *Jamaica Advocate*, 30 July 1904.
10. *Jamaica Times*, 6 March 1907.
11. *Our Own* was edited by S.A.G. Cox and published twice monthly in 1910 and 1911. Copies are preserved in the National Library, Institute of Jamaica. Its name was a rough translation of the name of the Irish nationalist organisation Sinn Fein. At this time, when belief in Britain's benevolence

prevailed, *Our Own*, in addition to its nationalistic message, often expressed loyalty to King and Empire.

12. *Our Own*, Vol. 2, No. 8, 15 April 1911.
13. Brizan, *Grenada*, pp. 314–5.
14. *Laws of Jamaica*: Law 22 of 1919.
15. Augier and Gordon, *Sources of West Indian History*, pp. 132–3.
16. *Report by E.F.L. Wood, M.P. on his Visit to the West Indies and British Guiana, December 1921–February 1922* (presented to Parliament June 1922), HM Stationery Office, London, 1922, Cmd. 1679.
17. Williams, *History of the People of Trinidad & Tobago*, pp. 219–20.
18. *Report by E.F.L. Wood*, pp. 87–8.
19. V.T. Daly, *A Short History of the Guyanese People*, Macmillan, London, 1975, pp. 288–93.
20. Beckles, *A History of Barbados*, pp. 156–8 citing the Representation of the People Act 1901. O'Neale died in 1936.
21. *The Blackman*, 1 April 1929, editorial.
22. *The Blackman*, 12 April 1929, editorial.
23. *The Blackman*, 2 January 1930, Manifesto of the Honourable Marcus Garvey D.C.L.
24. PRO: CO 318/436/6 and 442/4 File 71013 – Electors of the West Indies (1938).

Chapter 17

1. J.R. Green, *A Short History of the English People*, London, J.M. Dent, 1915, reprinted in Everyman's Library, 1926, p. 824, citing the Trade Union Act, 1871, and the Trade Union Act, 1875.
2. The Protection of Property Law, Law 30 of 1905. Section 1 of this law was amended by Law 8 of 1918 by adding to the categories of workers to which it applied persons employed to extinguish fires and protect life and property in case of fire and persons employed in conserving health by any parochial or municipal service. Similar legislation to the 1905 Jamaican law was probably approved by the Colonial Office for other Crown colonies. Further research on this is required.
3. Rodney, *History of the Guyanese Working People*, pp. 96 and 158; Ashton Chase, *A History of Trade Unionism in Guyana, 1900–1961*, Georgetown, New Guyana Co., 1964, pp. 36–7.
4. Walter Rodney, *History of the Guyanese Working People*, pp. 104 and 163. Referring to the Patriotic Club and Mechanics

Union, Rodney says that 'no details have come to hand on this ... venture'.

5. B. Samaroo, 'The Trinidad Workingmen's Association and the Origins of Popular Protest in a Crown Colony', in *Social & Economic Studies*, Vol. 21, No. 2 (June 1972), pp. 205–22.

6. H. Goulbourne, *Teachers, Education and Politics in Jamaica 1892–1972*, London, Macmillan, 1988, p. 64, citing *Handbook of Jamaica, 1895*, Kingston, Govt. Printing Office, p. 503.

7. Goulbourne's *Teachers, Education and Politics* contains an excellent history of teachers' organisations in Jamaica.

8. Interview with A.J. McGlashan, who had been a founder member of the printers' union, in February 1958.

9. George Eaton, 'Trade Union Development in Jamaica', in *Caribbean Quarterly*, Vol. 8, No. 1, citing interview by Hinchcliffe in *Daily Gleaner*, 17 April 1919. This union appears to have been revived for a brief period in or about 1919 as Local 16203 of the A.F. of L.

10. Public Record Office: CO 137/674, memo initialled G.G. The author is indebted to Richard Lobdell for the information that these are the initials of G. Grindle, later Private Secretary to the Permanent Under-Secretary of State, who subsequently became Governor of the Windward Islands.

11. Chase, *A History of Trade Unionism in Guyana*, pp. 38–42.

12. Fraser, 'Some Effects of the First World War on the British West Indies', London University, Institute of Commonwealth Studies, seminar paper presented March 1981, unpublished, pp. 4–5.

13. Samaroo, 'The Trinidad Workingmen's Association', p. 213, citing the *Port of Spain Gazette*, 29 March 1917, and the *Trinidad Guardian*, 27 May 1919.

14. Fraser, 'Some Effects of the First World War'.

15. Jos. N. France, 'Working Class Struggles of Half a Century', unpublished manuscript, 1968.

16. Eaton, 'Trade Union Development'; Richard Lobdell, 'Jamaican Labour 1838–1938', University of Wisconsin, 1968, unpublished, citing *Daily Gleaner*, 27 June, 22 August, 22 and 28 October 1918, and *Jamaica Times*,14 June and 23 August 1919; interviews with A.J. McGlashan and Edward Reid, contemporaries involved in these events.

17. Fraser, 'Some Effects of the First World War', p. 6.

18. Interviews with railwaymen Cyril Ivey, Edward Reid and Percy Aiken. The Workingmen's Co-operative Association published a pamphlet in 1919, a copy of which was given to the author by Aiken, but unfortunately this has been lost.

19. Chase, *A History of Trade Unionism in Guyana*; Carlyle Harry, *Hubert Nathaniel Critchlow*, Georgetown, Guyana National Service Publishing Centre, 1977, p. 17.
20. Fraser, 'Some Effects of the First World War', p. 6.
21. Samaroo, 'The Trinidad Workingmen's Association', citing the *Trinidad Guardian*, 14 November, 1919; Selwyn Ryan, 'Rise and Fall of the Barefooted Man', in *Trinidad and Tobago Index*, Winter 1966, No. 3.
22. The Trade Union Law, Law 37 of 1919, in Jamaica, and The Trade Union Ordinance, No. 17 of 1921, in British Guiana.
23. Wendy Charles, *Early Labour Organisation in Trinidad and the Colonial Context of the Butler Riots*, St Augustine, Dept of Sociology, University of the West Indies, 1978, pp. 10–12.
24. Charles, *Early Labour Organisation in Trinidad*, p. 13; Ryan, 'Rise and Fall', p. 9.
25. Lennox Pierre, *Quintin O'Connor*, Port of Spain, n.d.
26. Public Record Office: CO 104/52 – Grenada Legislative Council Minutes, 15 and 29 November 1933.
27. F.A. Hoyos, *Barbados, A History from the Amerindians to Independence*, Macmillan, London, 1978, p. 1981; Beckles, *A History of Barbados*, pp. 158–9.
28. *Daily Gleaner*, 4 April and 12 May 1930; *The Blackman* (Garvey's newspaper), 12 April 1930.

Chapter 18

1. Boland, *On the March: Labour Rebellions in the British Caribbean 1934–39*, pp. 44–50.
2. Boland, *On the March*, pp. 174–80, citing Report of J. Nicole, District Commissioner, 3 October 1934, Report of Commission of Inquiry into the 1935 Disturbances, 24 August 1936, Acting Governor Crawford Douglas-Jones to Cunliffe Lister, 24 January 1935, Governor G. Northcote to Secretary of State, 17 October 1935 – all in PRO: CO 111/726 File 60036.
3. W. Arthur Lewis, *Labour in the West Indies*, Fabian Society, London, 1939, pp. 12–13; Jos. N. France, 'Working Class Struggles of Half a Century', manuscript consisting of a collection of contemporary articles published in the *Union Messenger*, Basse Terre, St Kitts. The author is indebted to Fidel O'Flaherty for a copy of this manuscript; Boland, *On the March*, pp. 56–65; R. Hart, 'Origin & Development of the Working Class in the English-speaking Caribbean Area 1897–1937', in Cross and Heuman, *Labour in the Caribbean*, pp. 66–7.

4. W. Arthur Lewis, *Labour in the West Indies*, pp. 15–16; Ralph Gonsalves, 'The Role of Labour in the Political Process of St. Vincent (1935–1970)', University of the West Indies, Kingston (unpublished MSc thesis); Boland, *On the March*, pp. 69–76; R. Hart, 'Origin & Development of the Working Class', pp. 67–9.

5. Lewis, *Labour in the West Indies*, pp. 14–15; Boland, *On the March*, pp. 78–80.

6. K. Post, *Arise Ye Starvelings*, Martinus Nijhoff, The Hague, 1978, p. 262, n. 21, citing *Plain Talk*, 28 January 1938; R. Hart, *Rise and Organise*, Karia Press, London, 1989, pp. 16–17.

7. R.A. Lobdell, 'Jamaican Labor, 1838–1938', Madison, University of Wisconsin, 1968 (unpublished), p. 46, citing *Jamaica Times*, 4 July 1936.

8. Chase, *A History of Trade Unionism in Guyana*; Boland, *On the March*, pp. 182–3.

9. Kelvin Singh, 'The June 1937 Disturbances in Trinidad', in Roy Thomas, ed., *The Trinidad Labour Riots of 1937*, University of the West Indies, St Augustine, 1987, pp. 58–9, citing West India Committee circulars, 8 October and 31 December 1936: Company Reports.

10. K. Singh, 'The June 1937 Disturbances', p. 58; Susan Craig, 'Smiles and Blood: The Ruling Class Response to the Workers Rebellion of 1937', in Roy Thomas, ed., *Trinidad Labour Riots*, p. 94, citing W. Arthur Lewis, 'Notes on the Trinidad Report', British Labour Party International Dept. (confidential – mimeographed), p. 1.

11. K. Singh, 'The June 1937 Disturbances', p. 61, citing interviews with Butler.

12. K. Singh, 'The June 1937 Disturbances', pp. 62–3, citing *Trinidad & Tobago Disturbances 1937*, Report of the Commission, Cmd. 5641, 1938 (The Forster Commission).

13. Singh, 'The June 1937 Disturbances', pp. 62–6.

14. Singh, 'The June 1937 Disturbances', pp. 67–8, citing *Hansard*, 9 July 1937, pp. 252–8, 263 and 266.

15. *Trinidad Guardian*, 25 July 1937.

16. Susan Craig, 'Smiles and Blood', p. 114, citing PRO: CO 29/600 File 70307/15 – Fletcher to Ormsby-Gore, telegram (secret) 22 October 1937.

17. Although Nankivell was appointed Secretary of Labour, the employers in the oil and sugar industries refused to meet him and he was confined to dealing with government employees only. As his position had become untenable, he applied for a transfer out of the colony, and was appointed to the lesser post of Treasurer of Cyprus. He had obtained a house there

and was on his way to England to collect his family when he died on falling from a train in France. Suspicions persist in Trinidad that he was thrown from the train by agents of the oil industry. Whether he was murdered or was driven to take his own life by the course of events, is a question that his son Edmund has not been able to resolve. (Letter from Edmund Nankivell to the author, June 1997.)

18. Francis Mark, *The History of the Barbados Workers' Union*, Barbados Workers Union, Bridgetown, n.d. [1964?], pp. 1–8, citing a contemporary report by Rev. W.A. Beckles, editor of the *Weekly Advocate*; Beckles, *A History of Barbados*, pp. 163–8.

Chapter 19

1. *Jamaica Labour Weekly*, 9 July 1938.
2. A detailed account of the 1938 labour rebellion and the formation of the modern trade union movement in Jamaica is contained in the author's books *Rise and Organise*, and *Towards Decolonisation*, Chs 2–4, 7.
3. *West India Royal Commission Report 1938–39*, HM Stationery Office, London, 1945.
4. PRO: CO 318/443/6 File 71168 – Secretary of State to Officers Administering West Indian Governments, 30 January 1940.
5. *West India Royal Commission Report*, p. 198; PRO: CO 318/433/7 – Note of Information asked for by Citrine.
6. *West India Royal Commission 1938–39: Recommendations*, HM Stationery Office, London, 1940, pp. 15–16.
7. Boland, *On the March*, pp. 53, 66, 76, 124 and 189; W. Arthur Lewis, *Labour in the West Indies*, p. 14; Francis Mark, *The History of the Barbados Workers' Union*, p. 79.

Chapter 20

1. *West India Royal Commission Report*, HM Stationery Office, London, 1945, p. xiii.
2. PRO: CO 318/434/8 File 71175 – telegram, Secretary of State to Officer Administering Government, 8 August 1938.
3. *West India Royal Commission 1938–39: Recommendations*, HM Stationery Office, London, 1940, p. 25.
4. *West India Royal Commission 1938–39: Recommendations*, HM Stationery Office, London, 1940, pp. 25–6.
5. Brereton, *A History of Modern Trinidad*, pp. 192–3.

6. *Daily Gleaner*, 23 November 1942 – letter from E. Platt, a retired Army officer, reproducing this passage from Churchill's broadcast and expressing the hope that 'the leaders of the PNP and other anti-imperialists will ... realise that the British Empire is not to be given away ...'.
7. PRO: CO 318/452 File 71265, CO 318/455/2 File 71307 and CO 318/455/6 File 71317.
8. PRO: CO 137/849/42 File 68714 – Minute by Battershill, 16 November 1942.
9. PRO: CO 875/20/7 File 96595 and CO 137/850 File 68714/8.
10. Brereton, *A History of Modern Trinidad*, pp. 193–4, citing a 1945 Order in Council.

Chapter 21

1. Brereton, *A History of Modern Trinidad*, pp. 169–70.
2. Hart, *Towards Decolonisation*, Chapter 5.
3. *Pamphlets: Jamaica Political*, Vol. 1, *Outline of Policy and Programme*, Peoples National Party, 1939.
4. Hart, *Towards Decolonisation*, Chapter 27.
5. Hart, *Towards Decolonisation*, Chapter 33.
6. Sherlock, *Norman Manley: A Biography*, pp. 152 and 154, citing *Jamaica Hansard*, July 1947, pp. 393–4, 22 March 1949, p. 95, and 18 July 1950.
7. Beckles, *A History of Barbados*, pp. 170–8; Hoyos, *Barbados: A History from the Amerindians to Independence*, pp. 210–16. According to Hoyos, the voter's income qualification was in 1943 reduced to £20.
8. Beckles, *A History of Barbados*, pp. 178–89; Hoyos, *Barbados: A History*, pp. 217–24.
9. Cheddi Jagan, *Forbidden Freedom*, London, Lawrence & Wishart, 1954, 3rd edn, Hansib, London, 1994.
10. Cheddi Jagan, *The West on Trial: The Fight for Guyana's Freedom*, Michael Joseph, London, 1966.
11. Assad Shoman, *Party Politics in Belize*, Cubola Productions, Belize, 1987, pp. 21–2.

Chapter 22

1. PRO: T.220/359 File 1F 38/558/01 – Stanley to West Indian Governors, 14 March 1945.
2. PRO: CO 318/466//2 File 71295 (1946) – Memorandum by P. Rogers.
3. Report of the Founding Conference of the Caribbean Labour Congress, Barbados, 17-27 September 1945.

4. *Report: Conference on the Closer Association of the British West Indian Colonies*, Montego Bay, Jamaica, 11–19 September 1947, Cmd. 7291, HM Stationery Office, London, 1948.
5. Information concerning these discussions is contained in Colonial Office files in the Public Record Office under references CO 318/484, 318/485, 318/486, 318/487, 318/488, T.220/358, T.220/359 and CO 884/37 and in the *Report of the British Caribbean Standing Closer Association Committee 1948–49*, Advocate Co., Barbados.
6. Williams, *History of the People of Trinidad & Tobago*, pp. 240–1.
7. The proceedings of this conference were reported in the *Monthly Bulletin* of the Caribbean Labour Congress for June 1948, copies of which are in the National Library of the Institute of Jamaica and the Library of the University of Guyana.
8. Sherlock, *Norman Manley: A Biography*, pp. 180–7, citing John Mordecai, *The West Indies – The Federal Negotiations*, London, 1968.
9. PRO: CO 1031/4274, No.5, quoted in S. Ashton and D. Killingray, 'The West Indian Federation: Decolonization in the British Caribbean' – a seminar paper presented at the Institute of Commonwealth Studies, London University, 12 March 1998.

Bibliography

Caribbean Region

Augier, F.R. and Gordon, S.C. (eds) *Sources of West Indian History* (London, Longman, 1962).

Augier, F.R. and others, *The Making of the West Indies* (London, Longman, 1960).

Beachey, R., *The West Indian Sugar Industry in the late 19th Century* (Oxford, Oxford University Press, 1957).

Beckles, Hilary and Shepherd, V. (eds), *Caribbean Freedom: Economy and Society from Emancipation to the Present* (Kingston, Ian Randle, 1993).

Besson, J. and Momsen, J., *Land and Development in the Caribbean* (London, Macmillan, 1987).

Bicknell, R., *The West Indies as they are* (London, J. Hatchard & Son, 1836).

Bisnauth, D., *History of Religions in the Caribbean* (Kingston, Kingston Publishers, 1989).

Boland, O. Nigel, *On The March: Labour Rebellions in the British Caribbean 1934–39* (Kingston, Ian Randle, 1995).

Buckley, R.N., *Slaves in Red Coats: The British West India Regiments* (New Haven, Yale University Press, 1979).

Burns, Alan, *History of the British West Indies* (London, Allen & Unwin, 1954).

Caldecott, A., *The Church in the West Indies* (1898, reprinted Frank Cass Library of West Indian Studies, No. 14).

Coke, Thomas, *A History of the West Indies* (Liverpool, Nutall, Fisher & Dixon, 1808, reprinted Miami, Mnemosyne Publishing Co., 1969).

Craton, M., *Testing the Chains: Resistance to Slavery in the British West Indies* (Ithaca, NY, Cornell University Press, 1982).

Cross, M. and Heuman, G. (eds), *Labour in the Caribbean* (London, Macmillan, 1988).

Dunn, R.S., *Sugar and Slaves: The Rise of the Planter Class in the English West Indies 1624–1713* (Chapel Hill, NC, University of North Carolina Press, 1972).

Edwards, Bryan, *The History, Civil and Commercial, of the British Colonies in the West Indies* (London (2 vols), Stockdale, 1793, 4th edition (3 vols) 1801, 5th (posthumous) edition (5 vols – last 2 vols by anonymous author), 1819).

Gordon, S., *A Century of West Indian Education* (London, Longman, 1963).

Goveia, Elsa, *A Historiography of the British West Indies* (Mexico, Instituto Panamericana de Geografia e Historia, 1956).

Goveia, Elsa, *West Indian Slave Laws* (Kingston, Caribbean University Press, 1970).

Guerin, D. *The West Indies and Their Future* (London, Dennis Dobson, 1961).

Hart, Richard, *Slaves Who Abolished Slavery*. Vol. 1, *Blacks in Bondage* (Kingston, University of the West Indies, 1980).

Higman, B.W., *Slave Populations in the British Caribbean 1807–1834* (Baltimore, Johns Hopkins University Press, 1984).

Knowles, W.H., *Trade Union Development and Industrial Relations in the British West Indies* (Berkeley, CA, 1959).

Laurence, K.O., *Immigration into the West Indies in the 19th Century* (Aylesbury, Ginn & Co., 1971).

Lewis, Gordon, *The Growth of the Modern West Indies* (London, MacGibbon & Kee, 1968).

Lewis, Gordon, *Main Currents of Caribbean Thought: The Historical Evolution of Caribbean Society in its Ideological Aspects 1492–1900* (London, Johns Hopkins University Press, 1983).

Madden, R.R., *Twelve Months' Residence in the West Indies*, 2 vols (London, J. Cochran, 1835).

Murray, D.J., *The West Indies & the Development of Colonial Government 1801–1834* (Oxford, Oxford University Press, 1965).

Mordecai, J., *The West Indies – The Federal Negotiations* (London, Allen & Unwin, 1967).

Parry, J.H. and Sherlock, Philip, *A Short History of the West Indies* (London, Macmillan, 1971).

Pitman, F.W., *The Development of the British West Indies* (New Haven, Yale University Press, 1917).

Ragatz, L.J., *The Fall of the Planter Class in the British Caribbean* (New York, Century Publishers, 1928).

Sewell, W.G., *The Ordeal of Free Labour in the British West Indies* (New York, Harper, 1861; reprinted London, Frank Cass, 1968).

Sheridan, R.B., *Sugar and Slavery: An Economic History of the British West Indies 1623–1775* (Aylesbury, Ginn & Co., 1974).

Sheridan, R.B., *Doctors and Slaves: A medical and demographic history of slavery in the British West Indies* (Cambridge, Cambridge University Press, 1985).

Sherlock, Philip, *West Indian Nations* (London, Macmillan, 1973).

Singh, Bahadur (ed.), *Indians in the Caribbean* (London, Oriental University Press, 1987).

Smith, M.G., *West Indian Family Structure* (Seattle, University of Washington Press, 1962).

Southey, Thomas, *Chronological History of the West Indies* (London, 1827; reprinted London, Frank Cass, 1968).

Spackman, A., *Constitutional Development of the West Indies 1922–68: A selection from major documents* (Kingston, Caribbean University Press, n.d.).

Turner, Mary (ed.), *From Chattel Slaves to Wage Slaves* (Kingston, Ian Randle, 1995).

Wallace, E., *The British Caribbean: from the Decline of Colonialism to the end of Federation* (Toronto, University of Toronto Press, 1977).

Will, H.A., *Constitutional Change in the British West Indies 1880–1903* (Oxford, Clarendon Press, 1970).

Williams, Eric (ed.), *Documents of West Indian History 1492–1655* (Port of Spain, PNM Publishing Co., 1963).

Williams, Eric (ed.), *Documents on British West Indian History 1807–1833* (Port of Spain, Trinidad Publishing Co., 1952).

Williams, Eric, *From Columbus to Castro 1492–1969* (London, André Deutsch, 1970).

Williams, Eric, *Capitalism and Slavery* (Chapel Hill, NC, University of North Carolina Press, 1944; London, André Deutsch, 1964).

Wrong, H., *Government in the West Indies* (Oxford, 1923).

Bahamas

Albury, P., *The Story of the Bahamas* (London, 1975).

Craton, M., *A History of the Bahamas* (Waterloo, Canada, San Salvador Press, 1986).

Dodge, S., *Abaco: The History of an Out Island and its Cays* (Decatur, Illinois, 1983).

Johnson, Howard, *The Bahamas in Slavery and Freedom* (London, James Currey, 1991).

Barbados

Barton, G., *Prehistory of Barbados* (Bridgetown, Advocate Co., 1953).

Beckles, Hilary, *Black Rebellion in Barbados* (Bridgetown, Antilles Publications, 1984).

Beckles, Hilary, *Natural Rebels: A Social History of Enslaved Black Women in Barbados* (London, Zed Books, 1989).

Beckles, Hilary, *A History of Barbados*, (Cambridge, Cambridge University Press, 1990).

Bennett, J.H., *Bondsmen and Bishops: Slavery and Apprenticeship on the Codrington Plantation* ... (Berkeley, CA, 1958).

Frere, George, *A Short History of Barbados* (London, 1768).

Handler, J. *The Unappropriated People: Freedmen in the Slave Society of Barbados* (Baltimore, Johns Hopkins University Press, 1974).

Harlow, V.T., *A History of Barbados 1625–1685* (Oxford, 1926).

Hoyos, F.A., *Grantley Adams and the Social Revolution* (London, Macmillan, 1974).

Hoyos, F.A., *Barbados: A History from the Amerindians to Independence* (London, Macmillan, 1978).

Ligon, R., *A True and Exact History of the Island of Barbados 1647–1650*, 2nd edition (London, 1763; reprinted in Frank Cass Library of West Indian Studies No. 11).

Mark, F., *The History of the Barbados Workers Union* (Bridgetown, Barbados Workers Union, n.d. [1964?]).

Poyer, John, *A History of Barbados from the First Discovery ...* (London, Mawman, 1808).

Schomburgk, R.H., *A History of Barbados* (London, 1848).

Watson, Karl, *The Civilised Island, Barbados: A Social History 1750–1816* (Barbados, 1979).

Watson, Karl, *A History of Barbados* (Cambridge, Cambridge University Press, 1990).

British Guiana/Guyana

Adamson, A.H., *Sugar without Slaves: The Political Economy of British Guiana 1838–1904* (New Haven, CT, Yale University Press, 1972).

Brett, W.H., *The Indian Tribes of Guiana* (London, 1868).

Chase, Ashton, *A History of Trade Unionism in Guyana 1900–1961* (Georgetown, New Guyana Co., 1964).

Clementi, C., *A Constitutional History of British Guiana* (London, Macmillan, 1937).

Dalton, H.G., *The History of British Guiana*, 2 vols (London, 1855).

Daly, V.T., *A Short History of the Guyanese People* (London, Macmillan, 1975).

Jagan, Cheddi, *Forbidden Freedom* (London, Lawrence & Wishart, 1954; 2nd edition, London, Hansib, 1994).

Jagan, Cheddi, *The West on Trial* (London, Michael Joseph, 1966; revised edition, Berlin, Seven Seas Books, 1972).

Mandle, J.R., *The Plantation Economy: Population and Economic Change in Guyana 1838–1960* (Philadelphia, Temple University Press, 1973).

Menezes, M., *British Policy Towards the Amerindians ... 1803–1873* (Oxford, Clarendon Press, 1977).

Moore, B.L., *Race, Power and Social Segmentation in ... Guyana 1838–1960* (New York, Gordon & Breach, 1987).

Nath, Dwarka, *A History of Indians in British Guiana* (London, the author, 1950).

Northcott, C., *Slavery's Martyr* (London, Epworth, 1976).

Ramashoye, F., *The Development of Land Law in British Guiana* (New York, Oceana Publications, 1966).

Rodney, Walter, *A History of the Guyanese Working People 1881–1905* (Baltimore, Johns Hopkins University Press, 1981).

Rodway, J., *History of British Guiana*, 3 vols (Georgetown, J. Thomson, 1891–94).

Schomburgk, R., *A Description of British Guiana* (London, 1840).

Schomburgk, R., *Travels in British Guiana 1840–1844*, 2 vols, edited and translated by W.E. Roth (Georgetown, Daily Chronicle, 1922–23).

Seecharan, C., *Tiger in the Stars: ... Indian Achievements in British Guiana 1919–29* (London, Macmillan, 1997).

Thomas, Clive, *Plantations, Peasants and the State* (Kingston, University of the West Indies, 1984).

British Honduras/Belize

Ashcroft, N., *Colonialism and Underdevelopment: Processes of Political Economic Change in British Honduras* (New York, Teachers College Press, 1973).

Bancroft, H.H., *History of Central America*, 3 vols (San Francisco, History Co., 1883–87).

Boland, O. Nigel, *The Formation of a Colonial Society: Belize from Conquest to Crown Colony* (Cambridge, Cambridge University Press, 1976).

Boland, O. Nigel, *Colonialism and Resistance in Belize* (Kingston, University of the West Indies, 1988).

Burdon, J.A., *Archives of British Honduras*, 3 vols (London, Sifton Praed, 1935).

Caiger, S., *British Honduras: Past and Present* (London, Allen & Unwin, 1951).

Clegern, W.M., *British Honduras: Colonial Dead End 1859–1900* (Baton Rouge, LA, Louisiana State University Press, 1967).

Dobson, N., *A History of Belize* (London, Longman, 1973).

Gibbs, A.R., *British Honduras: An Historical and Descriptive Account of the Colony from its Settlement 1670* (London, Sampson Low, 1883).

Grant, C.H., *The Making of Modern Belize: Politics, Society & British Colonialism in Central America* (Cambridge, Cambridge University Press, 1976).

Shoman, Asad, *Party Politics in Belize 1950–1986* (Belize, Cubola Productions, 1987).

Jamaica

Bakan, Abigail, *Ideology and Class Conflict in Jamica* (Montreal, McGill-Queens University Press, 1990).

Bleby, Henry, *Death Struggles of Slavery*, 3rd edition (London, William Nichols, 1868).

Bleby, Henry, *The Reign of Terror ... Ex-Governor Eyre, George William Gordon & the Jamaica Atrocities* (London, William Nichols, 1868).

Beckford, William, *A Descriptive Account of ... Jamaica*, 2 vols (London, T. & G. Egerton, 1790).

Black, Clinton, *History of Jamaica* (London, Collins, 1958; new edition London, Longman, 1994).

Braithwaite, E.K., *The Development of Creole Society ... 1770–1820* (Oxford, Clarendon Press, 1971).

Bridges, G.W., *Annals of Jamaica*, 2 vols (London, John Murray, 1828; reprinted London, Frank Cass Library of West Indian Studies No. 1).

Bryan, Patrick, *The Jamaican People 1880–1902* (London, Macmillan, 1991).

Campbell, Mavis, *The Maroons of Jamaica 1655–1796* (Granby, Bergin & Garvey, 1988).

Clarke, Colin, *Kingston, Jamaica: Urban Development and Social Change 1692–1962* (Berkeley, CA, University of California Press, 1975).

Craton, M. and Walvin, J., *A Jamaica Plantation: The History of Worthy Park 1670–1970* (London, W.H. Allen, 1970).

Curtin, P.D., *Two Jamaicas: The Role of Ideas ... 1830–1865* (Cambridge, MA, Harvard University Press, 1975).

Dallas, R.C., *The History of the Maroons*, 2 vols (London, T.N. Longman & O. Rees, 1803).

Eisner, G., *Jamaica 1830–1930* (Manchester, Manchester University Press, 1961).

Foot, Hugh, *A Start in Freedom* (London, Hodder & Stoughton, 1964).

Gardner, W.J., *The History of Jamaica from its Discovery ... to the Year 1872* (London, Elliot Stock, 1874; new edition 1909; reprinted London, Frank Cass Library of West Indian Studies No. 17, 1971).

Hall, Douglas, *Free Jamaica 1838–1865* (New Haven, CT, Yale University Press, 1959).

Hart, Ansell, *The Life of George William Gordon* (Kingston, Institute of Jamaica, n.d. [1972]).

Hart, Richard, *Slaves Who Abolished Slavery*. Vol. 2, *Blacks in Rebellion* (Kingston, University of the West Indies, 1985).

Hart, Richard, *Rise and Organise: The Birth of the Workers &*
National Movements ... 1936–1939 (London, Karia Press, 1989).

Hart, Richard, *Towards Decolonisation* (Kingston, Canoe Press –
University of the West Indies, 1998).

Heuman, G., *Between Black and White: Politics and the Free Coloreds
... 1792–1865* (London, Clio Press, 1981).

Heuman, G., *The Killing Time: The Morant Bay Rebellion* (London,
Macmillan, 1994).

Higman, B.W., *Slave Population and Economy of Jamaica 1807–1834*
(Cambridge, Cambridge University Press, 1976).

Holt, T.C., *The Problem of Freedom: Race, Labor and Politics in
Jamaica and Britain 1832–1938* (Baltimore & London, Johns
Hopkins University Press, 1992).

Ingram, K.E., *Sources of Jamaican History 1655–1838* (Zug,
Switzerland, Inter Document Centre A.G., 1976).

Jacobs, H.P., *Sixty Years of Change 1806–1866* (Kingston, Institute
of Jamaica, 1973).

Johnson, Anthony, *J.A.G. Smith* (Kingston, Kingston Publishers,
1991).

Kaufman, M., *Jamaica under Manley* (London, Zed Books, 1985).

Leslie, C., *A True & Exact Account of Jamaica* (Edinburgh, A.
Kinkaid, 1739).

Lewis, M.G., *Journal of a West India Proprietor* (London, Murray,
1834).

Lewis, Rupert, *Marcus Garvey: Anti-Colonial Champion* (London,
Karia Press, 1987).

Long, Edward, *The History of Jamaica*, 2 vols (London, T. Lowndes,
1774; reprinted London, Frank Cass Library of West Indian
Studies No. 12).

Munroe, Trevor, *The Politics of Constitutional Development ...
1944–62* (Kingston, University of the West Indies, 1972).

Munroe, Trevor, *Jamican Politics: A Marxist Perspective in Transition*
(Kingston, Heinemann, 1990).

Munroe, Trevor, *The Cold War and The Jamaican Left 1950–55*
(Kingston, Kingston Publishers, 1992).

Manley, Michael, *The Politics of Change* (London, André Deutsch,
1974).

Manley, Michael, *A Voice at the Workplace* (London, André Deutsch,
1975).

Manley, Michael, *Jamaica: Struggle in the Periphery* (London,
Writers & Readers Publishing Co-op., n.d. [1980–81?]).

Manley, Michael, *Up the Down Escalator* (London, André Deutsch,
1987).

Nettleford, R. (ed.), *Manley and the New Jamaica: Selective Writings
& Speeches* (London, Longman, 1971).

180   FROM OCCUPATION TO INDEPENDENCE

Olivier, Sidney, *The Myth of Governor Eyre* (London, Hogarth Press, 1933).

Olivier, Sidney, *Jamaica, the Blessed Isle* (London, Faber, 1936).

Panton, D.K., *Jamaica's Michael Manley* (Kingston, Kingston Publishers, 1993).

Paterson, O., *The Sociology of Slavery* (London, MacGibbon & Kee, 1967).

Phillippo, J.M., *Jamaica, its Past and Present State* (London, John Snow, 1843).

Post, Ken, *Arise Ye Starvelings: The Jamaica Labour Rebellion of 1938 and its Aftermath* (The Hague, Martinus Nijhoff, 1978).

Post, Ken, *Strike the Iron: A Colony at War ... 1939–1945*, 2 vols (Englewood Cliffs, NJ, Humanities Press, 1981).

Roberts, G.W., *The Population of Jamaica* (Cambridge, Cambridge University Press, 1957).

Satchell, V., *From Plots to Plantations: Land Transactions in Jamaica 1866–1900* (Kingston, University of the West Indies, 1990).

Schuler, Monica, *Alas, Alas Kongo: A Social History of Indentured African Immigration into Jamaica 1841–1865* (Baltimore, Johns Hopkins University Press, 1980).

Semmell, B., *Democracy versus Empire: The Jamaica Riots of 1865* ... (1963; reprinted New York, Anchor Books, 1969).

Sherlock, Philip, *Norman Manley: A Biography* (London, Macmillan, 1980).

Sherlock, Philip and H. Bennett, *The Story of Jamaica*, (Kingston, Ian Randle, 1998).

Stephens, E.H. and J.D., *Democratic Socialism in Jamaica* (Princeton, NJ, Princeton University Press, 1986).

Turner, Mary, *Slaves and Missionaries: The Disintegration of a Jamaican Slave Society 1787–1834* (Urbana, IL, University of Illinois Press, 1982).

Underhill, E.B., *The Tragedy of Morant Bay* (London, Alexander & Shepeard, 1895).

Leeward Islands

Cox, Edward, *Free Coloureds in the Slave Societies of St. Kitts & Grenada* (Knoxville, University of Tenessee Press, 1984).

Dookhan, I., *A History of the Virgin Islands* (Kingston, Caribbean University Press, 1975).

Gaspar, D.B., *Bondsmen and Rebels: A Study of Master–Slave Relations in Antigua* (Baltimore, Johns Hopkins University Press, 1985).

Goveia, Elsa, *Slave Society in the British Leeward Islands* (New Haven, Yale University Press, 1965).

Hall, Douglas, *Five of the Leewards 1834–70* (Barbados, 1971).
Higham, C.S., *The Development of the Leeward Islands under the Restoration 1660–1688* (Cambridge, 1921).
Oliver, V.L., *History of the Island of Antigua* (1894).
Pares, R., *A West Indian Fortune* (London, Longmans Green, 1950).
Smith, K.B. & F.C., *To Shoot Hard Labour: The Life and Times of Samuel Smith, an Antiguan Workingman 1877–1982* (London, Karia Press, 1985).

Trinidad and Tobago

Basdeo, S., *Labour Organisation and Labour Reform in Trinidad 1919–1933* (St Augustine, Trinidad, University of the West Indies, 1983).
Brereton, B., *A History of Modern Trinidad 1783–1962* (London and Port of Spain, Heinemann, 1981).
Carmichael, G., *History of the West Indian Islands of Trinidad & Tobago* (London, 1961).
Craig, H., *The Legislative Council of Trinidad & Tobago* (London, 1952).
Fraser, L.M., *History of Trinidad 1781–1839*, 2 vols (Trinidad, 1891–96).
Hollis, Claud, *A Brief History of Trinidad Under the Spanish Crown* (Trinidad, 1941).
Mallet, F., *Descriptive Account of the Island of Trinidad* (London, 1797).
Millette, James, *The Genesis of Crown Colony Government* (Port of Spain, 1970; 2nd edition published under the title *Society and Politics in Colonial Trinidad* (London, Zed Books, 1985).
Ramdin, F., *From Chattel Slave to Wage Earner: A History of Trade Unionism in Trinidad & Tobago* (London, Martin Brian & O'Keefe, 1982).
Reis, Charles, *A History of the Constitution or Government of Trinidad*, 2 vols (Trinidad, 1929).
Ryan, Selwyn, *Race and Nationalism in Trinidad & Tobago* (Toronto, Toronto University Press, 1972).
Williams, Eric, *History of the People of Trinidad & Tobago* (London, André Deutsch, 1964).
Wood, Donald, *Trinidad in Transition: The Years after Slavery* (Oxford, Oxford University Press, 1968).
Woodcock, H.L., *A History of Tobago* (London, Frank Cass Library of West Indies Studies No. 28, 1971).

Windward Islands

Brizan, G., *Grenada, Island of Conflict* (London, Zed Books, 1984).

Breen, H.H., *St. Lucia, Historical, Statistical and Descriptive* (1844; reprinted London, Frank Cass Library of West Indian Studies No. 9, 1970).

DaBreo, D.S., *From the Beginning: A History of Grenada* (St Georges, Printers Ltd, 1973).

Honeychurch, L., *The Dominica Story* (London, Macmillan, 1995).

Searle, C. (ed.), *In Nobody's Backyard: Maurice Bishop's Speeches 1979–1983* (London, Zed Books, 1984).

Shephard, C. *An Historical Account of the Island of St. Vincent* (London, 1831; reprinted London, Frank Cass Library of West Indian Studies No. 23, 1971).

Young, Virginia, *Becoming West Indian: Culture, Self and Nation in St Vincent* (Washington D.C., Smithsonian Institute Press, 1993).

Young, William, *An Account of the Black Charaibs in the Island of St Vincent* (London, 1795; reprinted London, Frank Cass Library of West Indian Studies No. 18, 1971).

Index